* Volumes with an asterisk following the title are a part of the NCRLL set: Approaches to Language and Literacy
Research, edited by JoBeth Allen and Donna Alvermann.

(Continued)

ON
QUALITATIVE INQUIRY

Approaches to Language and Literacy Research

(AN NCRLL VOLUME)

GEORGE KAMBERELIS
GREG DIMITRIADIS

TEACHERS COLLEGE PRESS

Teachers College, Columbia University
New York and London

National Conference on Research in
Language and Literacy

Published by Teachers College Press, 1234 Amsterdam Avenue, New York, NY 10027

Published in association with the National Conference on Research in Language and Literacy (NCRLL). For more about NCRLL, see *www.nyu.edu/education/teachlearn/ research/ncrll/*

Library of Congress Cataloging-in-Publication Data

Kamberelis, George.
    On qualitative inquiry / George Kamberelis, Greg Dimitriadis.
        p. cm. — (Approaches to language and literacy research)
    (Language and literacy series) "An NCRLL volume."
    Includes bibliographical references and index.
    ISBN 0-8077-4545-6 (cloth : alk. paper). — ISBN 0-8077-4544-8 (pbk. : alk. paper)
        1. Philology—Research. 2. Logic. I. Dimitriadis, Greg, 1969-
    II. National Conference on Research in Language and Literacy. III. Title. IV. Series.
    V. Language and literacy series (New York, N.Y.)
    P51.K26 2005
    407.2—dc22   2004058122

ISBN 0-8077-4544-8 (paper)
ISBN 0-8077-4545-6 (cloth)

Printed on acid-free paper
Manufactured in the United States of America

12 11 10 09 08 07 06 05   8   7   6   5   4   3   2   1

Contents

From the NCRLL Editors

Do you wish you could go back to graduate school and take more research courses? Are you in graduate school and worried that you don't have the tools to become a researcher? Does your current project cry out for an approach that you aren't quite sure how to design? Have you ever wondered how and why people study conversations in classrooms, or what different approaches there might be to case study research, or how to employ critical race theory in designing a study?

If so, you are not alone. A recent survey of the membership of the National Conference on Research in Language and Literacy (NCRLL) indicated a strong need for a definitive source of information about different research approaches in the field. To respond to that need, NCRLL and Teachers College Press have joined forces to develop and publish the current collection—Approaches to Language and Literacy Research—with *On Qualitative Inquiry* as its introductory volume. Each subsequent book will address a particular research framework, tradition, or approach used by language and literacy researchers, authored by one or more prominent researchers. Topics and authors tentatively slated for future volumes include Arlette Willis on research informed by critical theories; Anne Haas Dyson and Celia Genishi on case studies; David Bloome, Nora Shuart-Faris, Stephanie Carter, Mary Beth Christian, and Sheila Otto on classroom discourse analysis; Dixie Goswami, Ceci Lewis, Marty Rutherford, and Diane Waff on teacher inquiry; Shirley Brice Heath on ethnography; David Schaafsma on narrative inquiry; and David Reinking and Barbara Bradley on formative experiments.

We believe the books in this collection will be useful to a wide range of researchers: graduate students, novice researchers, and experienced researchers who want to learn about an unfamiliar research tradition or methodology. Each volume will address theoretical assumptions and issues within a particular tradition (including different interpretations, applications, and methods), research questions that might be addressed using that approach, design possibilities, exemplars (with an annotated bibliography of studies), and a reference list for further reading. We are confident that this collection will make a major contribution to the field by connecting researchers to influential works of language and literacy scholars using a variety of approaches.

The current volume, *On Qualitative Inquiry*, maps the philosophical foundations and disciplinary histories of qualitative research and serves as a prelude to many of the practice-oriented volumes that will follow. Brilliantly conceived, it situates language and literacy research in the larger, multi-disciplinary field of qualitative inquiry. Kamberelis' and Dimitriadis' genealogy of the ideas that converged to spark the collective imagination of the larger research community from which qualitative inquiry emerged is intellectually provocative and highly useful. The authors' deep knowledge of their subject matter and their ability to bring such knowledge to life through diverse examples in language and literacy research are unparalleled. We trust that these ideas will engage each reader in generative ways, and provide a heuristic for investigating qualitative approaches to literacy research. Subsequent volumes will focus on the whys and hows of conducting literacy and language research within various qualitative and quantitative approaches.

JoBeth Allen and Donna Alvermann,
NCRLL Editors

Acknowledgments

We are most grateful to the NCRLL series editors (Donna Alvermann and JoBeth Allen), without whose insight, counsel, and patience this book would never have been completed. We would also like to thank the entire staff at Teachers College Press (and especially Carole Saltz, Carol Collins, and Karl Nyberg) for the outstanding job they did throughout the process of developing and producing the book.

Several reviewers of an earlier version of the book manuscript—Peg (Margaret) Finders, David T Cantaffa, and A. Jonathan Eakle—provided us with formative that were invaluable in making the book clearer, more accurate, and more accessible. We are deeply indebted to them for this work. Several other scholars—Stephen Bailey, Marta Albert, and Vanessa Machado—also read and responded to earlier versions of the book manuscript with care and insight, and we are grateful for the ways in which they helped us improve the work. Finally, we would like to thank Amy Ferry for her prompt and astute editorial assistance at many points along the way.

George would like to thank his colleagues and students in the Reading Department and the School of Education at the State University of New York at Albany, all of whom contribute to the ongoing creation of fertile spaces for intellectual work. He would also like to thank the National Academy of Education and the Spencer Foundation whose generous support through a postdoctoral fellowship funded some of the research and writing for chapters 1 and 2.

Greg would like to thank all of his colleagues and students in the Graduate School of Education and the Department of Educational Leadership and Policy at the State University of New York at Buffalo for their intellectual sustenance and support.

Logic and Structure of the Book

In the early stages of planning this book, we imagined our task to be twofold. First, we would map the epistemological and theoretical foundations of qualitative inquiry and how these foundations were appropriated and deployed in our field. Second, we would map the epistemological and methodological histories of the key qualitative approaches to language and literacy research (e.g., ethnographic, case study, life history, critical/feminist, discourse analytic, etc.) that would constitute the topics for other books in the series. This twofold task seemed easy enough. However, as we jettisoned outline after outline and chapter draft after chapter draft for the book, we realized that the challenge issued us was far greater than we had imagined. Different qualitative approaches to research (including language and literacy research) seemed to defy simple histories of development, direct linkages to foundational theories, clearly marked boundaries between and among each other, and their own unique methods (i.e., strategies and tactics for data collections and analysis). There seemed to be very little that any given qualitative approach to inquiry could truly call its own. Yet the various approaches continued to seem distinctly unique in many ways.

As our research progressed, we began to view qualitative inquiry (and its foundations) in a different way—as an extremely variegated and overlapping set of enterprises with internal contradictions and sometimes contentious relations with one another. We also began to regard qualitative researchers as a loosely coupled collective of inquirers united by little more than their general opposition to foundationalist or objectivist epistemological traditions—those traditions that maintain that truth is attainable through instrumental-technical means such as quantification and statistical analysis. Viewed from this new perch, the editors' invitation to write the book seemed both more complex and more daunting.

That concern notwithstanding, we began to explore why things seemed to be so multiple, complex, and even contradictory. Several possible reasons emerged. First, because objectivism and positivism continue to exercise considerable power within social science research, qualitative research continues to have a kind of stepchild complex and to be more than a little apologetic. Second, debates about epistemology and theory related to empirical research have often dissolved into debates about differences between quantitative versus qualitative methods of data collection and analysis. Among other things, this tendency has elided more important trajectories of thinking that are more epistemological and theoretical. Third, apparently for historical reasons, there has been a propensity to reduce all qualitative approaches to a single approach, usually ethnography. Since ethnography is but one of many quite different approaches to qualitative inquiry and since it is typically located within the discipline of anthropology alone, this propensity has detracted attention away from some very rich and powerful philosophy of science and epistemological work generated within philosophy, sociology, literary studies, communication studies, and other fields. It has also eclipsed the importance of methods other than ethnography such as grounded theory, narrative and life history research, symbolic interactionism, and conversation analysis that have grown up within some of these other disciplines. Fourth, this entity we call qualitative inquiry has grown and changed almost exponentially during the past few decades and continues to grow at an astounding rate. Fifth, before even adequately addressing assaults from the right (e.g., positivist/objectivist camps), qualitative research was assaulted from the critical left. These assaults called into question the tendency for qualitative researchers to seek and to trust "emic" accounts of "lived experience" at the expense of mapping the material and ideological conditions of experience that make these experiences possible in the first place. Finally, the general desire for clarity in defining what qualitative inquiry is all about has often resulted in glossing differences between various approaches and overdetermining otherwise useful categories.

Based on these issues and concerns, we decided to take a genealogical approach guided by a single question: What conditions of possibility—ideas, discursive and material practices, social and political forces—had to be in place for many and varied forms of qualitative inquiry to emerge, develop, and gain legitimacy when and how they did? Taking this approach opened up more productive spaces for exploring the relations between prevailing philosophical ideas and their effects on how and why social science might be done, as well as how various histories of doing social science within various disciplines and interdisciplinary contexts developed.

Genealogy: Thinking History Differently

What, precisely, is meant by genealogy, and what relevance does it have for understanding the philosophical and theoretical horizons of qualitative research (including research on language and literacy)? Whether or not he coined the term, Nietzsche (2003) deployed it late in the 19th century in his study of morality, *The Genealogy of Morals*. In this study, Nietzsche explored the arbitrary nature of what we consider to be immutable or timeless values—"good" and "bad." In particular, Nietzsche stressed the role of historical contingency in the ways certain values proliferated and came to be accepted as "common sense." He concluded that there is no "timeless" history, only a series of struggles in which the victors define what is accepted as true or real or natural or good.

It is precisely this notion of genealogy that Michel Foucault appropriated and developed in his famous work on institutions (including prisons, asylums, and schools) and discourses (especially the discourses of sexuality). For Foucault, all efforts to write traditional histories with clear teleologies are suspect. In place of traditional histories, he recommended writing genealogies. Genealogies are complex, even paradoxical. They foreground discontinuity at least as much as continuity, but they also attend to regularity in dispersion. We will unpack these goals one at a time. Genealogies show how the past was different from, strange in relation to, and even threatening to the present. Genealogies disrupt the comfortable, intimate relations that historians typically claim link the past with the present. They show that the present is foreign to and constitutes a break (often a violent break) with the past despite the efforts of traditional historians to suggest otherwise:

> History becomes "effective" to the degree that it introduces discontinuity into our very being—as it divides our emotions, dramatizes our instincts, multiplies our body and sets it against itself. "Effective" history deprives the self of the reassuring stability of life and nature, and it will not permit itself to be transported by a voiceless obstinacy toward a millennial ending. It will uproot its traditional foundations and relentlessly disrupt its

pretended continuity. This is because knowledge is not made for understanding; it is made for cutting. (Foucault, 1984b, p. 88)

Unlike traditional historical methods, genealogies aim "to record the singularity of events outside any monotonous finality" (Dreyfus & Rabinow, 1982, p. 106). They focus on fractures, recurrences and play, surface manifestations, accidents, unpredicted/unpredictable events, power relations, knowledge refraction and dispersion, and the constitutive effects of local practices and events.

While genealogies call attention to temporal discontinuity, they also attend to regularity in dispersion during particular time periods or epochs. So although all disciplines or social formations (and we view the domain of qualitative inquiry as a historically produced social formation) are dispersed because they are constituted at the intersection of multiple social and material forces, there is also a certain regularity in dispersion because these forces work not only within but also across multiple disciplines or social formations. For example, although medicine, law enforcement, education, and the Catholic church are very different social formations, each operates with remarkably similar discursive instruments of surveillance and control—the medical interview, the police interrogation, the examination, and the confession.

Because disciplines or social formations can never be grasped or understood in their entirety, Foucault advocated a syncopated rather than a totalizing approach to understanding them. This approach never pretends to capture the whole of any social formation and instead sets out to describe the uniqueness and oddities of its practices, the play and slippage among their relations, and the ways in which the social formation depends on the historical affordances of the times.

The goal of genealogy, then, is to study the past in order to understand and disrupt the present. The genealogist begins with a present phenomenon or social formation and tries to explain how it arose, how it developed, and how it gained legitimacy and power. The genealogist is also concerned with unmasking the processes that functioned (and still function) to render historically produced phenomena or social formations as natural and universal rather than as historical and local. Often, the genealogist finds that an origin lies in an unsuspected place or as a distinctly different phenomenon or social formation from what he or she had assumed; that the developmental trajectory of a particular phenomenon or social formation has been unpredictable and discontinuous; that the effects of a phenomenon or social formation are significantly dispersed; and that ostensibly different phenomena or social formations operate according to similar logics of surveillance and control. This is indeed the case when one looks at qualitative research, whether one investigates the genealogy of a particular study (e.g., Heath's [1983] ethnographies of Maintown, Roadville, and Trackton), a particular method (e.g., critical discourse analysis), or a particular foundational theory (e.g., phenomenology). The remainder of this book is an attempt to demonstrate this social-historical fact.

There are, as one might expect, several ways to "do" genealogies of qualitative inquiry. One approach might focus on a very specific artifact such as Shirley Brice Heath's *Ways with Words* (1983), a groundbreaking and extraordinarily influential study of literacy learning. Instead of asking predictable questions such as which theory grounded Heath's work or how her mentors influenced her study, a genealogist might ask a question such as: What collection of ideas and practices coalesced in the 1970s and 1980s that allowed Heath to draw upon naturalized constructs such as "community," "event," "bedtime story," and "socialization" and naturalized dichotomies such as "oral traditions" and "literate traditions" in her work? When taking this approach, the influences of social theorists such as Max Weber and Pierre Bourdieu, folklorists such as Roger Abrahams and Vladimir Propp, and linguists such as Dell Hymes and Charles Ferguson might turn out to be more important than one might initially imagine. Also important here might be knowledge of Heath's biography, including the specific personal and professional relations she enjoyed with her research participants and with professional colleagues, as well as the ways in which she located herself within various intellectual traditions. This is but one example of how a genealogical analysis might proceed. There are, of course, many others.

Deploying a genealogical approach seems particularly important at this particular historical juncture when multiple proliferations of qualitative inquiry are being used to study human social life. It also seems particularly appropriate at a time when the collective "common sense" of the fields of education and literacy studies seems to suggest that qualitative approaches are currently far more prevalent than quantitative ones, even while state and federal policymakers cast a suspicious eye toward educational research that is not "scientifically based" with experimental designs and replicability as key requirements. These apparently contradictory social facts are intriguing for the way in which they reflect the genealogical assumption that the proliferation and dispersion of discourses is complex and contentious, and typically occurs on highly contested terrain with high stakes and ever-changing forms of cultural capital (Bourdieu, 1998). Finally, a genealogical approach seems particularly apt to the task at hand because qualitative inquiry has emerged from being primarily a diverse set of discipline-based perspectives to being a transdisciplinary metadiscourse.

The emergence of various modes of qualitative inquiry has been particularly prevalent within certain fields such as anthropology and sociology for more than a century (see chapters 3 and 4). During the past several decades, however, there has been a tremendous amount of intellectual and pragmatic cross-pollination related to qualitative inquiry across a wide range of disciplines. For example, while anthropology emerged as a distinct discipline in the late 19th and early 20th centuries, it faced a validation crisis in the 1960s, brought on by pressures from within its own history of complicity with colonialism. It was also influenced heavily by the emergence of cognitive science, with its emphasis on the symbolic structures of the mind. Finally, it faced broader social pressures to become more relevant. Both of these forces were external to the discipline and led to a rapprochement of anthropology with education, specifically around issues of language socialization and use. The Ethnography of Communication (EOC) tradition was literally born of this rapprochement, allowing figures like Dell Hymes, Shirley Brice Heath, and Courtney Cazden to draw readily from multiple disciplinary resources to frame their work. Additionally, while many scholars (mostly from education) focused on "unmarked" language performances, others (mostly from anthropology and folklore studies) were also heavily influenced by literary studies that took up "marked" performances as their main objects of inquiry. EOC thus transcended traditional disciplinary boundaries, and in doing so paved the way for the creation of various transdisciplinary metadiscourses, including qualitative inquiry.

Another illustration: Traditionally, anthropology has been a solidly empirical discipline. Sociology, in contrast, has been marked by a split between creating social theory and conducting empirical research. The former focus emerged from an investment in continental philosophy, a line that ran from Weber and Durkheim through Marx to Foucault, Bourdieu, and Deleuze. Its main preoccupation involved conceptual thinking about the nature of reality and the constitution of research problems. Yet this work sat side by side with a rigorous empirical tradition. In the United States, for example, this empirical tradition began with the Chicago School of sociology, the work of Frederic Thrasher, Paul Cressey, and others. Over time, this tradition became more and more marked by modernist imperatives, as evidenced by the rise of grounded theory, ethnomethodology, and conversation analysis. Because it embodied a kind of abstract empiricism, conversation analysis, in particular, began to flourish in other disciplines as well, including communication studies and education, at a time when modernist imperatives ruled there, too.

This example suggests that it would be incorrect to assume that the disciplines of anthropology and sociology (or specific approaches or traditions within either of them) have not mutually informed each other for some time. Indeed, many recent studies have drawn together insights from anthropology and sociology within yet other disciplinary contexts. Good examples of this tendency are recent efforts to link ethnography (macroanalysis) and conversation analysis (microanalysis) in books such as Goodwin's (1990) *He-Said-She-Said: Talk as Social Organization Among Black Children* and Moermann's (1988) *Talking Culture: Ethnography and Conversation Analysis*. Both used fine-grained conversation analysis to understand how local social orders are developed and maintained. Both also used ethnographic analyses to situate findings from conversation analysis within and against understandings of the social, cultural, and historical contexts that partially constituted the possibilities of these local social orders in the first place. Importantly, the authors of these books are anthropologists who appropriate the tools of sociologists to work on transdisciplinary projects. For example, *He-Said-She-Said* deals with the nature and functions of peer interactions of urban children and is widely cited in education and even considered by many to be an educational study.

The tendency for social scientists to turn to models of literature and literary criticism at key moments in their disciplinary histories when threats of squeezing the "human" out of the "human sciences" are felt is yet another key aspect of disciplinary cross-pollination. As we will show in later chapters, scholars as diverse as Clifford Geertz, James Clifford, Ruth Behar, Norman Denzin, Mike Rose, Jonathan Kozol, Niko Besnier, Patti Lather, and Alison Lee, from disciplines as diverse as anthropology, sociology, linguistics, and education, all turned to literary studies in distinct ways and for distinct ends, and each wound up influencing contemporary qualitative inquiry in important ways. Influences associated with the "writing culture" movement and its fallout have been particularly powerful in this regard (see chapter 3). This movement brought questions of representation to the forefront of qualitative inquiry, giving rise to the development of a wide range of experimental forms of research writing, from poetry to drama to fiction to performance and beyond. These literary influences have indeed been felt across all qualitative traditions, and they have contributed in important ways to the emergence of qualitative inquiry as a legitimate and powerful force within the social sciences.

Beginning as a set of approaches largely developed within disciplinary boundaries, qualitative inquiry has indeed become a transdisciplinary metadiscourse, with national and international conferences, a wide range of journals, a steady stream of new books, and many book series. In fact, some publishing outlets now deal almost exclusively with books on qualitative inquiry. Perhaps the most important text here is the first edition of the *Handbook of Qualitative Research* (Denzin & Lincoln, 1994). In the introduction to the first edition of this book, the co-editors claimed, "Qualitative research is a field of inquiry in its own right. It crosscuts disciplines, fields, and subject matter. A complex, interconnected family of terms, concepts, and assumptions surround the term *qualitative research*" (p. 1). The collection was foundational in constituting the field. It brought together a wide range of scholars and social scientists from a diverse range of disciplines. It also provided a rubric for thinking through the history of qualitative research as a series of "moments," each of which could be found at play across a range of disciplines. The five moments identified by Denzin and Lincoln in the first edition of this volume were: first moment: the traditional period (1900–1950); second moment: the modernist phase (1950–1970); third moment: blurred genres (1970–1986); fourth moment: the crisis of representation (1986–); and finally, the fifth moment, the present, embodying the agendas of various "posts"—postmodernism, poststructuralism, postcolonialism. In the second edition of this volume, published in 2000, Denzin and Lincoln added two more moments. They call the sixth moment the "postexperimental" moment. It is driven by praxis concerns and involves connecting research and writing to the needs of a free and democratic society. The seventh moment is the "future," which they imagine will be increasingly motivated by concerns with local histories and struggles, ethics, politics, and praxis. They also suspect inquiry to be more performative, both in the field and in the ways in which research findings are communicated.

There have been many critiques of Denzin and Lincoln's history of qualitative inquiry. Raymond Morrow (2000), for example, criticized what he called the book's reductive split between "positivist" and "post-positivist" approaches. While admitting that the first edition is a helpful heuristic, Atkinson, Coffey, and Delamont (1999) argued that efforts to "tidy up" the field are problematic. They noted that "ethnographic research has always contained within it a variety of perspectives" (p. 467) and that there have been tensions between the aesthetic and the scientific throughout the history of the qualitative enterprise. Still others have argued that the book's "great chain of being" model elides much of the complexity that has characterized qualitative inquiry in all of its moments.

Such critiques are valid and worthy of our attention. However, two more things are worth our attention as well. First, Denzin and Lincoln (2000) included caveats throughout, acknowledging that they have offered up a smoothed-out and glossed-over history for heuristic purposes and that "the history of qualitative research is defined more by breaks and ruptures than by a clear, evolutionary, progressive movement from one stage to the next" (p. 1047). Second, and more important, the creation of this model (in spite of all its flaws) has been incredibly influential in constituting a field of inquiry with its own history and its own logics, outside of the histories and logics of any single discipline. Parenthetically, most significant social movements have been characterized by critical moments of overdetermination and essentialization, apparently because this is necessary to become visible in public and political arenas. Another way to view these critiques is that they have highlighted just how important and influential Denzin and Lincoln's model has been. Following Foucault, we might argue that the proliferation of critical commentary around this book only serves to underscore its central role in the constitution of a new and powerful discourse, the discourse of qualitative inquiry. As testimony to this claim, a second edition of *The Handbook of Qualitative Research* has been published, and the editors are in the process of producing a third.

The Handbook of Qualitative Research is just one marker of the proliferation and legitimation of qualitative inquiry as a distinct and important field. There are many other indices, such as the seven-volume *Ethnographer's Toolkit* (Schensul & LeCompte, 1999), another important attempt to promote a discourse about methods of inquiry that transcends disciplinary boundaries. Additionally, several new journals

have helped constitute this field. These include *Qualitative Inquiry,*
Ethnography, Qualitative Research Journal of Contemporary Ethnography,
and *International Journal of Qualitative Studies in Education.* The articles represented in these journals transcend disciplinary, racial, ethnic, gender, national, and paradigmatic boundaries. They range from
traditional ethnographies to theoretical treatises to various kinds of
experimental and performative texts. And they are written by scholars from across virtually all humanities and social science disciplines
including anthropology, sociology, psychology, social work, criminal
justice, business management, medicine, folklore, geography, history,
cultural studies, nursing, health studies, education, women's studies,
media studies, kinesiology, communication studies, literacy studies,
and English. Finally, despite or perhaps because of this tremendous
disciplinary diversity, all of these journals foreground the importance
of reflexivity and self-reflexivity with respect to locating specific research endeavors within epistemologies, theories, approaches to research, and research strategies. This is particularly important for the
ways in which these journals are partially responsible for constructing
the transdisciplinary metadiscourse of qualitative inquiry.

Rhetorical Orientations and Structure of the Book

Throughout this book, we move back and forth across more philosophical and more historical orientations for thinking about qualitative inquiry. We foreground key epistemological frameworks and
assumptions that have spawned and legitimated various modes of
qualitative inquiry and their concomitant research strategies. We also
show how these frameworks and assumptions have emerged, grown,
and changed within the cultural common sense of specific disciplinary contexts and of the human sciences research community generally
(as uneven and contentious as this community is). Whether adopting
primarily a philosophical or an historical orientation, we show how
key social and intellectual movements exerted powerful and pervasive effects on the epistemologies, theories, approaches to research,
and research strategies involved in various modes of qualitative inquiry. For us, mapping these social-intellectual processes involves
both troubling unpredictability and thrilling moments of insight.
What we mean by this will become clearer as we move forward.

    In the first major section of the book (chapters 1 and 2), we ad-
dress key philosophical concepts and traditions that underlie and

gave rise to various theories, approaches, and strategies of qualitative inquiry. Due largely to their focus on philosophical foundations, these chapters are organized paradigmatically (Bruner, 1986). In chapter 1, we map the interrelated levels of analysis that qualitative researchers must attend to simultaneously as they design and implement their studies. These include (a) epistemologies, (b) theories, (c) approaches or methodological frameworks, and (d) strategies and techniques for collecting and analyzing relevant information and artifacts. We also discuss some of the various ways in which the field of qualitative inquiry has been imagined and organized. In chapter 2, we offer what we believe to be the predominant "chronotopes" (see chapter 2, note 1) of inquiry that have informed and continue to inform qualitative inquiry across a broad range of disciplines, including language and literacy studies. Among other things, we demonstrate how all chronotopes engage with the Enlightenment project in different ways. We also show how each chronotope has been constituted historically as a unique assemblage of episteme/epistemology/theory/method and how each embodies a different set of assumptions about the world, knowledge, the human subject, language, and meaning.

In the next section of the book (chapters 3 and 4), we trace the histories of qualitative inquiry as they have emerged within anthropology and sociology—the two disciplinary spaces where the most and the most creative epistemological, theoretical, and pragmatic work has been conducted for the past century or so. In chapter 3, we demonstrate how anthropological approaches to inquiry developed through the integration of ideas and strategies from a broad range of disciplines including linguistics, anthropology, sociology, English literature, and even Germanic philology in highly specific and counterintuitive ways. We go on to discuss the Ethnography of Communication tradition in considerable detail. And we discuss the "remaking of anthropology" in the wake of postmodernism, poststructuralism, and postcolonialism. Throughout, we highlight continuities, breaks, and ruptures, and we note disciplinary paths taken and disciplinary paths that were avoided or foreclosed.

In chapter 4 we map the development of qualitative inquiry within sociology. We begin with a discussion of the structuralism of Émile Durkheim and the interpretivism of Max Weber, and then we show how the tension between these basic approaches has animated sociological discourse about inquiry ever since. Next, we discuss the development of more critical strands of sociological inquiry, rooted in

Marxist and neo-Marxist traditions. Finally, we address some of the ways in which postmodernism, poststructuralism, and postcolonialism have affected the nature and functions of sociological inquiry in recent decades. Throughout the chapter, we show how different theorists, different movements, and different traditions influenced each other while also competing for privileged places within sociologically oriented qualitative inquiry.

We conclude this book with a chapter composed of three distinct but related parts. In the first part, we revisit the idea that qualitative inquiry has become a transdisciplinary metadiscourse and discuss some of the consequences of this social fact. In the second part, we offer a set of annotations of key language and literacy studies conducted from within many of the different approaches to qualitative inquiry discussed in chapters 3 and 4. In the third part of the chapter, we argue that qualitative researchers can and should remain sensitive to the complex and uneven terrain of epistemologies, theories, approaches, and strategies that constitute the "blooming buzzing confusion" of qualitative inquiry while still adopting "postures" (Wolcott, 1992) that allow us all to get some work done. We theorize these postures in much the same way that Grossberg (1992) and Hall (1992) theorized theories. They are detours that help us ground our engagement with new empirical problems and allow that engagement to function as the ground for developing more adequate ways to study these problems. As Hall (1992) aptly noted, "the only [methods] worth having [are ones] that you have to fight off, not [ones] that you [use] with profound fluency" (p. 280). We imagine our task here, as throughout, to be about demystifying qualitative inquiry logics and practices for new researchers, helping them see their work as part of a complex and historically emergent field of inquiry.

CHAPTER 1

Into the Fray:
A Practiced and Practical Set of
Analytic Strata

L ike any mode of inquiry, qualitative inquiry is grounded in a set of philosophical and theoretical horizons or traditions. These horizons or traditions provide its assumptions, limit conditions, and tactical tools. The interpretive horizons or traditions within which qualitative research in the human sciences is embedded has been articulated by many different philosophers of science (e.g., Bernstein, 1983; Crotty, 1998; Packer & Addison, 1989; Taylor, 1979; Winch, 1963/1958). Although these and kindred scholars have described these horizons and traditions in slightly different ways, most have suggested that inquiry involves at least four dimensions or analytic strata: (a) *epistemologies*, (b) *theories*, (c) *approaches*, and (d) *strategies*. Most of the other books in this series outline specific approaches to qualitative research and their concomitant strategies. This book focuses more on epistemologies and theoretical frameworks. It is important, however, to unpack the meaning and relevance of these dimensions or analytic levels, as well as the relations between and among them, in this book. This latter task is particularly important because we argue that when designing and conducting research, one should work hard to develop principled alignments between and among epistemological positions, relevant theoretical frameworks, approaches to research, and strategies for collecting, analyzing, and interpreting data.

Epistemologies

Epistemologies are concerned with knowledge and how people come to have knowledge. Objectivism and constructionism are examples of epistemologies. In fact, they are probably the two "grand" epistemologies found in this book, as well as other books on the historical and philosophical foundations of social science inquiry. Objectivism posits an objective world that is inherently meaningful. Within an objectivist framework, quarks, trees, llamas, and sex all have meaning independent of their ascription by human beings and their cultural systems. When human beings render such objects/processes meaningful, objectivists argue that they have merely discovered inherent meaning. From this perspective, there are laws and truths that may be identified with precision and certainty. With the goal of discovering the essential nature of so called "primitive" cultures, much early ethnography operated according to the epistemological assumptions of objectivism.[1]

Constructionism poses a different view. Although constructionists agree on the existence of an objective world independent of our experience of it, they generally disagree that it has any inherent meaning. Instead, they argue that meaning is a function of our engagement with the world. Meaning is not discovered but is constituted or constructed in interaction with objective (but not inherently meaningful) reality. Among other things, this means that the meaning of reality is likely to be constructed differently as a function of the position or perspective taken by a culture, a social formation, or an individual person. Knowledge and meaning are always partial and perspectival (i.e., only known from some but not all perspectives). Thus there are a variety of meanings that might be ascribed to any object or process, all of which may be both reasonable and functional given the perspective from which they are viewed or known.

It should be apparent by now that much qualitative research is conducted against the backdrop of a constructionist epistemology. However, this particular articulation was not always self-evident. The specter of objectivism (and its theoretical counterpart, positivism) exerted a bridling effect on efforts within the social sciences to make the "interpretive turn," as the advent of qualitative approaches to research is sometimes called. One serious consequence of this effect was that for almost a century, interpretivists experienced a kind of legitimacy crisis and were pressured to justify their research as equally "objective" and "rigorous" as their more positivistic counterparts. It has only been in the last couple of decades that qualitative approaches to social science research rooted in constructionist epistemologies have gained scientific legitimacy, and the struggle for legitimacy continues in many domains, including language and literacy studies. In this regard, it was not until the late 1980s and early 1990s that qualitative studies of language and literacy began to appear in significant numbers in the major journals of the field. And even then, it was more common to see multimethod studies in which qualitative components played secondary roles.

Theories

Within the social sciences, theories constitute abstract sets of assumptions and assertions used to interpret and sometimes explain psychological, social, cultural, and historical processes and formations. Theories, however, are neither value-free nor universal. As Grossberg (1992) noted, their value is largely functional and heuristic. Theories are "detours" that help us ground our engagement with new problems and allow that engagement to function as a substrate for generating more theory. Theories are thus practices in two senses. First, they are quasi-formal conceptual tools-in-action. Rosenblatt's (1983) transactional theory of reading and Bourdieu's (1990) theory of social practice are examples of such tools. Second, theories are processes of trying out ways of making sense of phenomena of interest. They involve pragmatic commitments. Even though we know they are tentative, partial, and vulnerable to criticism, we need to posit theories with some authority to keep moving down the road of understanding.

Theories can occur at various levels of abstraction, with the most abstract ones blurring into the level of epistemologies. *Positivism* and *interpretivism* are two highly abstract social theories. Positivism is a theoretical perspective that has grounded philosophy and social theory at least since the Enlightenment. It was popularized by the work of Auguste Comte in the early 19th century. Since then, it has been appropriated, adapted, and refined by many philosophers and theorists including those affiliated with the Vienna Circle, various logical positivists such as Carl Hempel and Bertrand Russell, and postpositivists including Karl Popper and Thomas Kuhn. Indeed, there are almost as many variants of positivism as there are positivists. Although it is both unnecessary and beyond the scope of this chapter to outline all the variants of positivism and their differences, it will help here to outline the features of this theoretical orientation that are widely shared. Among other things, positivism is thoroughly entrenched in objectivism. Positivists assume a meaningful reality that is independent of experience. They argue that this reality can only be known through empirical observation. The nature of reality is discovered through induction, or the process of generating rules and laws from observed regularities. The "truthfulness" of these rules and laws is assured by what is called "a logic of verification." Repeated instances of the same outcome *verify* the universal truthfulness of the rule that describes or explains it. For example, if, as Galileo did, we drop hundreds of objects differing in mass from the Leaning Tower of Pisa and we find that they all reach the same final velocity, we have verified the fact that falling bodies achieve a maximum velocity independent of their weight. This, of course, contradicts Aristotle's law that falling bodies attain velocities proportional to their weight. Hmmm, if one set of laws that are justified according to a logic of verification are later replaced by a different set of laws that are also justified by the same logic, we would seem to have an epistemological problem on our hands.

As it turns out, such contradictions forced philosophers of science at the advent of the 20th century (e.g., Popper, 1959; Kuhn, 1970) to rethink this logic. What resulted was what is now commonly known as postpositivism. Although also an overly simplistic rendering, postpositivism is similar to positivism except for two key aspects. First, a logic of verification is replaced with a logic of falsification. Second, the process of *induction* is replaced by the process of hypothetico-deduction. But what are these? The problem with a logic of verification is that a single counterexample undermines it. The fact that water has always boiled at 100°C under certain conditions provides no logical verification that it will, with absolute certainty, boil at 100°C under the same conditions tomorrow. Positing that it will is an assumption, not an empirically proven fact. In the wake of this devastating news, Karl Popper proposed a solution, falsificationism, which holds that scientists should abandon attempts to verify theories and instead try vigorously to falsify them—a kind of theoretical survival of the fittest. A theory remains viable until it is falsified.

With this new logic of justification came a new process of conducting science. Hypothetico-deduction replaced induction as the predominant scientific method in the social sciences (and some natural sciences as well). According to this method, theories are proposed hypothetically, propositions are deduced from these theories, and these propositions are tested with every attempt to falsify them. Instead of inductively generating laws, science is a matter of "conjectures and refutations," the title of one of Popper's books on the philosophy of science. Despite these adjustments, postpositivism is every bit as objectivist and traditionally empirical as its predecessor, positivism. This would not be problematic if we could someday know with certainty that some form of the correspondence theory of truth—whether arrived at through verification or falsification—would hold up forever, but of course we cannot. Therefore, positivism and postpositivism are extremely vulnerable to criticism, and even bankruptcy.

Interpretivism is a yet more radical response to the internal inconsistencies of positivism. Like the term *positivism*, the term *interpretivism* refers to an assemblage of theoretical variants that guide approaches to qualitative research. Although each variant shares family resemblances with the others, each also embodies some unique methods and practices. Nevertheless, most approaches operate within a constructionist epistemology rather than an objectivist epistemology.

Following Alasuutari (1995), a useful way into thinking about qualitative inquiry is to define it by what it is not. Qualitative inquiry does *not* isolate single variables to test their effects using control groups versus experimental groups. It does *not* attempt to generate causal laws that are presumed timeless and universal. Instead, qualitative inquiry attempts to understand, interpret, and explain complex and highly contextualized social phenomena such as classroom cultures, avid readers, or peer group development and maintenance. In this regard, it tends to be motivated by "how" and "why" questions as much as, if not more than, "what" questions. Qualitative research may be more descriptive or more explanatory, but it always aims to demonstrate the complexity, texture, and nuance involved in how individuals and groups experience themselves and their worlds. Finally, qualitative research focuses on both the meanings and the practices involved in such experiencing.

Approaches

Approaches are systematic yet dynamic (i.e., changeable and changing) social scientific formations that provide loosely defined structures for conceiving, designing, and carrying out research projects. We use the term "approaches" rather than the more commonly used term, "methods," strategically here. Like "theories," in the popular imagination "methods" often falsely connote rigid templates of sets of techniques for the proper conduct of research. By using the term "approaches" we want to foreground the "practice" dimension of engaging in research. In contrast, Crotty (1998) used the term "methodology" and Wolcott (1992) used the term "illustrative types" to refer to what we call approaches.

Approaches to research involve specific and partially unique sets of guiding assumptions, strategies, and techniques that are used as analytic resources, as well as the ongoing activity of trying things out in the field and at the desk. Within a given approach, we use and adapt various techniques and strategies; we borrow and combine these techniques and strategies; we work with them; and we rework them. Like theories, approaches are more heuristic than real, and their primary function is to move us along in our attempts to understand the problems that interest us.

Ethnography, life history research, and grounded theory research are fairly well known examples of approaches to social scientific inquiry. We might choose an ethnographic approach if we are interested in mapping the systems of meaning and practice that constitute a particular social formation such as a classroom, a church, or a community center. We might choose a life history approach if we want to understand the socialization histories that contributed to women's marginalization in scientific pursuits. We might choose a grounded theory approach if we want to discover the key categories and relations among categories that seem to constitute and help explain a complex human activity such as how conflict emerges and is resolved in some workplace settings.

Strategies

Research strategies (or "methods" in Crotty's [1998] lexicon and "techniques" in Wolcott's [1992] vocabulary) are the specific practices and procedures that researchers deploy to collect and analyze data and to report their findings. Most scholars agree that qualitative research involves three basic kinds of data: observational data, interview data, and archival data. There are multiple strategies for collecting and analyzing these kinds of data both individually and collectively. Whether and how much to conduct interviews, to engage in participant observation, to videotape interactions, or to enact some combination of these and other data collection strategies are questions researchers must constantly ask themselves.

Once data are collected, there are a variety of analysis strategies that may be employed to interpret the data or to figure out what the data "mean." To illustrate the nature and function of different interpretive analytics, we discuss two such sets of strategies very briefly here—inductive analysis and discourse analysis. In chapter 4, we offer more comprehensive discussions of these strategies. In general, inductive analysis (e.g., Bogdan & Biklen, 1992; Glaser & Strauss, 1967; Merriam, 2001) involves analyzing multiple forms of data (e.g., texts, observations, interviews) to discover recurrent themes and thematic relations. Most forms of inductive analysis involve multiple and interrelated phases of coding or categorizing, along with various forms of preliminary analysis and cross-checking. Coding and analyzing data begin almost as soon as data collection begins, and the process continues throughout the final write-up.

Whereas inductive analysis is used to discover and map recurrent "macro" patterns that characterize writing practices, contexts, and politics, discourse analysis is used to examine the "micro" patterns embodied in specific verbal-visual interactions (usually represented in transcripts) to understand both the forms and functions of these interactions and the ways in which they both index and sustain recurrent "macro" patterns. Thus, discourse analysis often yields powerful exemplars of the various "macro" patterns found in any study. Conversely, these "macro" patterns can be used to understand and explain the "micro" patterns found within and across individual interactions.

There are many kinds of discourse analysis, ranging from conversational analysis (e.g., Atkinson & Heritage, 1984) to narrative analysis (e.g., Cortazzi, 1993; Wortham, 2001) to critical discourse analysis (e.g., Fairclough, 1989, 1992). Many researchers mix and match techniques and procedures from these different kinds of analysis, and indeed, the foregoing description will reflect this eclecticism. As we mentioned, a primary goal of discourse analysis is to show how specific verbal-visual actions and interactions both index and sustain general and durable patterns of action and interaction common to a given social formation.

In many research studies, some form of inductive analysis is often combined with some form of discourse analysis. Combining these two kinds of analysis strategies often allows researchers to develop particularly powerful insights and arguments about the nature of the social phenomena they are studying. In this regard, discourse analysis is especially useful for critically examining the often opaque relations between and among categories generated through inductive analysis. Good inductive analyses are enormously useful for conducting systematic and compelling accounts of the durable discursive and social practices that influence the emergence of specific texts and interactions.

With respect to reporting practices, findings and interpretations generated from each type of analysis are usually used to amplify, support, and complement each other. In most interpretive accounts of most social-material phenomena, multiple analyses and resulting interpretations are usually integrated more or less seamlessly into coherent, compelling, well argued, and adequately supported accounts.

Indeterminacy and Positioning in Qualitative Inquiry

We conclude this chapter with some thoughts about the practical problem of locating oneself within the complex, indeterminate landscape of qualitative inquiry and actually conducting research. We think that the way we have described and organized the analytic strata of inquiry is useful in this regard. It has heuristic power, largely because it is neither too indeterminate nor too overdetermined. It is useful for negotiating a complex array of ambiguous and polysemous terms—each defined in different ways by different theorists and in different ways by the same theorists at different times. Whether or not you like our terms or their organization, we hope you appreciate our efforts to be consistent in the ways we use them. And we urge you not to take them at face value but as tools for your own thinking and practice.

Designing and conducting a qualitative research study is (or at least should be) a strategic matter. In this regard, researchers seem to have little trouble choosing their epistemologies and "grand" or high-level theories. For example, many qualitative researchers of language and literacy position themselves within the epistemological framework of constructionism and the grand social theory of interpretivism. However, they often struggle more in choosing among relevant but less grand theories that operate a bit closer to the ground. Vygotsky's learning theory and Foucault's theory of power/knowledge are examples of such theories. We might frame a study using the former if we are interested in the productive aspects of socialization practices (e.g., Ochs, 1988). We might choose the latter if we are more interested in the reproductive (and perhaps oppressive) aspects of such practices (e.g., Luke, 1992).

Negotiating the relative commensurability between and among epistemologies, theories, approaches, and strategies is another issue researchers must address. This process is complicated by the fact that as we move from epistemologies to theories to approaches to strategies, the levels themselves seem to become more internally heterogeneous. Additionally, the sphere of influence of more abstract levels on less abstract levels becomes both wider and less predictable as we move from epistemologies to strategies. For example, while it is difficult to imagine a positivism not rooted in objectivism, it is not so difficult to imagine an ethnography framed within different interpretive theories or critical social theories.

Unfortunately, positioning oneself as a researcher is further complicated by a lack of strategic clarity in many texts about qualitative inquiry. These texts often blur the boundaries between and among epistemologies, theories, approaches, and strategies. This often results in claims and arguments that we find confusing. It is not uncommon, for example, to find social constructionism, symbolic interactionism, and ethnography all discussed as approaches to research. A more careful treatment of these terms, we believe, would render social constructionism as an epistemological framework that underlies many theoretical perspectives. It would render symbolic interactionism as a theoretical perspective or philosophical school that informs a range of approaches. And it would render ethnography as a research approach or methodology. As we see it, then, the task of the social science researcher is to determine the categorical status of terms such as social constructionism, symbolic interactionism, and ethnography and then to determine whether and how they might be constitutively related both historically and in practice. An example might help here. Grounded theory is one of the most widely used approaches to qualitative research in a variety of disciplines. By and large, grounded theory is rooted in a complex interweaving of constructs from the theoretical perspectives of postpositivism, hermeneutics, symbolic interactionism, and phenomenology. Its research strategies include participant observation, interviewing, the collection of archival data, descriptive statistical analyses, thematic analyses, and so on. Yet many of these methods are also used within other approaches such as ethnography, case study research, and life history research.

Another problem facing beginning researchers is the distinction between *quantitative* and *qualitative* research. Battles around this distinction became known as the "paradigm wars," and articles about these wars filled the pages of *Educational Researcher* and other respectable journals during the 1980s. We find the inclusion of the word *para-*

digm in this term ironic. A distinction between paradigms would seem to operate somewhere between the stratum of epistemology or theory, yet these "wars" were played out largely at the level of strategies, and complex differences in theoretical assumptions and forms of argument were often reduced to whether data were constituted by "numbers" or "stories." To us, constructing the difference between positivist and interpretivist perspectives at the level of research strategies does not hold up under close examination. We find it more productive to re-define the quantitative-qualitative distinction at the level of grand theory: positivist approaches and interpretive approaches.

Qualitative researchers often quantify social action as part of their interpretive work, and the results of statistical analyses require in-terpretation. The work of sociologist Pierre Bourdieu provides a nice example of the productive integration of qualitative and quantitative analysis. Working within a basically interpretive framework, Bourdieu has conducted some of the most rigorous research on the roles of so-cial class and the institution of education on social reproduction. In a famous series of studies, for example, he demonstrated how taste (preferred foods, leisure activities, cultural artifacts, etc.) is systemati-cally related to class position, arguing that this constitutive relation was fundamental to social reproduction. To construct his systematic and highly contextualized interpretations of this relationship, he used surveys and statistics as well as interviews, observations, and archival material. Despite his uses of quantification and statistical analysis, his reports constitute detailed narrative accounts about how these rela-tions are constituted, what effects they have, and why they might be so powerful, pervasive, and durable in the real lives of real people.

Another problem beginning researchers are likely to face is related to the overuse and misuse of the term *ethnography*. In other words, all kinds of qualitative approaches to inquiry are often referred to as eth-nographies. Although there is a grain of truth in this overdetermina-tion in the sense that many qualitative researchers use ethnographic strategies, this is far from the whole story. Just as qualitative research is informed by a wide array of theories, it is also conducted from within a wide range of approaches. To complicate things even more, many studies have been designed using a combination of approach-es. Finally, it is often difficult to separate the theoretical frameworks from the approaches used in particular studies because theories and approaches often develop historically in mutually constitutive ways. Nevertheless, most qualitative approaches share several common characteristics. They include the use of nonquantifiable data; they are highly contextualized and provide richly textured accounts of complex social phenomena; they deploy narrative rhetorical techniques to make their arguments; and they are more interested in verisimilitude, trustworthiness, and praxis than validity and generalizability. We unpack these characteristics in different ways throughout the book.

Finally, in relation to our claim that qualitative approaches to research have often been mapped in both careless and overdetermined ways, we want to mention that we also have problems with how many scholars use the terms *method* and *methodology*. It simply is not useful to indiscriminately refer to all sorts of things, including what we have called overarching theories that ground research (e.g., interpretivism, positivism), approaches to conducting research (e.g., ethnographic, life history), and specific research strategies (e.g., interviewing, observation), as methods or methodologies. If all of these things are methods or methodologies, we are at a loss to define in any exact or useful way what a method or a methodology is. We are not exactly sure what to do with these terms for the moment except perhaps to urge that they be used cautiously and defined carefully each time they are used. So in this book we have tried to avoid the terms *methods* and *methodologies* and to be very clear about what we mean by them when we have used them.

In the wake of all these difficulties, what practical advice do we have to offer researchers relatively new to the enterprise of qualitative inquiry? The answer is quite simple. Approach the enterprise with both wonder and skepticism. Appreciate the ways that others (including us) have attempted to understand and map the enterprise. Maintain a critical eye toward this work and a reflexive stance toward your own. Take a pragmatic stance toward inquiry, asking yourself not whether the epistemologies, theories, approaches, and strategies you read about are true but whether they might be useful for the kinds of research questions that interest you and the kind of work you want to do. Enter some of the many ongoing conversations and debates about aspects of inquiry still being worked on/out.

CHAPTER 2

Predominant Chronotopes of Qualitative Inquiry

In this chapter, we offer an account of what we see to be the prevalent *chronotopes* of inquiry that ground and inform most qualitative research. Our task in this regard is akin to the one undertaken by Birdwhistell (1970) in response to his students' queries about whether Margaret Mead and Gregory Bateson (both anthropologists) had a methodology. These queries led him to argue that theory-method complexes, which he termed "logics-of-inquiry," guide all research. Our task is also similar to Strike's (1974) construct of "expressive potential." Strike argued that all research endeavors are governed by an expressive potential that delimits the objects worthy of investigation, the research questions that may be asked, the units of analysis that are relevant, the analyses that may be conducted, the claims that may be made about the objects of investigation, and the forms of explanation that may be invoked.

Why Chronotopes?

Although similar to "logics-of-inquiry" or "expressive potentials," the construct of chronotopes[1] of inquiry also extends these constructs in important ways. To the best of our knowledge, Bakhtin (1981) borrowed the term *chronotope*, which literally means "time-space," from Einstein and applied it to the study of language and literature. For Bakhtin, chronotopes do not simply link particular times and spaces with specific cultural events. Instead, they delineate or construct sedimentations of concrete, motivated social situations or figured worlds (Holland, Lachiotte, Skinner, & Cain, 1998) replete with typified plots, themes, agents, forms of agency, scenes, objects, affective dispositions, kinds of intentionality, ideologies, value orientations, and so on. In this regard, chronotopes are like "x-rays of the forces at work in the culture system from which they spring" (Bakhtin, 1981, pp. 425–426). Chronotopes are normalizing frames that render the world as "just the way things are" by celebrating the prosaic regularities that make any given world, day after day, recognizable and predictable for the people who live in it (Morson & Emerson, 1990, p. 87). They connote specific ways to understand context and the actions, agents, events, and practices that constitute those contexts. Bakhtin was clear about the fact that chronotopes are not *a priori* structures but durable structuring structures (e.g., Bourdieu, 1990; Giddens, 1979) constituted within concrete histories of human activity across time and space. Among the ways in which he illustrated this idea was to show how the public square in ancient Greece or the family at the height of the Roman Empire were constitutively related to specific modes of rhetorical and literary activity common to those time-spaces.

Chronotopes are a lot like what cultural studies scholars (e.g., Grossberg, 1992; Hall, 1992; Hebdige, 1979; Willis, 1977) refer to as *cultural formations*—historically formed/informed and socially distributed modes of engagement with particular sets of practices for particular reasons. Chronotopes describe the lines of force that locate, distribute, and connect specific sets of practices, effects, goals, and groups of actors. Such articulations not only involve selections and configurations from among the available practices, but also a distribution of the chronotopes themselves within and across social time and space. To understand and describe a chronotope thus requires a reconstruction of its context—the dispersed yet structured field of objects, practices, agents, and so on by which the specific articulation reproduces itself across time and space. Chronotopic assertions are thus "stratagems" of genealogy. All chronotopes have their own "common cultural sense," "sensibilities," "tastes," "logics," and so on. These dimensions of being become embodied in the people who work within a chronotope such that they become part of the chronotope itself. What seems natural, proper, and obvious to individuals becomes aligned with what is the "common cultural sense" within the chronotope. For our purposes, then, *chronotopes of qualitative inquiry index durable historical realities that constitute what is common, natural, and expected by collectives of social scientists who conduct particular kinds of qualitative research.*

We have chosen chronotopes as the organizing trope of this chapter for a variety of reasons. First, we want to emphasize the historical/

institutional dimensions of the ~~foundational~~[2] schemes we propose. Second, we want to make clear that these schemes become internalized by researchers who then operate with them in tacit and highly embodied ways. Finally, we want to emphasize the fact that through these embodied practices, individual researchers affect and change the chronotopes themselves. Additionally, we have chosen to use the construct of the chronotope because it suggests structuring tendencies that function in transdisciplinary ways rather than within specific disciplines of domains of practice.[3]

Although other scholars might argue for slightly fewer or slightly more, we focus on four primary chronotopes of inquiry currently operating in powerful and pervasive ways within the contemporary scene of educational research, especially in relation to literacy studies. We settled on the following "names" for the chronotopes that we believe most commonly ground qualitative inquiry within education and literacy studies:

1. Objectivism and Representation
2. Reading and Interpretation
3. Skepticism, Conscientization, and Praxis
4. Power/Knowledge and Defamiliarization

All four chronotopes engage with the Enlightenment project mentioned in chapter 1 but in different ways—some more resonantly and some more dissonantly. Each chronotope embodies a different set of assumptions about the world, knowledge, the human subject, language, and meaning. Each also embodies or indexes a particular set of approaches/methods for framing and conducting research. Finally, in different ways and to different degrees, each has exerted considerable power in sustaining and reproducing particular logics of inquiry within our field and within the larger world of the social sciences. We propose this loosely coupled taxonomy simply as a heuristic for understanding some of the different ways in which qualitative inquiry is typically framed and how different frameworks predispose researchers to embrace different epistemologies, theories, approaches, and strategies.

In constructing a taxonomy of chronotopes, we admit to living a paradox—attempting to impose order on a dynamic, unstable, and unfixable theoretical space. With this paradox in mind, we offer the taxonomy less as a definitive account and more as a useful heuristic for understanding the discursively and materially constructed foundations of qualitative inquiry at a time when knowledge itself is a highly contested term. As we outline the elements of our taxonomy, we discuss how each chronotope theorizes perennial questions within the history of philosophy such as subjectivity, rationality, language, knowledge, and truth. Also important here is the fact that we do not define chronotopes by mutually exclusive and exhaustive sets of properties as in Aristotelian category systems. Instead, chronotopes are more like prototypic categories (e.g., Rosch, 1978). The boundaries between and among them are fluid rather than fixed. Each chronotope overlaps, leaks into, or slides over some others.

Simply looking at how much space we devote to each chronotope suggests that we privilege some over others. In some ways this is true. We believe that *Chronotopes II, III,* and *IV* are more commensurate with the goals of qualitative inquiry with its roots in the "interpretive turn" (e.g., Taylor, 1979) and in an historical epoch when even natural scientists question the limits of objectivity and acknowledge the interpretive dimensions of their work (e.g., Latour & Woolgar, 1986). We also believe that *Chronotopes III* and *IV* have the most purchase for conducting useful and effective research given the social, cultural, and political exigencies of "new times" (Hall, 1996).

Our typology also suggests something of a "great chain of being" (Lovejoy, 1970), with each chronotope we describe being more "advanced" than those that came before. In some ways this is true, too. However, although *Chronotopes I, II, III,* and *IV* do follow each other historically and although we do admit some "great chain of being" bias, there are other reasons why we attend more to some chronotopes and less to others. For example, the basic constructs and principles that make up earlier chronotopes are likely to be much more familiar and understandable to readers than the constructs and principles that make up later ones. Additionally, the basic *worldviews* embodied in the earlier chronotopes are likely to be more comfortable and less counterintuitive to readers than the worldviews embodied in the later ones.

While acknowledging our biases and intellectual preferences, we also want to argue that each chronotope is uniquely valuable as an epistemological "location" for conducting certain kinds of research. Also important to note here is that certain kinds of approaches to research seem to be (or could easily be) located in more than one chronotope, often in complex and contradictory ways. So, for example, it is possible to have more objectivist (e.g., Heath, 1983) and less objectivist (e.g., Abu-Lughod, 1993) ethnographies, each located within different chronotopic spaces.

Figure 1 previews discussions of our four chronotopes. As we unpack the figure, we devote increasingly more space to each chronotope we describe.

Figure 1. Predominant Chronotopes of Qualitative Inquiry

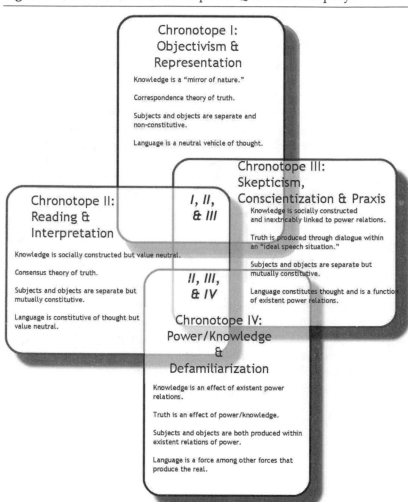

Chronotope I: Objectivism and Representation

This chronotope is the one most of us are familiar with through our exposure to the "scientific method" in school. It is predicated on the idea that "knowledge is a mirror of nature" (Rorty, 1979) and on a concomitant "correspondence theory of truth" and a "logic of verification." Conceiving knowledge as a mirror of nature presupposes an objective world that preexists and is separate from our knowledge of it. This claim poses no problem for most philosophers of science. However, it also presupposes the possibility of unmediated access to that world or the ability to know the world "in itself" rather than "for us." Neither the idea that knowledge is partial and perspectival nor that the activity of the scientist influences his or her findings (the Heisenberg Principle) has a place here. The theory of truth that best fits with this view of knowledge is a "correspondence theory of truth," which posits the possibility of directly and unproblematically mapping symbolic representations onto the facts in the world in a one-to-one fashion. With this theory of truth comes a "logic of verification," or the faith in the ability to verify knowledge through consistency across observations or the replication of experimental findings.

Approaches driven by a correspondence theory of truth derive from Descartes' dualism of mind and body. This dualism posits the individual human subject as radically separate from the external world and thus able to know this world "objectively" through the rational and/or technical-instrumental separation of subject and object. This separation is achieved in one of two ways. For rationalists or pure theorists, it is achieved through the systematic application of reason to achieve unmediated access to formal principles or the formal logic that makes possible the observables of the world. For empiricists, it is achieved through controlled observation and experimentation with the goal of "finding" interpretation-free brute facts.

According to the principles of *Chronotope I*, language is conceived as a neutral medium for accurately *representing* observed relations in the external world. It has neither constitutive capacity nor political valence, neither illocutionary force nor perlocutionary force (e.g., Searle, 1969). In other words, acts of language use do not embody and accomplish their speaker's or writer's intentions (e.g., apology, argument, accusation). Nor do they produce effects on their audiences (e.g., convincing, irritating, offending). They are unmediated, uninterested transmissions of fact.

Illustration from Research. A considerable amount of the qualitative research that is conducted in the field of language and literacy fits comfortably within the chronotope of objectivism and representation. E. D. Hirsch's (1987) work on cultural literacy is one example.[4] Within a cultural literacy framework, it is assumed that there is a neutral canon of key cultural knowledge that all students should know. It is also assumed that this body of knowledge exists outside of the individual subject and can be learned, usually through direct instruction and study. This neutral body of knowledge is transmitted to individual subjects through the neutral medium of Standard English. Finally, Hirsch asserts that if students lack a particular and prescribed set of cultural knowledge, then they will be unable to read and write adequately or function productively in society. The cultural knowledge that Hirsch has in mind is presumed to be "common culture" and not elite culture, even though it derives primarily from canonical works within a white, European-American, middle- to upper-class, heterosexist tradition.

Summary and Implications for Research Practice. As this exemplar suggests, the chronotope of objectivism and representation has several consequences for conducting research. Knowledge is regarded as entirely separate from power relations or any other dimensions of context. A radical separation of subject and object is assumed. Language and literacy practices are assumed to be neutral vehicles for representing equally neutral facts.[5] The real world and talking or writing about the real world are held radically separate. The idea that language might be able to shape or constitute thought, practice, or the circulation of power is eclipsed. Such a construal renders language and literacy practices as little more than conduits or vehicles for preexistent thoughts or conditions, and it occludes the idea that such practices have ontological substance and constitutive power themselves. Questions about whether our relations with and within the world are at least partially constituted by language and literacy practices become unimportant. Little, if any, conceptual room is allocated for political praxis or social change through language and literacy practices because fact and value are believed to be independent of each other. Instead, language and literacy practices are evaluated according to their relative *effectiveness* in representing *a priori* cognitive or communicative entities or events. Positing effectiveness as a primary (or sole) evaluative criterion galvanizes the tendency to view language and literacy as little more than simple conduits for communicating established perspectives or existing sets of conditions, and it eclipses processes of imagining the constitutive roles that these practices might play in the construction of knowledges, identities, and fields of social practice.

Accepting the separation of subject and object or language and world as "given" or "natural" positions the field of language and literacy studies as a second-order field of inquiry that is *de facto* subservient to more legitimate fields and dependent on their theories and methods for its existence. It is not surprising, then, that many of the constructs and methods deployed within research on language and literacy that is conducted within the chronotope of objectivism and representation derive from other disciplines such as psychology (e.g., schema, motivation), sociology (e.g., symbolic interactionism, conversation analysis), anthropology (e.g., speech event, participation-observation) or literary studies (e.g., reader response, genre studies). By drawing heavily on conceptual frameworks developed in other fields (especially psychology), research agendas often focus not on actual language and literacy practices but on internal or hidden *variables* such as readers' motivations (e.g., Turner, 1995) or writers' intentions (e.g., Flower & Hayes, 1981). When language and literacy research is located within the chronotope of objectivism and representation, one wonders exactly what language and literacy practices are involved and where they can be found. Are the reasons for practices always to be found outside of the practices themselves—in some hidden or deep structures or an Oz behind the curtain? Is nothing important evident in the surface of things? As we move through the discussions of all four chronotopes, we will show how actual, observable practices have become increasingly important as legitimate resources for explaining the nature and functions of language and literacy activities. And their increasing legitimation as both data and interpretive/explanatory resources has presented serious challenges to canonical ways of thinking about qualitative research practice.

Chronotope II: Reading and Interpretation

Not all approaches to research conducted within a modernist framework adhere to positivist epistemologies and their attendant assumptions. One framework that is modernist but not positivist is what we call *Chronotope II: Reading and Interpretation*. Grounded in social constructionist epistemologies, this chronotope is not predicated on a complete rejection of Enlightenment perspectives on knowledge, rationality, and truth, but it does rearticulate these perspectives to render knowledge, truth, and rationality as relative (or perspectival) rather than absolute. Such a move rescues these constructs from the hegemonic clutches of scientism and instrumental reasoning without jettisoning these perspectives altogether. Knowledge, reason, and truth are no longer conceived as the representational mirroring (through language and other semiotic media) of an already existing world. Instead, knowledge, reason, and truth are believed to be constructed through the symbolic acts of human beings in relation to the world and to others (e.g., Heidegger, 1962; Rorty, 1979). Concomitantly, science is no longer about verification within a correspondence theory of truth but about human interaction, communication, dialogue, and reasoned argument.

Modernism, then, embraces not only scientistic modes of reason grounded in objectivist epistemologies but also modes of reason that are linguistically (or semiotically) mediated and grounded in the experience of "being-in-the-world."[6] As we noted earlier, chronotopes are fluid, leaky, and flexible, and it is possible to have both objectivist-modernist articulations as well as interpretive-modernist ones. From this perspective, the existence of a real world external to human subjects is assumed, but faith in the timeless, universal nature of the world-knowledge relation and thus the possibility of generating representations that map that world in absolute or foundational terms is rejected. This shift from "brute facts" to semiotically mediated facts is far from trivial. Among other things, it marks the need to replace a correspondence theory of truth with a consensus theory of truth, which implies a human discourse community as the arbiter of knowledge and truth claims. Gadamer's (1968) work is instructive here. Gadamer argued that truth does not emerge through the application of technical tools or methods but within and through embodied engagement within a "horizon" of experience within a human community. He went even further to claim that truth will always elude capture by technical methods because knowledge is always semiotically and dialogically constructed. Truth is never an act of reproduction but always an act of production within the limited horizon of a community's texts and meanings. Because knowledge (and thus truth) always emerge out of the embodied, rich, and messy process of being-in-the-world, it is always perspectival and conditional.

Within the chronotope of reading and interpretation, the subject-object dualism of the Enlightenment project is also assumed, but subject and object are placed in dialogic tension. This tension is a hallmark of philosophical hermeneutics, which is the ~~foundation~~ upon which the chronotope of reading and interpretation was built. The term *hermeneu-*

tics derives from the Greek word *hermeneuein* with its obvious linkages to Hermes, the fleet-footed messenger of the gods. This derivation would suggest, then, that the origins of the chronotope of reading and interpretation lie in early Greek thought. Most philosophers of science and social theorists, however, would place the beginnings of the chronotope of reading and interpretation in 19th century German philosophy, especially the work of Schleiermacher and Dilthey. Although the term *verstehen* is often used as a generic term for interpretive social science (see our discussions of Weber and Durkheim in chapter 4), Dilthey (1976) has been credited with developing a specific *verstehen* approach to understanding. This approach basically refers to the process of understanding from another subject's point of view. The *verstehen approach*, according to Dilthey, is achieved through the psychological reenactment or imaginative reconstruction of the experiences of others. In other words, it is intersubjectivity achieved through empathy. The extreme psychologism of Dilthey's position has been challenged and tempered by other philosophers including Husserl, Heidegger, and Gadamer. Most contemporary uses of the term *hermeneutics* refer to the general process of coming to understand a phenomenon of interest (e.g., text, experience, social activity) or constructing an interpretation of such a phenomenon without placing such a heavy burden on intersubjectivity through empathy. Instead, hermeneutic or interpretive inquiries are predicated on understanding meanings and practices in relation to the situations in which they occur. Such modes of inquiry draw upon the notion of the "hermeneutic circle" as a unique and powerful strategy for understanding and knowledge-building. Using this strategy, understanding the "part" (a text, an act, a person) always involves also understanding the whole (the context, the activity setting, the life history) and vice versa.

Heavily influenced by this notion of the hermeneutic circle, qualitative inquiry conducted within the chronotope of reading and interpretation does not aim to generate foundational knowledge claims. Instead, it aims to refine and deepen our sense of what it means to understand other people and their social practices (including language and literacy practices) within relevant contexts of interaction and communication. Put in philosophical terms, these forms of inquiry link the Enlightenment or modernist project of discovering knowledge with a genuine interest in understanding and enriching the "life worlds" (Habermas, 1987) or "lived experience" of others (i.e., our research participants). Researchers operating within a chronotope of reading and interpretation espouse a linguistically mediated view of existence and knowledge wherein both are constituted (and not just represented) in and through human language practices. They study language practices such as conversation, storytelling, disciplinary writing, and the like in order to reveal and understand the contexts and ontologies that they index.

Although the historical roots of the chronotope of reading and interpretation may be traced to 19th-century German philosophy, it has grown exponentially during the past two decades. Interestingly, and a bit ironically, this trend was not particularly visible in the major language and literacy journals until just a few years ago, even though it has been quite visible in journals from allied disciplines (e.g., *Anthropology and Education Quarterly, International Journal of Qualitative Studies in Education*). It has also been quite visible for some time within dissertations, presentations at professional literacy conferences, and books. The fact that research conducted within the chronotope of reading and interpretation was resisted in our mainstream journals and had to be smuggled into our field through less mainstream venues is testimony to the powerful, pervasive, and long-lasting grip that the chronotope of objectivism and representation has had and still has on qualitative inquiry in our field. Nevertheless, the chronotope of reading and interpretation has become a powerful force in research on language and literacy.

Illustration from Research. Some of the earliest and most durable instances of literacy research representing this force grew out of the Ethnography of Communication (EOC) tradition (see chapter 3), with its focus on the relations among language, community, and identity. Shirley Brice Heath's (1983) now classic *Ways with Words*[7] is one of the best exemplars of this tradition.

In outlining the research strategies she used to conduct the research for her book, Heath (1982) virtually recreated earlier descriptions of the hermeneutic circle, arguing that her research involved "the collection of artifacts of literacy, descriptions of contexts of uses, and their spatial and temporal distribution within the life of members of the community" (p. 47). She went on to claim that she studied how people used literacy artifacts, the activities and events within which the artifacts were used, whether links were made between symbolic representations and their real-world equivalents, how artifacts were presented to children, and what children then did with them (p. 47). Clearly, she came to understand parts in relation to wholes and vice versa.

A central question that motivated Heath's research was "what were the effects of preschool, home and community environments on the learning of those language structures which were needed in classrooms and job settings?" (p. 2). Heath explored and documented language and literacy practices common in the homes of families in three different communities in the Piedmont Carolinas: a working-class Black community (Trackton), a working-class White community (Roadville), and an integrated middle-class community (Maintown). Based on findings from ten years of research, Heath argued convincingly for how the knowledges and "ways with words" of people living in these different communities were historically and socially constructed in very different ways. In Heath's own words, "the place of language in the cultural life of each social group is interdependent with the habits and values of behaving shared among members of that group" (p. 11). For example, the kinds of interactions that parents and children from the three communities engaged in while reading storybooks were linked to different ways of living, eating, sleeping, worshipping, using space, and spending time. These interactions were also linked to different notions of play, parenting, truth, and morality. More generally, Heath explained that "for the children of Trackton and Roadville . . . and for the majority of the mill workers and students in the Piedmont schools the ways [of the people of Maintown] are far from natural and they seem strange indeed" (p. 262). Importantly, these differences resulted in different consequences for children's success in school. Finally, Heath traced constitutive relations between the identities of people in these communities and their language and literacy practices. In this regard, Heath worked with teachers in the local schools—all of whom were from Maintown—to understand the "ways with words" of the children they taught and to adapt their classroom practices to be more culturally relevant. This process induced changes in the identities, knowledges, and language practices of teachers and students alike.

Central to the work of Heath and other researchers working from within the chronotope of reading and interpretation is the fundamental notion that language practices constitute both individual and community identities. All of these studies presuppose the central assumption that it is not biology or geography or universal structure that constitutes identity and community but the discursive construction of shared meanings and practices. In Heath's work, for example, the predispositions toward books and reading held by the children and parents of Roadville or Trackton have no *a priori* existence but are continually produced and reproduced through the specific language and literacy practices common to the respective communities. As important as these practices are, however, Heath (and others located within the chronotope of reading and interpretation) never address questions about the larger social, political, and economic forces that make specific language and literacy practices visible and available in the first place. These questions are more central to the chronotopes we discuss later in the chapter.

Summary and Implications for Research Practice. The chronotope of reading and interpretation is embedded within a social constructionist epistemology and deploys hermeneutics as its most common theory-method complex. From within this chronotope, language is theorized not as a vehicle for representing an already existent world but as the most powerful means available to human beings for constructing what is "really real" (Geertz, 1973) and fundamentally meaningful about that world. This chronotope holds onto the modernist notion of the individual rational subject but views this individual as fundamentally grounded in and constructed within the language and literacy practices of the speech and discourse communities in which he or she participates. From within the chronotope of reading and interpretation, scholars also reject the idea that science is fundamentally about prediction and control, technical-instrumental rationality, and the gradual accumulation of all knowledge. Instead, researchers operating within this chronotope are committed to reflexively participating in the "language games" (Wittgenstein, 1958) of hermeneutics and the communities that they study with a desire and a willingness to enter into the conversations they find there. From this perspective, ongoing dialogue between researchers and research participants is a primary requirement of knowledge production and understanding.

Chronotope III: Skepticism, Conscientization, and Praxis

Although the chronotope of reading and interpretation constituted the very foundation of early qualitative research, it came under attack for failing to deal adequately with the power-laden political contexts in which presumably "open dialogue" occurs and "genuine understanding" is constructed. In other words, classical interpretivism rooted in hermeneutics did not address the ways in which dialogue can readily become complicit with the hegemonic structures of power in which it is always embedded. Historically, for example, many ethnographers have also been missionaries or military personnel whose "dialogue" with natives was motivated largely by religious and colonial interests masquerading as paternalistic (or maternalistic) benevolence. This so-cial fact is true even into the middle of the 20th century, when ethnogra-phers shifted their gaze from "exotic" natives in distant places to equal-ly "exotic" natives in American inner cities (e.g., Blacks, Asians, Jews, etc.). Accusations about the absence of attention paid to ideology and domination within the chronotope of reading and interpretation pro-moted the development of more critical forms of interpretivism within the Enlightenment or modernist project. We refer to these forms under the rubric of a chronotope of skepticism, conscientization, and praxis.

The roots of a chronotope of skepticism, conscientization, and praxis can be traced to linkages between the hermeneutic tradition and various strands of critical social theory within the tradition of neo-Marxism during the middle of the 20th century. The name for the chro-notope itself is a play on the term "hermeneutics of suspicion," which was introduced by Paul Ricoeur (1970) to refer to modes of interpreta-tion that are radically skeptical about whatever is presumed to be the truth. Building upon Ricoeur's basic insights, John B. Thompson (1990) constructed a systematic theory-method complex, which he called depth hermeneutics. Echoing the classic line attributed to Karl Marx, Ricoeur and Thompson argued that ideologies often "operate behind people's backs," which makes it impossible to escape completely the bonds of "false consciousness." Gadamer (1972) had something similar in mind when he claimed that, more than our judgments, our interests or our prejudices[8] constitute who we are. Built largely upon the neo-Marxist concerns with ideology and ideology critique, the goal of a critical or depth hermeneutics is to deconstruct or unmask the "real-ity" or "truth" of prejudicial understanding and to reveal the contin-gency, relativity, and historicity of consciousness, other people, and the world. Finally, we included Freire's (1970) term "conscientization" in the name of this chronotope to underscore its *praxis* orientation. For Freire, "conscientization" refers to critical reflection and its articulation with social action to enact individual and collective emancipation.

Like the chronotope of reading and interpretation, the chronotope of skepticism, conscientization, and praxis is grounded in social con-structionist epistemologies. Unlike the chronotope of reading and in-terpretation, the chronotope of skepticism, conscientization, and prax-is embraces the challenge of interrogating how ideology functions to "naturalize" and privilege some forms of knowledge and being-in-the-world over others. It also embodies an imperative for democratic social change. Operating within this chronotope, researchers assume that surface-level meanings and actions hide deep structural conflicts, contradictions, and falsities that function to maintain the status quo.

The Neo-Marxist Foundations of Chronotope III. To better understand the chronotope of skepticism, conscientization, and praxis warrants a detour into neo-Marxism. Certain neo-Marxists including Antonio Gramsci (1971), George Lukács (1971), and Louis Althusser (1971) challenged the economic determinism of traditional Marxism, arguing that power derives not so much from base economic conditions but from cultural ideologies, which are only informed by economic/political configurations (e.g., feudalism, capitalism, socialism). Another group of neo-Marxist thinkers known as the Frankfurt School theorists concerned themselves with understanding what they believed to be a set of constitutive relations among capitalism, epistemology, and politics. Although steeped in modernism, many Frankfurt School theorists were downright suspicious about the Enlightenment vision of an increasingly free and more democratic society through technical-instrumental rationality (i.e., science). In the words of Horkheimer and Adorno (1988), "in the most general sense of progressive thought, the Enlightenment has always aimed at liberating men from fear and establishing their authority. Yet the fully enlightened earth radiates disastrous triumph" (p. 3). The radical skepticism of the Frankfurt School did not so much mark a break with the Enlightenment or modernist project as an extension of it, which included a radical critique of the technical-instrumental rationality that had become so central to the project. Frankfurt School theorists were fundamentally concerned with interrogating why the presumed social progress of the project had resulted in "the fallen nature of modern man" (Horkheimer & Adorno, 1988, p. xiv), and the goal of their work was to rescue and reanimate "the hopes of the past" (p. xv).

Frankfurt School theorists did not attempt to disrupt the subject-object dichotomy central to Enlightenment and modernist work, however. Indeed, they struggled to preserve the idea that individuals are both rational and free, but wanted to demonstrate how these inalienable characteristics had become distorted and corrupted by what Adorno (1973) called "identity logic." "Identity logic," according to Adorno, is radically subjectivistic and embodies the desperate human need to eliminate the distance between subject and object. It is rooted in the hubristic desire to know "things-in-themselves," to experience firsthand what is indexed by the notion of a "correspondence theory of truth." The propensity for mastery and control, which is implicit in

Adorno's "identity logic" and which was central to the Enlightenment project's notion of human freedom (and freedom from suffering), was viewed by Adorno and other neo-Marxists as the primary cause of the Enlightenment's demise and the disintegration of a logic of verification within the logical positivist tradition. Recall here our discussion of Karl Popper from chapter 1, especially his replacement of a logic of verification with a logic of falsification.

Although Adorno often "affirm[ed] the wildest utopian dreams of the Enlightenment project" (Bernstein, 1992, p. 43), he thought that equating human reason and technical-instrumental rationality would negate the possibility of a critique of ideology and critical self-reflexivity. In this regard, he saw lived experience and material reality as far richer and more complex than could ever be captured by human thought and language. To imagine otherwise, he believed, was wrongheaded and arrogant. Worse than this, he argued, such arrogance eclipsed people's capacity for reflexivity and self-reflexivity in human thought and action.

The work of Frankfurt School scholar Jürgen Habermas perhaps went the farthest in laminating an emancipatory logic onto the basic modernist project. In his theory of communicative action, Habermas (1984, 1987) offered a critique of modernism, which shifted the locus of human agency from the Cartesian ego to the possibilities of dialogue inherent in language itself. Importantly, this shift entailed a concomitant shift in the locus of agency from the individual to the social.[9] Finally, he rejected the technical-instrumental rationality of the Enlightenment without rejecting rationality itself, an issue we take up below.

Habermas's (1984, 1987) theory of communicative action is both a theory of rationality and a theory of society. In this regard, he viewed rationality as a social, dialogic process with both political and ethical valences. According to this view, rationality is not a property of the transcendental ego or individual subject. Instead, it is produced within "ideal speech situations" wherein people engage in communicative acts that are free, unconstrained, dialogic, and therefore undistorted. Ideal speech situations are defined or constituted by four "validity claims." Whatever speakers say must be (a) meaningful, (b) true, (c) justified, and (d) sincere.[10] Truth is the goal or promise of this model, and it is defined in terms of agreement or consensus achieved through critical dialogue and debate. Rational consensus is determined on the basis of who offers the better argument with the most adequate evidence and warrants. Reasoned argumentation is thus the ultimate court of appeal.[11]

Habermas's insistence on the importance of the ideal speech situation was rooted in his ethical and political commitments. Because he believed that the colonizing forces of capitalism were rooted in technical-instrumental rationality, he rejected this form of rationality and posited two alternatives: (a) practical rationality and (b) emancipatory rationality. Practical rationality (or Habermas's version of praxis) is the means by which people reach mutual understandings through unfettered dialogue. Emancipatory rationality is a mode of thinking/being that allows people to escape the lures of hegemony and oppression through self-reflection. By acknowledging the workings of these three forms of rationality in social life, Habermas was able to account for how language is a constitutive force *both* in generating shared understandings (and thus truth) *and* in the exercise of power and domination. Social movements such as second-wave feminism, the civil rights movement, and the ecology movement are good examples of how Habermas's rational, emancipatory, de/recolonization project has been concretely realized in history. In our own field, one might argue that "whole language" pedagogies, Gravesian versions of the "writing process" pedagogies, and many incarnations of the "critical literacy" pedagogies are all grounded in Habermas's practical and emancipatory forms of rationality. Not surprisingly, these pedagogies have been assaulted by hegemonic regimes rooted in and legitimated by technical-instrumental rationality.

The Praxis Turn. The general interest in practical reason or praxis has a long history in philosophy. Aristotle (e.g., Nichomachean Ethics, Book VI) contrasted poesis with praxis, arguing that poesis involves instrumental action that results in *making* or *producing* things, whereas praxis involves action that results in acting or doing things with and for others that promote moral goodness and "the good life." Thus praxis always has to do with what people *do* in relation to each other to enhance their respective lives. Aristotle also believed that through these acts, people promote the democratic goals of the state.

More generally, the term *praxis* has often been used to refer to the general process of linking knowledge and action to enhance the possibilities of *communitas*[12] and to make the world a better place to live in for all people. For the most part, knowledge has remained the privileged term in this binary, but practical knowledge, not knowledge for its own sake, has been emphasized. Since the so-called "crisis of representation" in anthropology (e.g., Marcus & Fischer, 1986; chapter 3 of this book), praxis has often been used to refer to the practical and dialogic/reciprocal relationships that researchers may forge with research participants. Within these relationships researchers have often imposed mandates on themselves to work with research participants to help them improve the conditions of their lives (e.g., Lather, 1991, 1997). Less common, but at least as important, is a political sense of praxis such as that developed by Gramsci (1971). This sense of praxis unites theory and practice in such a way that neither is subservient to the other. Researchers and research participants enter into reciprocal relationships wherein the common work experience has to be as much a venue for both intellectuals and workers to advance their points of view and interests. Reciprocal relationships must lead to the development of common goals, and these goals must in some ways express the transformative possibilities of a dialogic community.

Illustration from Research. A considerable amount of research in language and literacy in the past two decades has been conducted within the chronotope of skepticism, conscientization, and praxis. Following Habermas's lead, many language and literacy scholars have focused on the relations among language and literacy, power, identity, and society. These scholars have shown that social formations such as families, classrooms, schools, community-based organizations, and the like are not only sites for making and sharing meaning but also sites for exercising power and control through processes of meaning distortion. Knowledge and identity, according to these scholars, are produced within these sites through and within complex sets of power relations. Language and literacy practices function ideologically to produce and reproduce systems of power and domination, although these systems seem neutral and "natural." A chronotope of skepticism, conscientization, and praxis is required to expose the deep structural inequalities these systems occlude. Because language and literacy are posited as constitutive social forces within this chronotope, possibilities for increased democratization are directly associated with the discursive construction of alternative constructions of self, knowledge, social life, and world.

The work of Paulo Freire (e.g., 1970) is a classic example of research conducted within the chronotope of skepticism, conscientization, and praxis.[13] Indeed, this is why we included his construct of *conscientization* in the name of this chronotope. Freire was a Brazilian educator who developed and organized grassroots literacy programs among the peasants of northeastern Brazil in the 1960s. Due to the unparalleled success of these programs, the Brazilian government adopted them to launch a nationwide literacy campaign designed to "solve" the illiteracy problem in the country. Within a year, however, the Brazilian government was overthrown by a military coup and the literacy campaign ended. Freire was exiled, but spent the rest of his life working on "pedagogies for the oppressed" in Europe and North America. A hallmark of his programs was the elicitation of words (and concomitant ideas) that were fundamentally important in the lives of the people for whom the programs were designed. He called these words "generative words." He spent long periods of time in communities trying to understand their interests, investments, and concerns in order to elicit comprehensive sets of generative words. These words were then used as the starting point for literacy learning. They were paired with pictures that represented them and discussed by people in the community. Freire encouraged the people to dissect the meanings of the words in their lives and to put them together in a variety of different ways. The goal of these activities was to help them feel in control of their words and to be able to use them to exercise power over their lives. Thus, Freire's literacy programs were designed not to teach functional literacy but to raise people's critical consciousness (or *conscientization*) and encourage them to engage in praxis, which is critical reflection inextricably linked to political action in the real world. Freire was clear to underscore the fact that praxis is never easy and always involves power struggles, often violent ones. We will return to Freire's theory and work in chapter 4.

Importantly, Freire (1970) insisted that the unending process of emancipation must be a collective effort. Central to this process is a faith in the power of dialogue, defined as collective action/reflection. Dialogue, fellowship, and solidarity are essential to human liberation and transformation. "We can legitimately say that in the process of oppression someone oppresses someone else; we cannot legitimately say that in the process of revolution, someone liberates someone else, nor yet that that someone liberates himself, but rather that men in communion liberate each other" (p. 103). Only dialogue is capable of producing critical consciousness and praxis. Thus, all educational programs (and especially all language and literacy programs) must be dialogic. They must be spaces wherein equally knowing subjects engage in dialogue, struggle, and conflict in efforts to transform themselves and their worlds. Freire contrasted such educational enterprises with more traditional educational enterprises, "banking" models, which regard students as empty accounts into which educators must deposit knowledge. Such models operate according to monologic rather than dialogic logics, and serve the interests of the *status quo*.

Summary and Implications for Research Practice. Chronotope III is unquestionably modernist because issues of human freedom and emancipation lie at its core. Freire's work is certainly testimony to this social fact. However, it also represents a more radical break with the chronotope of objectivism and representation than was achieved by the chronotope of reading and interpretation because it calls into question the radical separation of subject and object characteristic of Enlightenment thinking without completely rejecting it, and more effectively problematizes how social life is constructed within flows of ideology, control, and domination. Although *Chronotopes II and III* share the idea that language and literacy constitute (rather than simply represent) reality, *Chronotope III* more effectively accounts for the ways in which discourse, ideology, and power interact and often work against the production of freer, more democratic, and more ethical forms of social life.

Still, this chronotope also reconstructs the Enlightenment project by placing the constitutive power of discourse practices at its very center (e.g., Habermas, 1984, 1987). Indeed, a powerful assumption of the chronotope of skepticism, conscientization, and praxis is the idea that technical-instrumental rationality will never produce freedom and democratic responsibility. These Enlightenment goals will only be achieved through the interrogation of the socially constructed nature of systems of oppression that limit people's ability to be reflexive about the social, cultural, and political conditions that seem "naturally" to constitute their lives. Only when they are able to peek at "the ideologies that operate behind their backs" will people be able to develop *conscientization* and engage in praxis designed to change the conditions of their worlds and their positions within them.

Chronotope III has spawned new modes of qualitative research practice such as collaborative action research (CAR) and participatory action research (PAR), both of which have been taken up extensively within the language and literacy field. These modes of action research involve concrete and practical efforts to change the social world for the better through improving shared social practices, shared understandings of these practices, and the material conditions in which these practices occur. They are *de facto* critical in that they aim to understand why things are the way they are and to imagine and enact ways to make them better. They are also critical because they involve groups of people (usually positioned in different ways, such as public school teachers and university researchers) changing their practices, evaluating the processes and effects of these changes, and entering into new cycles of change. Although CAR and PAR focus on improving social life through research on concrete social problems, they are always in relation to wider social structures and processes and the asymmetrical relations of power they usually entail.

More generally, *Chronotope III* marks a distinct move toward actualizing what Denzin and Lincoln (2000) have called key imperatives of "sixth and seventh moment" qualitative inquiry. Four of these key imperatives are particularly relevant for our purposes here. The first imperative is a commitment to morally sound social science inquiry rooted in praxis—research practice that is politically strategic, that moves beyond both a sense of dialogic impotence and outright rage to connect theories and methods with concrete action in the world to make a difference in terms of collective moral development, social justice, and the goals of democracy. The second imperative is methodological syncretism. Rather than privileging a single method or approach to the practice of inquiry, researchers are encouraged to use whatever techniques, strategies, and frameworks are required to conduct the best research possible and to produce research accounts that embody verisimilitude and that are poetic, transgressive, unfinalizable, and transformative. The third imperative is the production of open, nonrepresentational texts—texts that are as creative, dynamic, multiple, and unfinalized as the research activity they index. The fourth imperative involves the cultivation of sacredness in research practice. To engage in sacred inquiry requires a return to more embodied, organic, participatory, communal ways of thinking. It involves creating lives with others and with the many worlds of our experience through loving, imaginative, exploratory, critical sense-making reflection, which informs our future actions and experience (p. 6). *Chronotope IV*, to which we now turn, moves even further toward actualizing these sixth and seventh moment imperatives.

Chronotope IV: Power/Knowledge and Defamiliarization

When most people think about "critical" qualitative research, they presume that it is always framed within postmodern and/or poststructural[14] epistemologies and theories. Although we argued against this generalization in the previous section, critical qualitative research has been increasingly grounded in postmodern and poststructural perspectives. Because power/knowledge and defamiliarization are constructs that are central to these perspectives, we have used them to characterize the next chronotope we discuss. Partly because of its almost exclusive alignment with postmodernism and poststructuralism rather than modernism and structuralism, this chronotope is partially discontinuous with the chronotope of skepticism, conscientization, and praxis.

Power/Knowledge and Games of Truth. Perhaps the hallmark of postmodern and poststructural critical theorists is the extent to which they debunk modernist notions of knowledge, arguing that knowledge is always related to power. For example, they reject Habermas's (1984, 1987) dialogic/consensus model of knowledge made possible by the inherent potential of language to afford an "ideal speech situation." Contra Habermas, Baudrillard (1983), Foucault (1977), Lyotard (1984), and others warned that consensus is a hopeless vestige of modernism that actually elicits complicity with totalizing regimes of knowledge and truth, and they set out to demonstrate the ways in which knowledge and power are co-constitutive. Foucault's (1975, 1977, 1990) genealogies of madness/the asylum, criminality/the prison, and the discourses of sexuality, for example, showed how what is considered true or false is dependent on specific "games of truth" or "regimes of power" upon which the possibilities of making any and all knowledge claims depend. Different games of truth afford and allow different knowledge claims. For example, Foucault (1990) raised several doubts about the presumed "repressive hypothesis" of modern society beginning with the Victorian age:

> First doubt: Is sexual repression truly an established historical fact? . . . Second doubt: Do the workings of power, and in particular those mechanisms that are brought into play in societies such as ours, really belong primarily to the category of repression? . . . Third and final doubt: Did the critical discourse that addresses itself to repression come to act as a roadblock to a power mechanism that had operated unchallenged up to that point, or is it not in fact part of the same historical network as the thing it denounces (and doubtless misrepresents) in calling it "repression"? (p. 10)

Foucault went on to claim that these doubts about the repressive hypothesis "are aimed less at showing it to be mistaken than at putting it back within a general economy of discourses on sex in modern societies since the seventeenth century" (p. 10). And he argued that this relocation ushers in new (and more important) questions about sexuality such as "Why has sexuality been so widely discussed, and what has been said about it? What were the effects of power generated by what was said? What are the links between these discourses, these effects of power, and the pleasures that were invested by them? What knowledge (*savoir*) was formed as a result of this linkage?" (p. 10).

Positing knowledge as existing within games of truth as Foucault has done here in relation to sexuality requires moving beyond most social constructionist formulations. Some scholars (e.g., Bourdieu, 1990) believe they have moved too far, obscuring the very real social fact that although they are historically produced and thus changeable, games of truth are also very durable and resistant. This criticism notwithstanding, most social constructionist formulations do seem to gloss over the constitutive role of power in the production of knowledge and truth, especially in relation to the microprocesses of everyday life. In other words, they still view power as something "out there," and are not very insightful about how power inhabits everyday practices and how knowledge and truth are effects of this kind of power. Thus, to understand the concept of knowledge within the discourse of power/knowledge and defamiliarization requires understanding how Foucault believed that power works.

Foucault focused primarily on power's "capillary existence: the point where power reaches into the very grain of individuals, touches their bodies and inserts itself into their action and attitudes, their discourses, their learning processes and everyday lives" (1980, p. 39). He argued that power operates directly and in concrete ways not mediated by consciousness, representation, or ideology because these things are already effects of power. Power is "a multiple and mobile field of force relations where far-reaching, but never completely stable effects of domination are produced" (1980, p. 102). Power "traverses and produces things, it induces pleasure, forms of knowledge, produces discourse. It needs to be considered as a productive network that runs through the whole social body, much more than as a negative instance whose function is repression" (1984a, p. 61).

In arguing that power is productive and circulates among people in everyday practices, Foucault did not deny that hegemonic structural regimes of power exist. These regimes do exist. In fact, they are foregrounded in *Chronotope III*, and they do exert their own effects. However, these regimes are produced by and act back upon the whole constellation of specific local strategies and relations of power that constitute the micropractices of everyday life. In other words, although it is the case that some people and groups are dominant over others as a function of various institutional processes, dominance itself is sustained within micropolitical processes "of different origins and different locations" (Foucault, 1977, p. 138). Power operates concretely through what Foucault called "technologies of the self." This means that people are always complicit in the construction of asymmetrical relations of power and assigning differential value to various subject positions, even when they are attempting to challenge or subvert oppressive power relations (or these asymmetries). In saying this, we do not mean to dismiss the fact that institutional affiliations and the power that accrues to people through them is insignificant. Institutional affiliations do indeed contribute to power asymmetries, but they do not determine them once and for all. Nor do we want to suggest that institutional dimensions of power are separate from the power that is produced within the micropolitics of everyday life. The concrete practices in which people engage and in which power is produced and circulates are always situated within larger, institutionally informed arrangements of power, and these arrangements often "operate behind our backs," disposing us to position ourselves in specific ways and not other ways.[15] We are, to a considerable degree, effects of power. Yet it is too simple to view the production of subjects deterministically. We are not determined even if our agency is limited and constrained. Nor does power simply accrue to us as a function of our institutional affiliations even though we may ascribe power to each other through particular positions of status, authority, or institutional affiliation. Power is always a matter of *both* being positioned by proximal and distal social forces *and* responding to being positioned in unique and agentic ways.

In addition to showing how power is relational and productive, Foucault was able to show how power and knowledge are always intimately linked rather than inherently separate. Thus, he coined the compound term "power/knowledge." Within this framework, all knowledge claims index not Truth with a capital T or even local truths but "truth effects," which are produced, legitimated, and "naturalized" within specific "regimes of truth" or "discourses." Among other things, knowledge produces normative categories, prescriptions for behavior, ways of seeing, and relations of power such as those that obtain between women and men, patients and doctors, teachers and students, citizens and the police. Importantly, since knowledge and truth effects are always linked to power and since it is impossible to step completely outside of the "regimes of truth" that constitute them, utopian forms of praxis characteristic of the chronotope of skepticism, conscientization, and praxis are rendered impossible, or at least ineffective. Instead of theorizing praxis in classical Marxist or neo-Marxist revolutionary terms, Foucault theorized it as material, local, pragmatic, and relational. This focus on the material and the local constitutes a backlash against some postmodern and poststructural work, which foregrounds cultural work such as praxis in terms of texts and text interpretation and ignores the institutional regulation of culture and social formations, as well as the nondiscursive or spatial/material dimensions of existence. We return to this issue later in the chapter.

Reimagining the Subject. Besides reconceptualizing knowledge in relation to power, postmodern/poststructural critical theorists went much further than modernist critical theorists in decentering Enlightenment notions about the *human subject* and displacing the locus of rationality from the mind of this subject. For example, although Habermas (1984, 1987) rejected the idea of the Cartesian subject and argued for viewing rationality not as a possession of the individual subject but as a dialogic social process rooted in the potential for an "ideal speech situation" inherent in language, he still viewed subjectivity as coherent and progressive. For postmodern/poststructural critical theorists, the subject is neither autonomous nor coherent nor teleological in nature. Instead, the subject is constructed within various "discursive systems" or discourses that normalize what it means to be a subject in the first place (Foucault, 1977, 1980, 1990). These discourses are not linguistic and textual alone but involve habituated and largely unconscious ways of thinking, talking, feeling, acting, and being. Discourses are practical "grids of specification" (Foucault, 1977, 1996) for classifying, categorizing, and diagramming the human subject in relation to the social. Discourses are forms of power that both literally and metaphorically inscribe/produce the individual and the collective social body. Indeed, the residue of such production processes litters our vocabulary: "the culturally literate citizen," "the naturally literate child," "the educated gentleman," "the child author," "the reader of romance," "the functional illiterate," and "the academically prepared student." These classifications are almost always also classed, raced, and gendered.

Revisioning notions of the subject in relation to Foucault's work on discourses and power/knowledge requires viewing them not in expressivist or representational terms but in material terms. Notions of the subject shift from semifixed, autonomous essences to sites of articulation for multiple subjectivities that are continually constituted and reconstituted in relation to other subjectivities through various discursive and material practices (e.g., Laclau & Mouffe, 1985). Anzaldua (1987) referred to such sites of articulation as *mestiza* sites (an Aztec word meaning torn between ways), and she argued that individual and collective selves are "product[s] of the transfer of the cultural and spiritual values of one group to another. Cradled in one culture, sandwiched between two cultures, straddling all three cultures and their value systems, *la mestiza* undergoes a struggle of flesh, a struggle of borders, an inner war" (p. 78). Both individual and collective subjects are constantly engaged in inner wars because they are always being produced at the intersection of multiple discursive and material forces.

Foregrounding issues of power and its relation to knowledge even more overtly, Alcoff (1988) and other theorists have used the construct of "positioning" to construe identity. According to this perspective, raced, classed, or gendered identities involve being positioned at the intersection of various identity axes within a changing historical context of identity markers. Subjects assume responsibility for their positioning within a moving historical context, choose how to interpret their positioning, and imagine how to alter the context that made such positioning available in the first place. This way of thinking about subjectivity seems to avoid reducing agency to the intentions of a homunculus while also escaping antihumanist assaults, which negate the possibility of human agency at all. In this view, the subject is reconceptualized as the activity of positioning oneself within (and against) existing social, cultural, and material forces that make some subject positions more visible (and readily attainable) than others.

At first blush these views of the subject may seem absolutely relativistic, but this is not the case. Subjectivity itself is produced in and through sedimented institutional discourses that provide both the possibilities for and limits of our lived experiences. Additionally, we have uniquely sedimented life histories that involve myriad predispositions and habits. Unfortunately, from a critical perspective, these predispositions and habits induce a propensity for being unreflective about ourselves, our languages, and our worlds. The attendant "sutured" (Lacan, 1977) nature of our existences in relation to institutionalized and naturalized discourses and practices is largely responsible for our solipsistic folk belief that what we speak and write derives from "our own" minds. However, if we reconceptualize discursive practices as self-deconstructive rather than as self-expressive, then we are more able to see the many complex, conflicting, and contradictory discourses within which our subjectivities (and social worlds) are produced. Put another way, we are more able to see how discursively saturated, socially situated, materially saturated, and political the very notion of subjectivity is in the first place.[16]

The idea that discourses speak through us more than we speak with them raises serious issues about human agency. Where is agency if not in the minds and hearts of individual people? The chronotope of power/knowledge and defamiliarization does not entirely reject the idea that people have agency when they speak, read, and write. However, this chronotope is predicated on two important social facts that temper the privileging of freedom and agency characteristic of the Enlightenment project. First, language and literacy practices always occur within larger social, cultural, and historical contexts that exist independently of any specific instance of these practices. Second, individuals *have* intentions precisely because they are always already situated within institutionally informed discourses, and thus these intentions are themselves effects of these discourses, at least to some extent. Intention is not created *ex nihilo* from the subject. It is largely a function of our condition as hailed or interpellated subjects. The importance of this view of subjectivity and intentionality for scholars of language and literacy is to serve as a constant reminder that language and meaning do not exist in people's minds but in the multiple and interrelated set of discourses within which people are always already situated. Thus, it is always an empirical problem to account for the actions that people take.

So, within *Chronotope IV*, language and literacy practices are intentional, but not in the traditional sense of this term. Although individuals have intentions, these intentions are always already constructed within particular games of truth in the first place and then appropriated by individuals who are themselves constructed within the same games of truth. This is a troubling yet compelling circularity. Discourses always speak through people as much if not more than people willingly appropriate and revoice these discourses in anything close to an "ideal speech situation." The subject of language and literacy practices is always both an enunciative position and a product or effect of discourse.[17] Individuals participate in the struggle to construct discourses of self, others, and world but always from within the limits of the discourses that simultaneously produce them.

Language is productive. Although we have already touched upon the views of *language and discourse* central to the chronotope of power/knowledge and defamiliarization, we want to return to this topic and address it more explicitly here. The roots of understanding language and discourse within this framework seem to lie in postmodern notions of deconstruction. Importantly, however, like Habermas' communicative ethics, deconstruction never entirely escaped from the inherent dualism of transcendental philosophy or the foundational status of subjective experience. Again, Foucault offered some insights that allow us to address/redress these problems. So we will outline the contours of deconstruction and then show how Foucault identified and responded to some of its inherent weaknesses.

Deconstruction decentered traditional notions of the relations between signs and their referents (e.g., Saussure's signifiers and signifieds). Derrida (1976), for example, made the provocative claim that there is nothing outside of language (or semiotics more broadly conceived). Extending the "negative dialectics" of Adorno (see chapter 4 of this book), he argued that we can never make the relation between the sign and its referent identical. In uncompromising terms, this claim brought into high relief the possibility that the referents of all signs and symbols, including those of natural language, are not objects in the world, but other signs and symbols. Unmediated knowledge of the referents in themselves is a radical impossibility. No particular signifier (sign) can ever be regarded as referring to any particular signified (referent). Baudrillard (1983) extended this idea further with his construct of the "simulacrum." According to this construct, the sign is actually more real than the reality it represents. The real forever recapitulates the imagined. Postmodernity, Baudrillard argued, is "hyperreal." We do not live in reality but "hyperreality," where everything is simulation and objects seduce subjects rather than subjects rationally choosing objects. What he meant here is that the boundary between the real and the imaginary has been dissolved. Reality is no longer a court of appeal for experience and knowledge. The "more real than real" has become existence itself. In an age of hyperreality, signs exert more power and influence over people than material reality, and reality itself is experienced as mysterious and illusionary to a large extent.

Not all postmodern/poststructural theorists focus on language and text as the pivot points for their critical work.[18] Moreover, we believe that reducing everything to language and text is highly problematic. It constitutes what might be called a kind of structural entrapment induced by a Saussaurean view of language as an autonomous and universal system rather than as an abstraction from actual language practices (something like Saussure's *"parole"* or Bakhtin's *"utterance"*) that has become reified. Despite their insights about the productive power of signs (especially language), theorists who celebrate the deconstruction of presence and a kind of disembodied unlimited semiosis fail to avoid or decenter the inherent dualism of transcendental philosophy and the foundational status of subjective experience. For example, the subject-object binary is merely replaced by a subject-discourse binary in which the former term is located in the latter.

Foucault recognized these problems and sought ways to solve them. For example, as we already mentioned, whenever Foucault used the term "discourse," he was not referring to language alone but to a whole constellation of discursive and material practices that produced and reproduced the *status quo*.[19] Moreover, he rejected the idea that human existence could be reduced to anything like labor (e.g., Marx) or meaning (e.g., phenomenology and hermeneutics). For Foucault, not everything is discourse, and discourse is to be considered as one material force among other material forces, all of which contribute to the production of human existence. Note that we are now using the term *discourse* not as a synonym for "regimes of truth" but in the more everyday sense of language practice. With regard to this usage, Foucault saw critical readings of language or text—even deconstructive readings—as limited in the sense that they elide the productive power exerted by all kinds of other forces. Instead, he saw language and text as existing as facts or data among numerous other facts or data. Language and text are important to Foucault not as a play of discursive codes but only to the extent that they are forces among other forces that produce "truth effects" in the world. Thus, in the place of a theory of text and text interpretation, Foucault insisted on a theory of *contexts*. Within this theoretical perspective, mapping contexts replaces interpreting texts as the primary task of research. One consequence of this shift is that it makes valuing and judging possible once again, moving us from ludic to pragmatic forms of poststructuralism.

For example, discourse that is conceived in terms of *meaning* in the first three chronotopes is replaced by a concern for how discourse emerges, gains legitimacy, and functions to produce what we believe to be true. Foucault called this dimension of discourse its mode of existence and effectivity. Discourse is no longer viewed in dialogic terms but in terms of a constant struggle (he even uses the metaphor of war)[20] and therefore in terms of power. Moreover, although discourse practices emerge in response to particular historical needs, they are also seen to produce unintended and never-imagined effects because they become connected with a multiplicity of historical forces to form larger apparatuses of production. Thus, analyzing discourse is not a matter of searching for the underlying codes that govern human behavior. It is a matter of carefully mapping topologies or contexts, much as the chronotopes that organize this chapter map a history of ways to imagine and enact qualitative inquiry genealogically.

Defamiliarization. Research conducted within a chronotope of power/knowledge and defamiliarization is not a matter of deconstructing one set of language practices or one discourse and replacing it with a better one (the primary goal of the chronotope of skepticism, conscientization, and praxis). Instead, research is conducted to expose the possibilities and consequences of various discourses, with their attendant ideologies, practices, and preferences. The form of analysis used to do this work is often called conjunctural analysis, and it involves scrupulously mapping an event—say a literacy event—for the multiple, and often contingent, discursive and material forces that intersected to produce the event and its truth effects. Conjunctural analysis also involves mapping other events to demonstrate how things were and thus can be otherwise, asking: What happened? What were the effects of what happened? What could have happened given the intersection of a different contingent set of forces? It is thus radically empirical in the sense that it resists explaining events with ready-made constructs or theories. Conjunctural analysis is conducted in the spirit of Wittgenstein's famous dictum to "look" rather than to "think," by which he meant that philosophers and researchers often mistakenly rush to fit their data into some prefigured model or theory before looking closely at what they have.

The construct of defamiliarization becomes important for exploring the tactics at the heart of conjunctural analysis, and for understanding the ways in which *Chronotope IV* reflects a sharp break from the other chronotopes, especially with regard to the nature and process of research, and the stances of researchers toward the "objects" of their research. In his efforts to imagine an ethnography for the late 20th and early 21st centuries, Clifford (1988) talked about a "hermeneutics of vulnerability," which foregrounds the ruptures of fieldwork, the multiple and contradictory positionings of researchers and research participants, the imperfect control of the ethnographer, and the utility of self-reflexivity. In one sense, self-reflexivity involves making transparent the rhetorical and poetic work of the ethnographer in representing the object of her/his study. In another, perhaps more important, sense, self-reflexivity refers to the efforts of researchers and research participants to engage in acts of defamiliarization in relation to each other. In this regard, Probyn (1993) discussed how fieldwork always seems to result in being "uneasy in one's skin" and how this experience often engenders a virtual transformation of the identities of both researchers and research participants even as they are paradoxically engaged in the practice of consolidating them. This is important theoretically because it allows for the possibility of constructing a mutual ground between researchers and research participants even while recognizing that the ground is unstable and fragile. Self-reflexivity as defamiliarization is also important because it encourages reflection on ethnography as the practice of both knowledge gathering and self-transformation through self-reflection and mutual reflection with the other. Importantly, these acts of defamiliarization can help people recognize the fragmentary, historically situated, partial, and unfinished nature of their "selves" and promote processes of self-construction/reconstruction in relation to new discourses and others.

Illustration from Research. Comparatively little research in the field of language and literacy has been conducted from within a chronotope of power/knowledge and defamiliarization. Moreover, most, but not all, of the research that has been conducted from within this chronotope has come from Australia. The work of Allan Luke, Carmen Luke, Bronwyn Davies, Colin Lankshear, Alison Lee, and Michele Knobel are key exemplars in this regard. To illustrate the character and purpose of such research, we have chosen to showcase Allan Luke's (1992) study of first-grade literacy practices in an Australian elementary school as processes of inscribing literate practice upon children's bodies.

Luke framed his study within a synthesis of Foucault's discourse theory and Bourdieu's critical sociology to show how first-grade literacy instruction is a material/social practice that produces children who have a distinct bodily/linguistic/literacy "habitus." Luke argued that this production process is accomplished through various classroom "technologies of the self," which are practices by which individuals perform operations on their own bodies that constitute forms of self-regulation within prescribed/inscribed discourses (Foucault, 1988, p. 18). Luke adopted Foucault's notion of the "technologies of the self" to show how the locus of the production of "disciplined subjects" or "docile bodies" lies not in institutional metanarratives about the literacy development of children but in "those practical discourses inscribed in classroom literacy events" (p. 118). Stated even more strongly, he argued that early literacy training is a site of body mapping or body writing. Power/knowledge is actually inscribed on children's bodies through everyday discursive and material practices such as directing the attention of children's gaze to the book, requiring them to sit up straight and face straight ahead, and expecting and requiring round robin and choral reading, which induce specific and durable dispositions (or habiti) toward literacy and literate practices. According to Foucault (1977), four techniques of docility and three techniques of training function together to produce "docile bodies." The techniques of docility are (a) the distribution of individuals in space, (b) control of activity, (c) the capitalization of time, and (d) composition of forces, by which he meant the mutually reinforcing articulation of multiple disciplining practices. The three techniques of training are (a) hierarchical observation, (b) normative judgment, and (c) examinations/evaluations.

To unpack the import of these assertions, Luke reported findings from analyses of an intensive study of the discourse/material practices that occurred during "shared book experiences" (e.g., Holdaway, 1979) in first-grade classrooms in two urban Australia schools. Luke's analyses revealed that nearly all of the techniques for producing particular kinds of reading "subjects" were at work. For example, children's postures, movements, and visual gazes were policed and directed/redirected when they moved outside of the teacher's discursive/material frame for the activity (e.g., "sit up straight," "face the front," "on your bottoms, please, so that we can all see," "how *we* look," "where *we* look"). Children were conscripted to read *with* the teacher and *like* the teacher, thus collectivizing their eyes, mouths, and bodies. In this regard, Luke noted that the pervasive use of the pronoun "we" functioned as an instrument for drawing children into particular ways of speaking, acting, and being, particular ways of being a "subject." By transposing "I" and "we" as she directed individual and collective readings of stories, the teacher fused individual and group subjectivities, thus eliding the differences between them. Not all differences were elided, however. Children who internalized the discipline of collective readership were the ones chosen for solo readings. Children who did not seldom, if ever, were chosen as solo readers, and they were often reprimanded and thus excluded from equal participation in the presumed interest of the collective "we" (e.g., "Shhss, Kylie, *we* don't need help. Be quiet. Evelyn, you read the next page.").

By offering a poststructural discourse analysis of early literacy training, Luke provided a very different kind of map of "shared book experiences" than is typically provided in research on early literacy learning. His map foregrounded how the gaze of institutional power was inscribed within individual children so that they became both objects and subjects of a particular discourse or literacy. Through a certain "means of correct training" (Foucault, 1979) embodied in everyday practices, the children in his study were hailed to become specific kinds of readers and classroom citizens with specific kinds of naturalized dispositions toward reading and participating in the public sphere. "Particular postures, silences, gestures, and visible signs of 'being in' the collective body [were] on display. Proxemics, the organization of space and the delimitization of space and time in the classroom [were] encompassing aspects of the gaze" (p. 123). Whether children sat up straight and remained "on their bottoms," how they participated in reading aloud collectively, and how they responded to the turn-taking rules prescribed by the teacher were all monitored and sanctioned according to liberal humanist and normative/normalizing psychological grids of specification with their attendant prohibitions about appropriate and inappropriate behavior. Within these grids, the size, age, position, and official status of the teacher, along with his or her superior knowledge and power about both reading and teaching, invested the teacher with moral and epistemological authority.

Additionally, the teacher's superior positioning in the classroom was inscribed on "the canvas of the student body" (p. 123). As students appropriated the prescribed reading practices of "shared book experiences" (e.g., gaze, posture, pronunciation, cadence, oral interpretation, listening practices, and meaning-making strategies of the teacher), they "agreed," in a sense, to becoming particular kinds of "subjects." Moreover, subjectivity itself was constituted as a function a collective identity, a "we." Importantly, these children were not simply repressed but produced in such a way as to eventually desire particular kinds of and reading practices and subjectivities as readers.

Summary and Implications for Research Practice. Importantly, Luke's goal in this report was not to target and disparage the particular approach to literacy instruction he observed. Instead, his goal was to defamiliarize the familiar and to show power/knowledge at work.

He sought to reveal that "the truth claims of pedagogy and research themselves [are] discourse constructions with tangible, political consequences" (p. 123). He also sought to show that determining "truth effects" is a necessary step toward demonstrating that other truth effects have and might be produced. Since we can never escape the reality of truth effects, the goal of conjunctural analysis is to expose their historical roots and "naturalized" etiologies so that we might imagine how cultural and social realities could be otherwise.

To accomplish these goals, he had to avoid the received logic of the Cartesian mind/body dualism and focus on how cultures produce morally regulated, literate subjects by inscribing their bodies in and through quotidian language practices. He also had to take seriously the body "as a political object of literacy and linguistic research" (p. 125). Other researchers who locate themselves within the chronotope of power/knowledge and defamiliarization must also adopt these habits of mind for interrogating school literacy practices, programs, and sites, no matter how "child-centered," "natural," or "transformative" these practices, programs, and sites purport to be. Ironically perhaps, more ostensibly radical forms of pedagogy often simply replace "technologies of power" (e.g., the command, the reprimand) with "technologies of self" (e.g., the internalized gaze, the investment in the appropriate).

Besides providing a different map for reading classroom literacy events, research like that conducted by Luke indexes key continuities and discontinuities between modernist and postmodernist/poststuctural critical perspectives. Both are concerned with issues of dominance and resistance, but in very different ways. Modernist critical work such as that of the Frankfurt School has tended to focus on capitalist relations of domination that are reproduced through communicative practices. In other words, the totalizing logic of capitalism is used to explain oppression, and resistance is always interpreted *within* this logic (e.g., Eckert, 1989; McLaren, 1998; Willis, 1977). Consistent with the tenets of a chronotope of skepticism, conscientization, and praxis, this work typically concludes that resistance often ends up being complicit with and reproductive of the hegemonic systems and structures within which it occurs.

In contrast, a chronotope of power/knowledge and defamiliarization foregrounds the inherent contingency, instability, and vulnerability of totalizing logics, thus partially escaping the tendency to privilege systems and structures of domination. From this perspective, language and literacy practices can never produce a seamless sense of social life and society—even if this sense is deemed liberatory—because they inherently entail constant struggles for power and legitimacy. This approach to studying language and literacy practices does have a praxis subtext, but one far less utopian than those associated with the chronotope of skepticism, conscientization, and praxis. It does not aim specifically to empower individuals and groups who have previously been marginalized and left out of the extant dialogues. Instead, it aims to disarticulate and rearticulate the dialogues themselves and the very power relations that sustain them, thus affording possibilities for producing new kinds of human subjects and not just helping already existent subjects escape the bonds of false consciousness by piercing veils of ideology.

Summary and Conclusions

In this chapter, we have attempted to show that different approaches to qualitative research in language and literacy have been rooted in different chronotopes that were produced historically and constituted at the intersection of episteme, epistemology, theory, and methodology. In doing so, we have tried to show that no single episteme lines up with any single epistemology, theory, or methodology. Modernism, for example, may be articulated with positivism or with social constructionism, hermeneutics, and even social critical theory. Just as we noted in the last chapter that Bourdieu is a consummate qualitative researcher who deploys numbers and statistics to construct complex and nuanced interpretations, we showed in this chapter that thinkers like Habermas were both decidedly modernist but also antipositivist and critical.

In closing, we want to reiterate some issues we noted at the beginning of the chapter. The taxonomy we have used to organize our argument is not meant to be read as a taxonomy in the classic Aristotelian sense. Instead, it should be used as a heuristic device that helps move us down the road in our thinking about the complex and nuanced ways in which particular epistemes, epistemologies, theories, and methods have coalesced to become regimes of truth that inform inquiry practices in powerful and pervasive ways. Importantly, we did not find these "regimes of truth" lying around in the basement of a philosophy department; we produced them. They are neither "real" in any universal sense nor mutually exclusive. Together, however, they constitute a useful continuum for thinking about how different articulations or assemblages of subjectivity, rationality, language, knowledge, and truth emerged historically, became durable chronotopes, and continue to affect in very powerful ways how qualitative inquiry is imagined and practiced within literacy studies, education, and the social sciences. Imagined as points positioned on a continuum, the chronotope of objectivism and representation embodies many traditional Enlightenment logics such as Descartes' rational subject and a correspondence theory of truth, while the chronotope of power/knowledge and defamiliarization probably goes the furthest in disrupting these particular logics and replacing them with alternatives.

Translating these ideas into research practice, perhaps what is most important is to generate as good a fit as possible between research questions or objects of interest and where to locate oneself on this continuum of chronotopes. As we noted in chapter 1, this requires deep reflection on the relations among various epistemologies, theories, approaches, and strategies. In some ways, each chronotope is uniquely valuable for pursuing some research projects more than others. But this is a bit of an overstatement. Seldom is a researcher ever really located within a single chronotope. Additionally, depending upon their values and goals, two different researchers might choose to locate ostensibly the same research project within different chronotopes. For example, although Heath (1983) located herself quite firmly in *Chronotope II*, one could imagine locating similar work in the Piedmont Carolinas within *Chronotopes III* or *IV*. Indeed, certain critiques of Heath's work have suggested that this might have been a good idea. Similarly, Luke's (1992) work in Australian elementary schools could readily have been conducted within *Chronotope I* or *Chronotope II*. Indeed, many accounts of read-alouds and story discussions have been written that claim to be more noninterpretive and politically neutral. In closing, we simply urge readers to keep in mind that where one locates oneself epistemologically has important consequences for what one sees and how one explains what one sees.

CHAPTER 3

A Selective History of
Inquiry in Anthropology

In this chapter, we examine trajectories of qualitative research logics that have emerged within the discipline of anthropology during this century—logics that have exerted very powerful effects on how research on language and literacy has been conducted. Like all disciplinary histories, we imagine anthropology as a historically produced social formation that aligns with different chronotopes in different ways at different times. We begin with an account of some of the early tensions in the field of anthropology, which were typically played out as debates about the relative scientific or interpretive orientation the field should espouse. A large portion of the chapter is then devoted to the Ethnography of Communication (EOC) tradition. We devote considerable attention to EOC for several reasons. This tradition emerged at about the same time as the civil rights movement and second-wave feminism and may be read as a general response to a *crisis of relevance* (Denzin & Lincoln, 2000), a crisis that explicitly resonated with these political pressures and demands. In short, anthropology needed to become more relevant and more attuned to the pragmatic, political exigencies of the times.

After mapping the history of effects that the EOC tradition has had on qualitative inquiry, we turn our attention to this second crisis—the *crisis of representation*. This crisis practically defined anthropology during much of the 1980s and 1990s, and it continues as a powerful force within anthropological debates over various modes of inquiry and their discontents. The crisis of representation (Clifford & Marcus, 1986; Marcus & Fischer, 1986) challenged the long-held representational politics and practices of traditional anthropology, which posited that Western researchers could accurately capture and represent "exotic non-Western others" in their texts. This challenge shook the very foundations of anthropology, still grounded in Enlightenment epistemologies, including in a correspondence theory of truth—the idea that we can both *discover* and *represent* the facts and laws of an *a priori* objective reality. *Representations* were no longer viewed as "mirrors of nature" (Rorty, 1979) but as constructions of experiences and events filtered through the "terministic screens" (Burke, 1966) of their authors.

We end the chapter with what Denzin and Lincoln (2000) have called the *crisis of evaluation* and *the crisis of praxis* within anthropology. When researchers' accounts are viewed not as mirrors but as manu-facturers of reality that at best embody a strong form of verisimilitude, then traditional forms of evaluating research accounts (e.g., validity, reliability, generalizability) are no longer relevant. Instead, research ac-counts must be assessed along more pragmatic lines—whether they are useful, whether they restore the forward movement and productivity of human activity that has become bogged down or no longer productive (Packer & Addison, 1989), and whether they function to expose and transform hegemonic regimes of truth and asymmetrical power rela-tions (Deleuze & Guattari, 1987; Lather, 1991). Thus, evaluation strate-gies based on verisimilitude, emotionality, personal responsibility, an ethic of caring, political praxis, dialogic research practice, and multi-voiced texts must replace those based on positivist notions of validity, reliability, and generalizability (Denzin & Lincoln, 2000, p. 10).

The *crisis of evaluation* led to a *crisis of praxis*—the articulation of theory and practice designed to make the world a better and more equitable place for all to live. As such, the crisis of praxis constitutes a challenge to the privileging of discourse in theory and research (i.e., the idea that everything can be reduced to a text and that changing representational forms will in turn change material reality). Instead, a praxis orientation insists that research function as a political force to change material conditions so that economic and symbolic forms of capital are distributed more equally (Denzin & Lincoln, 2000, p.17). Throughout all of our discussions of traditions and crises, we em-phasize the evolving "common sense" about what anthropology, as a discipline, "is" and what anthropologists as exemplars of qualitative research more broadly conceived "do."

Anthropology in the Twentieth Century: From Sapir to Hymes to Heath and Beyond

In mapping connections between anthropology and education, the figure of Edward Sapir stands as a kind of founding father. Sapir is perhaps best known for his widely popular book, *Language*, though he wrote broadly and prolifically on a range of subjects. Like his mentor Franz Boas, Sapir was dedicated to collecting descriptions of different languages and creating large corpuses of such material, replete with grammars and phonological systems. Sapir himself committed several such grammars to print, including in his dissertation, *The Takelm Language of Southwestern Oregon* (1909). After graduating from Columbia, Sapir took an appointment in the Department of Sociology and Anthropology at the University of Chicago. It was not uncommon at the time for both of these disciplines to be housed in the same department. At this time, anthropology as a field was firmly situated in *Chronotope I*, dominated by Boas's approach, which drew largely on physical anthropology and archaeology and resonated with the kind of work then done in philology. Sociology, by comparison, was more typically concerned with the vitality of social life as currently lived (especially in cities), and it relied on more traditional field-based, naturalistic research methods of data collection and analysis.

While Sapir continued to pursue his interest in studying and recording languages at Chicago, he also turned his attention to other intellectual interests, especially the symbolic nature of culture. In this regard, he was amazingly eclectic. For example, he was a musician and music critic, a literary critic, and an accomplished poet. Perhaps most importantly for our purposes here, he helped to set the agenda for those working in cultural psychology (see articles such as "Why Cultural Anthropology Needs the Psychiatrist" [originally published in 1938]).

Sapir, then, seems to have initiated a constructionist or interpretive turn in anthropology consistent with *Chronotope II*, yet the field remained primarily objectivist, and this objectivism remains evident in some anthropological work even today. Moreover, Sapir himself practiced both more objectivist and more interpretive forms of anthropology depending on his objects of inquiry. Perhaps because of its astounding depth and breadth, Sapir's work has been picked up by many different scholars in many different fields, often for opposing or contradictory purposes. As Hymes (1985) wrote in a collection of Sapir's writings, "Sapir has become the most admired and respected predecessor to linguists of almost all persuasions" (p. 600). In fact, scholars as diametrically opposed as Noam Chomsky and Dell Hymes have claimed Sapir as an intellectual ancestor. For Chomsky, Sapir was someone who was interested in the "deep structures" of natural language, and thus a predecessor of the study of transformational grammar that Chomsky founded. For Hymes, Sapir opened up critical questions about the variability of language practice in concrete settings, a key focus for the field of Ethnography of Communication, of which Hymes was a founder.

Indeed, structural forms of linguistics, including transformational grammar, came under heavy attack in the late 1960s and early 1970s by Hymes and others. The EOC tradition was less interested in the universal structures of grammar and more interested in interpreting and understanding actual language practices as they unfolded in situated acts of communication. Compared with Chomsky, EOC scholars were interested in a very different side of Sapir—the side interested in the variability of language practices, especially as these practices were constitutive of other kinds of everyday social and cultural practices.

Ethnography of Communication: Linguistics in a New Key

Hymes began publishing his first articles in the early 1960s, arguing against abstracting language practices from their social contexts. In doing so, Hymes brought linguistics into contact with broader social and cultural concerns and other fields of study—including education, where more applied research was the norm. In this regard, Hymes delivered the germinal paper "Functions of Speech" on his first visit to Harvard's Graduate School of Education. He argued in this paper that social life shapes communicative competence from birth onward and that children's knowledge of and facility with different kinds of language forms (or speech genres) vary as a function of socialization experiences related to gender, ethnicity, family, community, and religion. More generally, Hymes pushed for a broader rapprochement between linguistics and other disciplines such as education, psychology, and sociology. Indeed, he foresaw the transformation of linguistics from its original association with philology, foreign languages, and anthropology to its later interdependence with psychology, education, cognitive science, philosophy, discourse studies, and performance studies, of which education would be its most receptive new home.

Hymes and the EOC tradition were hugely influential in shifting the focus of linguistic inquiry from a more objectivist orientation (*Chronotope I*) to a more interpretive one (*Chronotope II*), and thus in reimagining the purview of linguistics. Hymes viewed "grammar" as one among many other analytic categories such as "phonology," "semantics," "pragmatics," and even "social structure" that can be abstracted from situated activity, but are of relatively little use in understanding that activity itself. More generally, EOC's insistence that understanding language and how it works requires exploring it unfold in situated social activity—typically realized through relatively stable patterns of talk and social interaction—prompted scholars to attend more reflexively to their modes of inquiry.

In 1980, Hymes wrote a book on anthropology and education called *Language in Education,* which urged that more attention be paid to language "performances" as opposed to language structures and linguistic competence. This argument later became a central tenet of the EOC tradition. Theoretically, it implied a switch in the "unit of analysis" in language and literacy research from the synchronic to the diachronic dimensions of language—from language as a formal system to language as practice. The distinction between structure and performance had been around at least since the 18th-century work of Saussure (1959), who framed it with the terms "*la langue*" and "*la parole.*" The former was used to describe the "deep structure" of language systems in terms of their least parts and rules of combination. The study of "*la langue*" required no consideration of context and its effects. In contrast, "*la parole*" was used to refer to actual language use in concrete, situated contexts of communication. With few exceptions, modern linguistics had traditionally been more interested in language structures and systems than in the variability and contingency of actual language practices, which they assumed were predictable because they are based on *a priori* linguistic structures.

The Emergence of New Approaches to Research

As one approach for studying real-time situated patterns of talk and social interaction, Hymes (1974) proposed a heuristic captured in the acronym or mnemonic of SPEAKING: Situation, Participants, Ends, Acts, Keys, Instrumentalities, Norms, and Genres (p. 62). SPEAKING is a classificatory heuristic that can help researchers understand almost any speech event in richly contextualized ways. It allows them a ready-to-hand interpretive tool for describing the sets of interpersonal relationships and the sets of interpretative frames used to accomplish specific communicative goals within specific speech events and contexts of situation. Using the SPEAKING heuristic in comparative ways also allows researchers to account for the kinds of cultural and historical variability that occur across communicative situations in real space and real time.

An example of the SPEAKING heuristic in use might help here. Let's say the speech event in question is an academic counseling encounter (as opposed, for example, to a job interview or a telephone conversation). Given this speech event, participants will have specific expectations about each dimension of the SPEAKING heuristic. In this case, the *situation* is an academic advising meeting taking place in a university. *Participants* include the student and her advisor. The *ends* are to help the student choose the optimal path while also observing the university's rules and policies. The *acts*, or act sequences, involve the ways in which the participants jointly identify relevant issues or problems and work to resolve them. Indexed by various metacommunicative strategies such as smiles, phatic interchanges, handshakes, considerable eye contact, etc., the *key* is usually formal but friendly. The *instrumentality* is face-to-face spoken language. The *norms* include the advisor withholding personal opinions and leaving decision making to the student. And the *genre* is a hybrid somewhere between a formal interview and an informal conversation.

The move from privileging structure to privileging performance in linguistic anthropology, illustrated in SPEAKING, implied a move toward more "naturalistic" research methods like those that had always been common within cultural anthropology but were seldom appropriated for studying language and literacy practices. Behaviorist, structuralist, and phenomenological approaches grounded pretty firmly in *Chronotope I* gave way to more ethnographic approaches grounded more in *Chronotope II*. Recall here that although linguists like Sapir were interested in language variability, they typically drew upon analytic methods from literature and philology, as well as intensive work with individual "native informants" in controlled settings, to do their work. Data collection seldom involved "naturalistic" encounters but "often formal and contrived . . . almost always different from the settings within which people usually interact" (Gumperz & Hymes, 1972, p. 7). This strategy often led to the construction of prescriptive or descriptive grammars, which yielded little useful information about actual language practices and their effects. The shift from viewing language as representational to viewing it as performative was far from trivial, but marked an epistemological shift that redirected researchers' attention away from "brute facts" and other characteristics of *Chronotope I* and toward socially and semiotically mediated facts and other characteristics of *Chronotope II*.

When applied to research on language and literacy, the ethnographic methods used by Hymes and other EOC researchers are enormously useful for discovering how particular speech acts and speech events function in particular social contexts, as well as how they vary across contexts. Yet these methods also had to be adapted to be most effective for understanding situated language practices as opposed to whole cultures as systems of meanings embodied in symbols (Geertz, 1973). Observation and participant observation could help researchers understand the roles and functions of speech through close observation of specific speech events, such as storytelling, classroom talk, and other ritual events. But EOC required researchers to choose focal speech events strategically and to spend more time in the field than linguists were used to in order to document and understand how specific social and cultural factors influence speakers' "natural" performances. EOC emphasized learning firsthand what it means to be a competent participant of a particular social group, and paid close attention to the consequences of being more or less able to move across multiple social groups fluidly, flexibly, and competently. The powerful influence of the EOC tradition on linguistic anthropology, especially in relation to education and literacy studies, was particularly strong in the 1970s and 1980s, when language-based ethnographies became one of the most popular forms of inquiry within language and literacy studies. The work of Susan Philips (1972, 1983) is exemplary in this regard. Philips spent years studying communication patterns on the Warm Springs Indian Reservation, especially in school contexts. She developed and refined her understandings of these communication patterns for a decade and finally published findings from her work in book form as *The Invisible Culture: Communication in Classroom and Community on the Warm Springs Indian Reservation* in 1983.

Among other things, Philips noted that children on this reservation tended to speak very little in class. Even more importantly, they became more and more reticent as their time in school went on. Based on these observations, Philips conducted a comparative study of classrooms in all-Indian schools on the reservation and classrooms in a mixed Indian–white school, using "participant observation" as her main data collection strategy. Through participant observation, Philips isolated the ways in which participation structures (or the structures of face-to-face interaction) differed in the two different settings, noting that the "social conditions that define when a person [typically] uses speech in Indian social situations are present in classroom situations in which Indian students use speech a great deal, and absent in the more prevalent classroom situations in which they fail to participate verbally" (1972, p. 371). Particularly interesting was the fact that she found that Indian students were less likely to communicate in settings where they were asked to communicate individually in front of other students. Also interesting was the fact that students were less likely to speak when communication was controlled by the teacher. Importantly for our purposes in this book, the adaptation of participant observation for the focused study of situated language and literacy practices marked a milestone in how much of the research in our field has been conducted ever since.

Reimagining the Research(er) as an Agent of Change

As research conducted from within an EOC perspective became increasingly popular, many scholars began arguing that language practices are inherently political practices and that the role of the linguist is an inherently political and politicized one. Researchers who had previously conducted primarily descriptive studies began to design studies that were more critical, signaling a shifting allegiance from *Chronotope II* to *Chronotope III*. Hymes, for example, focused some of his attention on how the construction and uptake of narratives function to distribute power unevenly in education settings, which in turn results in different kinds and amounts of learning. Drawing largely on the field of ethnopoetics for their analytic strategies, for example, Hymes and Cazden (1980) showed how similarities and differences between the narrative styles of teachers and students had profound effects on what different students learned. More specifically, they argued that some students were evaluated unfairly because their narrative styles of presentation differed from their teachers, who were neither competent in using these styles nor aware of the knowledge children possessed and were trying to display. This more critical kind of research was taken up by many of Hymes and Cazden's students, including Sarah Michaels. Her 1981 article, "Sharing Time: Children's Narrative Styles and Differential Access to Literacy," is perhaps the most oft-cited and most famous exemplar.

The point we want to underscore is that a crucial shift within the EOC tradition, from more descriptive studies to more critical ones, occurred in the 1980s. More explicitly political orientations to research grew as well. At least a generation of language and literacy scholars in education have taken up these concerns in various ways. Among the most important work along these lines was done by Shirley Brice Heath and published in her 1983 book, *Ways with Words*. Although Heath's work is perhaps most resonant within education and literacy studies, Heath was trained as a linguist and her dissertation advisor was Dell Hymes. Like the work of Hymes, Cazden, and Michaels, Heath's work had a strong political subtext. Her dissertation, for example, which was published as a book in 1972, bore the title, *Telling Tongues: Language Policy in Mexico Colony to Nation*.

The politicization of research in the field extended beyond the founding scholars of the EOC tradition and their protégés. Although occasionally present in reading and English education journals (e.g., *Research in the Teaching of English* and *Reading Research Quarterly*) from the 1980s, politicization was particularly evident in scholarly monographs and books. Thus, we see the beginning of a growing rift in the field at about the time *Ways with Words* was published from which we can infer a disruption of the "fact-value" distinction common to the Enlightenment separation of science from politics. Research on language and literacy (and especially its variability across cultures and contexts) conducted using ethnographic research strategies was challenging the more psychological and scientistic research that had been more typical for several decades, under the aegis of both behaviorism and cognitivism. The EOC tradition was beginning to influence educational research in profound, though not always highly visible, ways, and Heath's work was firmly planted within this tradition.

In an article published just before *Ways with Words* and, more ironically, just before the famous *A Nation at Risk* monograph (1983), Heath (1982) reflected on what an EOC approach might bring to the study of language and literacy. Importantly, Heath's study would be one of the first that looked at the nature and functions of print literacies. In her construct of the "literacy event," Heath in a sense redefined how reading and writing were conceived—not so much as discrete skills but as language practices that also involve the use of printed artifacts. Such new ways of considering literacy also were seen in collections such as *The Acquisition of Literacy: Ethnographic Perspectives* (Schieffelin & Gilmore, 1986). Drawing on her work in the Piedmont Carolinas (much of which is reported in *Ways with Words*), Heath wrote a chapter for this text in which she outlined a set of research strategies for ethnographic studies of language and literacy:

> A first step would be the collection of artifacts of literacy, descriptions of contexts of uses, and their spatial and temporal distribution within the life of members of the community. The internal style of each artifact and the abilities of those who produce these should be considered part of the context. How are these artifacts presented to children? What activities and explanations surround their use? Do questions directed to these children about these artifacts emphasize the acquisition of labels and description of discrete characteristics of items? Are there links made between these representations and uses of their real-world equivalents? (p. 47).

As we noted in chapter 2, Heath developed and used these research strategies during the decade she conducted research on the language practices of three communities in the Piedmont Carolinas (Roadville, Trackton, and Maintown) to see how home language and literacy practices either reinforced or were at odds with the practices rewarded in school. In practice, however, these strategies seemed to be more informal than the rather prescriptive paragraph above might suggest. Ethnographic in its execution, her collection of empirical data was largely linked to the specific positions she held within the communities she studied, as well as to the specific goals of her project. She had grown up in the Piedmonts and returned there to teach in a teacher preparation program. "In the years between 1969 and 1978," she wrote, "I lived, worked, and played with the children and their families and friends in Roadville and Trackton. My entry into these specific communities came through a naturally occurring chain of events. In each case, I knew an old-time resident in the community, and my relationship opened the community to me" (Heath, 1982, p. 5). She also noted having participated in many official and unofficial activities in these communities. While participating in these various activities, she composed field notes and sometimes audiotaped events, a practice that had just begun to rise in prominence within educational research:

> Often I was able to write in a field notebook while minding children, tending food, or watching television with families; otherwise, I wrote fieldnotes as soon as possible afterwards when I left the community on an errand or to go to school. In the classrooms, I often audiotaped; we sometimes videotaped; and both the teachers and I took fieldnotes as a matter of course of many days of each year. (p. 9)

Heath's use of informal, long-term participant observation is akin in many, if not all, ways to the informal research practices of early anthropologists, working before the formal codification of its "methods." She was well aware of the tensions and attendant anxieties of being betwixt and between more scientistic and more interpretive approaches in her work, as well as the contingent nature of all anthropological work.

Through the study itself, Heath demonstrated the ways in which middle-class family language practices prepared young people for schoollike literacy activities. Objects and ideas were often talked about in decontextualized ways, as they are in school, and framed within secondary genres such as the Initiation-Response-Evaluation sequences, "known answer" questions, and extended explanations. Working-class Black and White parents, in contrast, did not socialize young children to use language in this fashion. Ideas and objects were often experienced and talked about in tacit and highly embodied ways, embedded within the warp and weft of everyday life. Because these children were apprenticed in their homes to value and to use language and literacy in ways that were not common in school, they experienced difficulty adapting to the ways of school. Moreover, their own "ways with words" were seldom valued or validated in school, and over time they learned less and less and school became more and more alienating. Heath's landmark study and studies like it opened up a range of questions and concerns about language, learning, and the functions and effects of specific institutional settings. In true anthropological fashion, many of these studies were comparative, usually comparisons of literacy and learning between and across school and nonschool contexts.

In addition to opening up questions and concerns about domains of inquiry on the frontier of research in language and literacy, work like Heath's also raised questions about the possibilities and limitations of using anthropological methods to conduct research in these domains. Echoing the concerns of Hymes with which we opened this chapter, in the introduction to their edited book, *Children In and Out of School* (1982), Perry Gilmore and Allan Glatthorn noted that "we believed strongly that ethnography, with its inherent sensitivity to people, to culture, and to context offered the promise of valuable new practical insights that could lead to the improvement of schools" (p. 3). They went on to say that much of the baggage of anthropology and anthropologists would need to be left behind:

Ethnographers who find their roots in anthropology tend to view the transmission of culture as their own special purview. . . . Such an approach not only confronts issues of turf but risks, for ethnographers, denying in practice that which is basic to their science and which holds the promise of usefulness. . . . What ethnography should bring to education is not answers, but a listening, learning posture that—based in respect for informants—leads to the explication of the important, unaddressed questions. (p. 5)

Ongoing Proliferations of the Ethnography of Communication Tradition

At around the time Heath's classic work was published, Courtney Cazden (1982) usefully summed up emergent themes that were beginning to register within the EOC tradition as it struggled to figure out exactly how to deploy the anthropological research tradition within educational settings. Specifically, she argued that educational research concerned with language and literacy practices (and their effects) needed to wrestle with four basic issues: (1) the continuity or discontinuity between school and home in children's lives; (2) the importance of understanding *in situ* language performance, children's folklore, and youth culture; (3) the importance of researcher/practitioner collaborations; and (4) the relative purchase of microanalytic and macroanalytic approaches to educational research, as well as the potential ways in which they might be integrated.

As it turns out, Cazden's insights were prescient, as language and literacy research has increasingly tended to focus on out-of-school literacies during the past few decades (e.g., Barton & Ivanic, 1991; Baynam, 1995; Finders, 1997; Heath & McLaughlin, 1993; Hull & Schultz, 2002; Knobel, 1999). More and more research has also focused on "naturally" occurring literacy activities in the context of children's everyday lives (e.g., Goodwin, 1990; Hicks, 2002; Wells, 1985). Within qualitative inquiry, more generally, Denzin and Lincoln (2000) argue convincingly that we have been experiencing a "performance turn" for at least a decade and probably longer. Within this turn, not only has more attention been paid to the practices and performances of everyday life but also to fieldwork and writing as performative activities. Similarly, both within language and literacy research and within qualitative inquiry more generally, there has been a press to understand how relationships between researchers and research participants actually affect the outcomes or findings of research. Finally, within anthropological research generally (especially research that focuses on language and literacy), working to understand the co-constitutive relations between macrosocial forces (e.g., race, class, or gender ideologies) and microsocial practices (e.g., patterns of moment-to-moment talk and interaction) has become much more common. Among other things, this has meant that researchers have developed more syncretic approaches to research, often combining traditional ethnographic strategies with strategies from discourse analysis. Indeed, there is even an emerging subfield of anthropology built around this particular syncretism that calls itself "the linguistic anthropology of education" (e.g., Kamberelis & Jaffe, 2003; Wortham & Rymes, 2002).

Let us briefly elaborate on each of Cazden's insights, and offer specific examples of how each has been taken up within our field. The first issue Cazden raised was the critical role of continuity versus discontinuity between school and home in the lives of young people, especially in terms of their resonance with school tasks and their prospects for school success. Very often the kinds of communicative practices privileged in school are based on a normative White European model. As a result, communicative mismatches occur, mismatches that are often mistaken for cognitive deficiencies. This has been perhaps the most lasting and enduring set of ideas to emerge from the EOC tradition, and it set the framework for much of the language and literacy research conducted during the past two decades.

The second issue Cazden called attention to was children's folklore or children's culture. Interestingly, many early anthropologists of language were folklorists. Worth recalling here is the fact that the EOC tradition has always been centrally concerned with language "performance" as opposed to language "structure." Although they viewed all communication as performance, folklorists were particularly concerned with performances "marked" by individuals and communities as unique or special and that were usually related to ritualistic events. The specific interest in children's folklore and children's culture that Cazden highlighted—chants, jump rope activities, riddles, and trading time activities—was constitutively linked to this larger set of interests in performance.

The third issue Cazden brought up was the need for more collaboration among teachers and researchers. Much early anthropology was comparative and descriptive, and the researcher operated as a kind of "lone ethnographer" (Rosaldo, 1989). As the anthropological approaches to research became more common in education (and other fields), however, more attention was paid to the nature and functions of participatory action research, or how researchers and practitioners could engage in dialogue and collaborative work both to enhance student learning and to enact educational reform. Among other things, this meant bringing typically unmarked and unconscious teaching and research practices to higher levels of self-reflection. Additionally, since the "crisis of representation" (e.g., Clifford & Marcus, 1986; Marcus & Fischer, 1986), which we discuss later, the press to align and integrate the ideologies, practices, and educational research with those of classroom teaching became very powerful. As the logic goes, if teachers were more involved in research on issues important to them, then they would both develop stronger research skills to benefit them in assessing others' work, and recognize and increase their abilities to enact change. Similarly, if research were rooted in practice, then teachers would increasingly use research to inform their practice.

The final issue that Cazden highlighted was the need to integrate macroanalytic and microanalytic approaches to educational research. One of the benefits of microanalysis is that it affords access to complexities that are not available though more holistic ethnographic analyses. Conversely, one of the benefits of ethnographic analysis is its ability to reveal more macrosituational dimensions of social life (as well as material conditions, social and cultural structures, and fields of power), which are less accessible through microanalysis. Because each technique operates at different levels or orders of data, they are complementary, and combining them can be analytically powerful.

Of course, this kind of integration was always lurking within several research traditions concerned with language and literacy practices. There were efforts, for example, within the EOC tradition and the conversation analytic tradition (see chapter 4) to move away from what C. Wright Mills (1959) called the "abstracted empiricism" of fine-tuned, microlevel studies largely disconnected from broader social and cultural concerns and issues. Indeed, while much of this work was concerned with face-to-face microlevel practices, many early anthropologists of communication argued that there was a need to understand these processes in terms of how they are embedded in larger social and cultural processes at the community or cultural level. Even more broadly, there was a need to link microlevel practices with macroanalytic structural forces that contributed to their conditions of possibility in the first place. Literacy researchers were among the scholars who responded to this call most effectively (e.g., Hornberger, 1997; Rymes, 2001; Street, 1995).

Coda: Inquiry Logics and the Ethnography of Communication Tradition

The genesis and ongoing development of the EOC tradition have exerted powerful effects on the development of qualitative research logics within anthropology. Straddling the boundary of *Chronotope I* and *II* while stepping toward *Chronotope III*, EOC scholarship began to problematize many key epistemological certainties. In particular, EOC opened up important interpretive trajectories in the study of language and language use. Scholars and researchers no longer focused on idealized language grammars and structures taken out of context. Rather, the focus shifted to situated and variable speaking practices. Language was now seen as socially mediated and performative. Although EOC scholars seldom went as far as to claim that language produces reality in any radical sense (and thus can never be neutral), they no longer viewed language as simply representational.

Given this view of language, scholars within the EOC tradition varied in the extent to which they viewed knowledge as socially constructed but generally neutral. Most agreed with Geertz that cultural symbols (e.g., narratives, myths, rituals, dreams, iconography) are windows into a society's collective cognitive structures, naturalized rules of conduct, and patterns of social interaction. Furthermore, they believed that by studying the meanings of the multiple and related symbolic forms of a culture, the anthropologist could render the "logic" of the culture from the "native's point of view." When knowledge is conceived in this way, a consensus theory of truth tends to be predominant. Truth is a matter of consensus within a particular interpretive community.

Because of the press to address the crisis of relevance, some EOC scholars went a bit further than this, positing knowledge as somehow related to power and truth as produced in dialogue across difference. EOC work within education was often of this kind, as EOC scholars began taking on issues of power and inequality, particularly around questions of schooling. The individual and collective works of Del Hymes and Courtney Cazden are but two examples of how EOC helped move anthropology from a primarily descriptive enterprise to one that took up pressing political questions. As Hymes's (1972) prophetic *Reinventing Anthropology* made clear, one could no longer claim a kind of transcendent objectivity in relation to one's research. Anthropologists had to make clear decisions about the directions their work would take—specifically, whether or not it would support progressive social and political agendas.

By and large, EOC scholars held on to a phenomenological view of the subject as separate from but in dialogue with other subjects (and objects). While the relationship between "facts" and "values" was called into question, the notion that one could unproblematically gather "facts" was not. They retained an inherent trust in accounts of experience (their own and those of their participants) as valid and true, and they held on to the idea that one could clearly separate oneself from one's object of study. There was little agonizing over the writing process or the possibility of speaking for others. Few scholars spent much time troubling over the relations among signs, concepts, and referents. Texts were taken as self-evident, and traditional notions of validity, reliability, and trustworthiness maintained their hegemonic hold. In short, the aims and goals of anthropology were called into question, but its tried-and-true practices were not. These tendencies, however, would change profoundly over the next two decades.

Responding to the Crisis of Representation: Writing Culture and Beyond

So far, we have sketched an important trajectory of thinking about the content and methods of anthropology, especially in relation to studying language and literacy—from Sapir to Hymes to Heath and beyond. Among other things, we noted that the politics of schooling and the roles of language and literacy within classroom practice emerged as important sites for anthropology as its exotic "fishing holes" dried up and as it sought to make itself more "relevant" to the world. Despite the continued development, refinement, and expansion of research methods within anthropology, objectivist epistemologies continued to exert a strong influence on the field while it also became more interpretive (*Chronotope II*) and more critical (*Chronotope III*). Heath's *Ways with Words* is a notable embodiment of these tensions. While explicitly written as a realistic descriptive ethnography (a kind of hybrid of *Chronotope I* and *Chronotope II*), an obvious subtext of this book is critical (*Chronotope III*). For example, in no uncertain terms, Heath signaled the need to align the "ways with words" of families and communities with the "ways with words" of school and society so that school might function more equitably and productively for all students and families. Moreover, her decade-long involvement in transformative work with teachers in the Piedmont Carolinas is clearly reminiscent of Freire's transformative work with Brazilian peasants. Finally, the fact that the effects of much of Heath's work unraveled after she left the Piedmont Carolinas suggests some of the limitations of *Chronotopes II* and *III* for engaging in effective political work, thus indexing some of the insights of *Chronotope IV*. Working for social change that becomes self-sustaining is both fragile and problematic work. Looking across the historical trajectory of Heath's work in the Piedmont Carolinas, it seems clear to us that even though objectivist and interpretive epistemologies remained powerful within anthropology as a discipline in the 1970s and 1980s, changing research practices in the field as well as new social and political forces at work in society began to erode this power. EOC, for example, with its stress on the political dimensions of fieldwork, began to disrupt the relatively nonreflexive nature of anthropological inquiry. As the field continued to develop through the 1980s, it became even more self-reflexive—even hyper-self-reflexive—ushering in many uncertainties and doubts, both epistemological and pragmatic. Indeed, the 1980s were a time of enormous growth and ferment within anthropology as a field, and this time was captured in the moniker the *crisis of representation*. The *crisis of representation* refers, in general terms, to the doubt that language can offer an "accurate view and confident knowledge of the world" (Marcus & Fischer, 1986, pp. 14–15).

During the mid-1980s, anthropologists (and qualitative researchers across disciplines) experienced this crisis when they began to realize that fieldwork did not consist of a "Lone Ethnographer" who "rode off into the sunset in search of 'his native,'" endured and passed a series of trials, underwent his rite of passage by enduring his "fieldwork," and after collecting his "data" returned to his home to write a "true" account of the "culture" (Rosaldo, 1989, p. 30). Researchers were forced to respond to many criticisms about how anthropologists were writing about "others" in particular Third World cultures from the perspectives of Western sociology and political science, and thus constructing these others with and within the constructs and languages of these perspectives (e.g., Clifford, 1988; Said, 1979). Gone were the days when ethnographies were viewed as authoritative accounts, written and sanctioned by (usually White male) anthropologists. Instead, ethnographies were reimagined as *textually* constructed *partial* representations of what was actually encountered and created. All representations were considered inherently problematic—constructions of their authors often deployed (even if unintentionally) in the service of some hegemonic regime (e.g., colonialism, education as social reproduction, etc.). Far from being objectively oriented "Lone Ethnographers," anthropologists contributed to the cultures that they "observed," and they developed relationships that also contributed heavily to their analyses and to what ended up on paper.

This crisis foregrounded the constitutive role of researcher both in the conduct of fieldwork and in the representation of the people and cultures they researched. Researchers increasingly began to consider such issues as the socioeconomics and politics of their research and how these affected the relationship between the researchers and the researched. Researchers became more self-reflexive and began to consider their own positionings as researchers. As a first response to correct the problems now seen, anthropologists (and qualitative researchers from various fields) changed the focus of the research process from one that centered on fieldwork to one centered on the act of writing and the production of ethnographic accounts. Instead of researchers speaking for others, they allotted spaces in their textual productions for others to speak for themselves. That is, they attempted to give voice to the previously silenced research subjects by adopting new textual strategies (e.g., including personal narratives, the use of extended quotations, adding appendices containing "raw" data). Clifford & Marcus's (1986) anthology, for example, often foregrounded personal narratives in writing up research, claiming that this served a crucial reflexive function that opened up new ways of doing field work. This new kind of field work stressed that research is an invention, not a representation of a cultural setting, and that reimagining research as invention forces inquirers to interrogate their own locations as well as how they construct the "other." Clifford (1986) urged that ethnographic researchers spend more time elaborating a "specification of discourses" of who speaks and writes, when and where, with whom, and under what constraints (p. 13).

A hallmark of the *crisis of representation*, then, was the realization that writing is not epiphenomenal. Instead, "language . . . is a constitutive force, creating a particular view of reality and of the self"

(Richardson, 1994, p. 518). Different genres of writing and different semiotic media (writing, photography, video) afford different kinds of access to experience and the world. Challenges to viewing writing (and other semiotic forms) uncritically as representational (and not performative and productive) led to critiques of anthropological work conducted by anthropologists in earlier times. Indeed, the work of Clifford and others can be seen both as an extension of and challenge to the "hermeneutic turn" heralded by anthropologist Clifford Geertz, among others.

Beginning in the mid-1960s, Geertz argued for what became known as "symbolic anthropology"—the study of the multiple and related symbolic forms of a culture, which help render the "logic" of the culture from the "native's point of view." Geertz's landmark book, *The Interpretation of Cultures* (1973), argued that culture was "semiotic," that "man is an animal suspended in webs of significance he himself has spun." The study of culture was, in essence, the study of those webs, and for Geertz, reading cultures was like reading texts. The analysis of culture was "therefore not an experimental science in search of law but an interpretive one in search of meaning" (p. 5). From this perspective, anthropology was redefined as the construction of other people's constructions of their realities, achieved through "thick description"—a notion that all but defined a generation of anthropologists (Ortner, 1999). A key example here is Geertz's famous treatment of the Balinese cockfight in which Geertz described this ritual event in detail and nuance and shows how its meaning and relevance can only be understood against the backdrop of a storehouse of cultural knowledge. It is a story, to evoke Geertz, that the anthropologist "strains to read over the shoulders of those to whom they properly belong" (Geertz, 1973, p. 452).

A faith in the representational dimensions of language was central to the hermeneutic turn heralded by Geertz and others. By the 1980s, various critiques of Geertz's work had emerged. In the introduction to *Writing Culture*, for example, James Clifford (1986) wrote, "We begin, not with participant-observation or with cultural texts . . . but with writing, the making of texts. No longer a marginal, or occulted, dimension, writing has emerged as central to what we do both in the field and thereafter." He went on to note, "The fact that it has not until recently been portrayed or seriously discussed reflects the persistence of an ideology claiming transparency of representation and immediacy of experience" (p. 2).

But the move from experiential validation to validation through good representation was not radical enough for Clifford and his colleagues. While scholars like Geertz reimagined fieldwork as text-making and thus world-making, their critiques of traditional ethnography were not deconstructive. Geertz, for example, still held on to the idea that "accurate" representations were possible. The ethnographer's primary task was still to expand her "horizon of vision" through experience with exotic others and to inscribe their worlds from "their point of view" as accurately as possible. Simply acknowledging that ethnographers "write" and "write others" was not nearly reflexive enough for Clifford and others, who were more interested in decentering the authority of the text, in the discursive production of texts and their effects, in questions of power and its role in whose voices inhabited texts, and in whether representations could be considered a form of knowledge at all. As Clifford (1988) noted, "With the recent questioning of colonial styles of representation, with the expansion of literacy and ethnographic consciousness, new possibilities for reading (and thus for writing) cultural descriptions are emerging" (p. 53).

The *crisis of representation* thus led many researchers to question traditional writing conventions and genres and to experiment with alternative forms of representation. Margery Wolf (1992), for example, addressed these concerns and interrogated their implications in *A Thrice Told Tale: Feminism, Postmodernism & Ethnographic Responsibility*. She summed up her critique of the crisis of representation thus: "To my thinking, if there is any crisis in ethnography, it is a growing uncertainty about our dual responsibility to our audiences and our informants" (p. 137). Theoretically, Wolf called attention to the fact that different writing conventions can give us different perspectives on a single strip of reality. Pragmatically, she offered her readers three different constructions of her field work in Taiwan: an ethnography, a short story, and her raw field notes. Importantly, Wolf's work challenged the ways anthropologists have used language uncritically to represent reality even as she maintained that one can say something meaningful about the "other," not just about the "self." Her writing is mutivocal, and the realities she opens up are multiple.

Worth noting here is the fact that critiques about the politics of representation were quite different from the critiques of anthropology spawned by the crisis of relevance we discussed earlier. Whereas critiques that motivated the development of EOC were located within *Chronotopes II* and *III*, these later critiques were located primarily within *Chronotope IV*. Although Dell Hymes was concerned about how the work of anthropologists was deployed in the service of imperialism and Western domination, for example, he still viewed power as "out there," located in political systems and particularly well-positioned and powerful social actors. With such a conception of power, possibilities for social change were also located in these distal social forces. So although political questions were continually raised, they did not affect the actual research practices of anthropologists very much. Later critiques of the anthropological project by James Clifford, Renato Rosaldo, Ruth Behar, and others were rooted in a very different notion of power (the Foucaultian notion of power we discussed at length in chapter 2), and they called into question objectivist epistemologies and their concomitant research and representational practices in even more compelling ways.

Armed with Foucault's insistence on the productive nature of power and discourse, many anthropologists since the *crisis of representation* have argued that researchers do not simply enter a field, discover the truth about a culture, and write it up objectively. Instead, one always enters as an interpreting agent among many interpreting agents, and fieldwork is largely a matter of negotiating the relative purchase of these interpretations. Researchers are always already "writing" or "producing" cultural practices and culture itself, and it is impossible ever to write a definitive account of any, either. One can only write an account that is one interpretation (fiction) among many interpretations (fictions). Indeed, many theorists and researchers in *Writing Culture* and other texts that followed it looked at classic ethnographic texts for the ways they employed literary tropes—such as those of travel writing—to construct their accounts. In doing so, the contributors deconstructed the classic accounts of culture that supported traditional anthropological practices. Culture was now seen as increasingly messy, without the fictitious cohesion that anthropologists had apparently laminated on top of them: "Cultures are not scientific 'objects' (assuming such things exist, even in the natural sciences). Culture, and our views of 'it,' are produced historically, and are actively contested. There is no whole picture that can be 'filled in' since the perception and filling of a gap lead to the awareness of other gaps" (Clifford, 1986, p. 18).

Clifford went on to say that "culture is contested, temporal, and emergent. Representation and explanation—both by insiders and outsiders—is implicated in this emergence" (p. 19). This realization opened the door to questions about ideology and the practice of anthropology itself, questions about why particular cultures have been represented in particular ways over time and to what political ends. Often these concerns gelled around the "orientalizing" project of anthropology and how it has worked in the service of imperialism (Said, 1979). Anthropologists became acutely aware that "their" cultures had typically been represented as seamless, coherent, timeless wholes while "our" cultures had always been represented as more complex and dynamic.

Beyond the Crisis of Representation: Reimagining the Field and Fieldwork

The seminal ideas of the *crisis of representation* have been taken up by a range of anthropologists during the past two decades. In a series of influential essays, for example, Rosaldo (1989) wrote about the "erosion of classic norms," the ways that functional appeals to transcendent norms no longer hold in this radically shifting and complex world. He also critiqued the ways anthropologists have traditionally assumed a functional approach to culture, and have been complicit in the ways that cultures work to limit their members with and into a codified set of norms. To redress these problems, Rosaldo argued that we must view culture "in motion," likening culture today to a "garage sale" where artifacts circulate in wide and often unpredictable ways:

> The image of anthropology as a garage sale depicts our present global situation. Analytical postures developed during the colonial era can no longer be sustained. Ours is definitely a postcolonial epoch. Despite the intensification of North American imperialism, the "Third World" has imploded into the metropolis. Even the conservative national politics of containment, designed to shield "us" from "them," betray the impossibility of maintaining hermetically sealed cultures. (p. 44)

Rosaldo focused our attention on the ways that culture is increasingly unstable, on the flow of cultural transactions that have all but eroded traditional boundaries and borders between and among cultures and nations. These transactions have registered, he noted, on the everyday practices and experiences of peoples who need to be viewed with a similarly flexible set of tools, with what he calls a "processural perspective" (p. 103). "Insofar as it is concerned with how people's actions alter their forms of life, social analysis must attend to improvisation, muddling though, and contingent events" (p. 103). Using the garage sale as a metaphor for culture suggests a world that is never finalized, that is always open to change, that is always emergent.

The garage sale metaphor also suggests serious implications for how theorists and researchers think about the key anthropological constructs of the *field* and *fieldwork* (Eisenhart, 2001). As we noted at the beginning of the chapter, the press to problematize and reimagine the field and fieldwork resulted from what Denzin and Lincoln (2000) have called the *crisis of evaluation* and the *crisis of praxis*, which followed directly on the heels of the *crisis of representation*.

These latter crises suggested epistemological frameworks within which researchers' accounts are seen to produce, rather than represent, reality. Within such frameworks, traditional forms of evaluating research accounts (e.g., validity, reliability, generalizability) are neither relevant nor adequate. New strategies for evaluating research accounts are required, strategies that are both more pragmatic and more generative. Instead of trying to justify the truth value of accounts or to argue for their replicability, researchers focus on developing strategies for showing how their accounts help to restore or enhance the forward movement and productivity of human life (e.g., Packer & Addison, 1989), and to expose and transform hegemonic regimes of truth and asymmetrical structures of power (e.g., Deleuze & Guattari, 1987; Lather, 1991). Researchers become less concerned with producing accounts with validity, reliability, and generalizability and more concerned with producing accounts that embody verisimilitude, emotionality, personal responsibility, care, praxis, and plurivocality (Denzin & Lincoln, 2000, p. 10).

The *crisis of evaluation* helped spawn the *crisis of praxis*. This crisis involved the resurrection of some key tropes of Marxist social theory, especially Marx's insistence on the articulation of theory and practice designed to make the world a better and more equitable place for all to live (i.e., praxis). Additionally, the *crisis of praxis* challenged the postmodern tendency to privilege discourse and its concomitant tendency to neglect material conditions and their constitutive effects. Within a praxis orientation, research is viewed as one among many political forces that actually change material conditions so that power and other social and material goods are distributed more equally (Denzin & Lincoln, 2000, p. 17).

In sum, then, as important as it was in initiating a key epistemological shift away from *Chronotopes I* and *II* and toward *Chronotopes III* and *IV*, the *crisis of representation* did not disrupt the epistemological foundations of anthropological inquiry enough for some anthropologists. More specifically, the almost exclusive emphasis on textual representation eclipsed the equally pressing issue of challenging research practice in the field and the constitutive function of power relations between researchers and research participants that led to the text's production in the first place. Challenging the veracity of texts and interrogating the processes of textual production does not necessarily lessen the power differentials between the researcher and the researched. In fact, "the emphasis on the textual operations may further centre the researcher's self in relation to the text" (Probyn, 1993, p. 68).

More and more, for example, ethnographic work has come to focus on how agents (anthropologists and their informants) collude in the emergence of particular versions of self and/in particular cultures (Behar, 1993; Lather, 1997; Sparkes, 1994). While this work has sometimes been concerned with how research is "written up" (echoing the concerns of Clifford and others), it has focused more often on power relations and power differentials in the field and how they inform the ethnographic project. Thus, many contemporary anthropological accounts provide readers with descriptions or "case studies" of how people have attempted to deal with complex ethical and personal situations in the field. This work has not so much sought to forge "cultural norms" or "typified cases," but has stressed the partiality of culture and the complexity of the research project itself.

Ruth Behar's groundbreaking book, *Translated Woman: Crossing the Border with Esperanza's Story* (1993), is a good example of this reorientation. Behar's most important work in this book involved her efforts to document the life history of a single woman in Mexico named Esperanza. Hers was not a "typified" account but a particular one. Behar made Esperanza's own goals transparent from the outset of her work. She stressed that Esperanza had a vested interest in narrating her life history (or "story") because she wanted it recorded and retold as a "story." Behar acknowledged this collusion from the very beginning. "What I am reading is a story, or set of stories, that have been told to me, so that I, in turn, can tell them again, transforming myself from a listener to a storyteller" (p. 152). Thus, the book containing Behar's account of Esperanza is constituted as multiple fictions worked out in dialogue.

The shared story that emerged and passed from storyteller to storyteller was negotiated across many axes, including those of gender and power. What developed in the narrative was "a constructed mirroring of the lives of the two women, so that the ethnographer's voice is not only revealed to us but also makes itself vulnerable to the reader through its own intimate confessions" (Socolovsky, 1998, p. 73). It is interesting to note how Behar reflected upon the fact that her identity was constructed differently by herself and others as she crossed the border between Mexico and the United States. In the United States, Behar was "Cubana, born in Cuba, raised in a series of noisy apartments in the sad borough of Queens, New York, that smelled of [her] mother's sofrito." She "spoke Spanish at home, learned English in school, where [she] was in the 'dumb class' for a while until [she] could speak" (Behar, 1993, p. 320). However, "in Mexico [she was] gringa because [she went] to Mexico with gringa privileges, gringa money, gringa credentials, not to mention a gringo husband and gringo car" (p. 321). Esperanza recognized and exploited the social facts of Behar's gringa identity as she negotiated the flow of power and goods that would flow back and forth between the two women.

Indeed, Behar's work illustrates the complex ways in which power circulates between researchers and research participants. As Behar became Esperanza's familial intimate and partner in a relationship of care, Esperanza assumed more control over Behar's data collection methods and even the goals of Behar's research. Esperanza also made increasing demands on Behar's time and financial resources. For example, the price tag for material goods that Esperanza requested (demanded?) from Behar increased considerably over time—from a soft drink to a cassette player to a television set to a new pump for her well. Indeed, the forms of reciprocity and exchange that occurred between Behar and Esperanza seemed necessary to create a space for praxis, where researchers and research participants work critically and collectively in various spaces of struggle with few, if any, guarantees about exactly where their work will lead or what it will produce.

In sum, Behar's work is a nice example of how both the conduct of fieldwork and the collection of life histories are always situated between the actions and constructions of the "researcher" and "researched" in ways that are driven by the continual emergence of microlevel power relations. Behar's revisioning of life history research was one of several groundbreaking epistemological and methodological responses to the complexities of the contemporary research scene.

Like Behar, other researchers have foregrounded the relationship between the "researcher" and the "researched" with an eye toward creating more dialogic relationships (and texts) through increased self-reflexivity and more developed forms of praxis. Fine (1995), for example, insisted that researchers all too often ignore the power that they have and use in representing others, and she cautioned against the monolithic, static identities that such representational practices seem to create. To redress this problem, Fine called for increased self-reflexivity and multivocality, within which the self/other dichotomy is explored, merged, and divided. She theorized this self/other dichotomy using the metaphor of the hyphen. The hyphen represents the space between the researcher and the researched. By "working the hyphen," Fine contended that researchers can create opportunities for those involved in the research (self and others) to explore what is happening between them. In this regard, she argues for a more dialogic approach than Richardson.

It is important to Fine not only to recognize the hyphen, but also to allow others to have a say in how they are constructed and represented. Becoming meta-aware through conversations about whose story is being told and why, as well as whose story is not being told and why, and whose interpretations are being privileged, allows researchers to work the hyphen, engage the boundaries of relationships and how they are represented in texts, and create more dialogic and egalitarian accounts:

> When we opt, as has been the tradition, simply to write *about* those who have been Othered, we deny the hyphen. Slipping into a contradictory discourse of individualism, personalogic, theorizing, and decontextualization, we inscribe the Other, strain to white out Self, and refuse to engage in contradictions that litter our texts. (p. 72)

Fine's aim here is for researchers to understand how narratives work politically, to understand how the traditions of social science work to inscribe, and to reflect on how these traditions can be reworked to resist acts of othering (p. 75).

For Fine, discussing these issues and negotiating decisions about whose knowledge and what aspects of relationships will be represented in texts is crucial. Self-reflexivity, then, constantly calls the positionality of the researcher into question instead of taking such positionality for granted and works to create alternatives for representing others. Although Fine argued for alternative forms of representation, her argument implies that accurate representations are possible if there is sufficient self-reflexivity and dialogism. As mentioned earlier, several researchers disagree with this possibility (e.g., Lather, 1991; Lather & Smithies, 1997; Lenzo, 1994; Probyn, 1993; Roman, 1993).

Leslie Roman's (1993) response to the complexities of fieldwork is particularly interesting. She is a praxis-oriented researcher who argues for what she calls "double exposure" (p. 280). Double exposure is her term for the dialogic interaction between her political beliefs and theoretical commitments and her research practices. Importantly, Roman pays much more attention to the actual act of research than to the representation of the researched. She discusses how "practical ethical dilemmas and conflicts shaped and transformed [her] feminist materialism, while this emergent theory and politicized consciousness in turn caused [her] to rethink [her] ethical stances" toward the women she worked with in her study of young punk women (p. 280). She believes that the phrase "double exposure" represents how ethnographers need to self-consciously and reflexively expose how their prior beliefs and structural positionings and interests (e.g., class, gender, race, age) partially constitute the empirical evidence for or against their descriptions and analyses of their research subjects (p. 281). Too few ethnographers, she argues, explicitly locate themselves within "analyses of the larger material conditions and power relations" that produce tension in the field (p. 283). Like Fine, she argues that ignoring these forces can perpetuate the fiction that researchers' experiences are not mediated by the conditions under which they work and their own political and theoretical commitments. Roman, in sum, believes it is necessary to acknowledge that her work involves making political and moral decisions and that its main goal is to help empower the people she works with.

Patti Lather and her colleagues have pushed the "limit conditions" of inquiry even further in their work. Lather and Smithies (1997), for example, explored the lives, experiences, and narratives of 25 women living with HIV/AIDS in their book *Troubling the Angels*. This book is filled with overlapping and contradictory voices that grew out of 5 years of focus group interviews conducted in the context of support groups in five major cities in Ohio:

> In the autumn of 1992, we met with one of the support groups to explore what questions we should use in the interviews. The women attending this meeting were spilling over with excitement and ideas; their talk became a dialogue of issues and feelings and insights. Group process was producing a form and level of collaboration that could not be remotely

duplicated in one-on-one interviews, so the decision was made to maintain the group format for most of the data collection. (p. xix)

Lather and Smithies also met and talked with these women at birthday parties and holiday get-togethers, hospital rooms and funerals, baby showers and picnics. The participation frameworks for interaction changed constantly across the project. In what she calls a "post-book," Lather (2001) acknowledged experiencing at least two "breakdowns" as she bore witness to the women's experiences and stories and was forced to negotiate her own relationships to pain, loss, and death (p. 210). In both "strategic" and "found" ways, more organized occasions for "collecting data" constantly blurred into the "practices of everyday life" (deCerteau, 1984). Among other things, this social fact transformed the very nature of the focus groups these researchers conducted, rendering them more like rich and powerful conversations among people who cared deeply for one another. Yet Lather and Smithies are careful to work against the tendency to sentimentalize or romanticize their roles or their work in what Lather (2001, p. 212) referred to as a "recalcitrant rhetoric" constantly working against *verstehen* or empathy. They remained aware that the goals and rewards of their participation were very different from the goals and rewards of their research participants. Their participants, for example, wanted to produce a "K Mart" book that chronicled their lived experiences and was presented as a collection of naïve realistic autobiographies or autoethnographies. Lather and Smithies were more interested in theorizing their participants' experiences and foregrounding their political (especially micropolitical) dimensions and effects. These competing goals were constantly negotiated in focus groups, and the resulting book embodies a productive, if uncomfortable/uncomforting, tension between the two.

Coda: Inquiry Logics in the Wake of the Crises of Representation, Evaluation, and Praxis

While the EOC tradition pushed anthropology into *Chronotopes II* and *III*, anthropologists in the wake of the triple crisis of representation, evaluation, and praxis took qualitative inquiry more squarely into the terrain of *Chronotope IV*. Perhaps most importantly, the relations among signs, concepts, and referents were called wholly into question. Classic anthropological texts were seen as select fictions among many possible fictions, produced with and within available rhetorical and literary techniques. The anthropologist's authority and traditional claims to objectivism, legitimated by long-term fieldwork, were disrupted by new theories that posited both power and discourse as generative rather than representational. Anthropologists no longer were thought to naively *discover* culture and the exotic other but to *produce* them in and through their writing.

With challenges to representational theories of language came challenges to traditional notions of validity, reliability, and trustworthiness. Now seen as effects of power/knowledge and regimes of truth, anthropological accounts no longer could lay claim to any kind of objectivity. Anthropological work was seen both as constructive and political. Writers like Clifford and Marcus pointed out that non-Western cultures were typically rendered as seamless, autonomous wholes, which made them now appear oddly out of time, place, and history. Upon reanalysis, these cultures also looked not only peculiarly Western but remarkably like the cultures from which their ethnographic writers hailed. Traditional ethnographies had clearly been complicit with the ideologies and practices of colonialism. Facts had always been (and would always be) highly politicized facts—effects of power and thus "interested" or "prejudiced" in Gadamer's (1972) sense of these terms.

Unlike the critiques spawned by the crisis of relevance, which were aimed outward, the critiques spawned by the triple crisis looked largely inward (at least at the beginning) toward the practices of anthropology and (often) its impossibilities. As anthropology scrambled to redefine itself in the wake of these critiques, it developed many new and exciting strategies for conducting ethnographic work, and with these new strategies came new insights. The relational and rhetorical tactics enacted by Behar, Fine, Roman, Lather, and other researchers, for example, brought to light the very complicated and sometimes troubling micropolitics that are part and parcel of research practice in our time. Their work has taught us that there are no easy separations between "researcher" and "researched." Produced within complex discursive and material relations of power/knowledge, both are theorized as positions in dialogue. No longer can anthropologists claim privileged places from which to objectively experience and report on culture and others. More than ever, we realize that fieldwork experiences often disrupt and transform the identities of both researchers and research participants even as they are paradoxically engaged n the practice of consolidating them. Whatever common ground is constructed between researchers and research participants is unstable and fragile.

These kinds of productive responses to the crises of representation, evaluation, and praxis took us beyond its initially paralyzing effects and back into "the field," but in ways much more attuned to its contingencies and complexities. From these new epistemological positions research was reimagined as always already scientific, creative, relational, political, and ethical work. The key point here is that anthropological work since the mid-1980s has dramatically changed how we think about the nature and functions of qualitative inquiry. Far from visiting distant lands and returning with objective tales from the field, anthropologists are now centrally concerned with research practices that help them deconstruct and reconstruct epistemological issues, interrogate the relative purchase of both lived experience and theory, locate ethics squarely within the purview of research practice, engage in fieldwork in ways that exploit its potentials for social and political transformation, and become more attuned to the sacred dimensions of being with others in the field.

Summary and Conclusions

Contemporary anthropology has been in a state of flux for some time now. As noted, the 1960s and 1970s were times of social ferment and unrest, and anthropologists had to reexamine and rethink the field's complicity with imperialism and colonialism. Dell Hymes's 1972 collection, *Reinventing Anthropology*, was perhaps the clearest distillation of these impulses. The old colonialist claims that had traditionally supported anthropology—the presumed authority to travel to distant lands to study "native others" for one's fellow anthropologists—were called inextricably into question by the global social movements that had marked the previous decade. Anthropologists, it seemed, would have to negotiate new kinds of relationships with new kinds of constituencies, including those in places more close to home, including schools. In short, anthropology needed to become more relevant and more attuned to the pragmatic, political exigencies of the times.

Relocating anthropology within *Chronotopes II and III*, the EOC tradition emerged at this time as a key site where these concerns would be drawn together and played out. This was evidenced, for example, in the release of two key collections—*Functions of Language in the Class-*

room (1972), edited by Courtney Cazden, Vera John, and Dell Hymes, and *Children in and out of School* (1982), edited by Perry Gilmore and Allan Glatthorn. These collections featured small, interdisciplinary groups of scholars, all of whom "believed that school problems could be better explained by differences in language use between home and school" (Cazden, John, & Hymes, 1972, p. vii). Scholars represented in both collections deployed ethnographic tools in the service of social justice agendas such as making the cultural capital of education more readily available to all children with the hope of closing the achievement gap between Black and White students.

The national social justice agendas that Hymes and others responded to have been replaced by the more local but equally pressing agendas of the "posts," and these agendas have spawned new sets of concerns: deconstructing anthropology's past, struggling with the politics of representation, producing more adequate theory, and more effectively enacting praxis-oriented research strategies and practices. Indexing the impulses of *Chronotope IV*, Clifford (1988) noted, "One may approach a classic ethnography seeking simply to grasp the meanings that the researcher derives from represented cultural facts. Or, as I have suggested, one may also read against the grain of the text's dominant voice, seeking out other half-hidden authorities, reinterpreting the descriptions, texts, and quotations gathered together by the writer" (p. 53). Anthropologists now read texts not so much for their truth value but for the "work" they do to construct power/knowledge.

Indeed, anthropologists working in and within the sixth and seventh moments of qualitative inquiry (Denzin & Lincoln, 2000), are deeply committed to the key impulses of *Chronotope IV* and are heavily influenced by critical social theorists such as Michel Foucault and Gilles Deleuze, as well as spatial theorists such as Henri LeFebvre (1991) and Edward Soja (1989). As we explained in chapter 2, within *Chronotope IV*, all knowledge, including cultural representations, is seen to be produced within discourses of power/knowledge. Unmediated experience and uninterested knowledge are impossibilities. While earlier anthropologists like Geertz had called attention to the centrality of writing and text construction in anthropological work, Clifford and others called into question the very relationship between text and experience, claiming not only that anthropologists textualize culture and others but also that there is no such thing as a stable representative text. Blurring the lines between and among literature, literary criticism, journalism, and anthropology had eliminated that possibility. At best, texts could be read in relation to other texts but never as "mirrors of nature" (Rorty, 1979). Representation itself is a political act.

Besides problematizing representational theories of language by drawing on the impulses of *Chronotope IV*, anthropologists have also been working to challenge traditional notions of validity, reliability, and trustworthiness and to produce more generative theoretical and epistemological stances, especially in relation to subjectivity and intersubjectivity. Scholars like Lather, Behar, Roman, Fine, Clifford, and Rosaldo have continually identified the tensions and pushed the limits of thinking about the micropolitics of fieldwork and the production of anthropological knowledge.

Under increasing pressure to define and reinvent itself, anthropology's responses have not mapped onto larger social and political debates in simple ways. The boundaries between and among natural science and social science, anthropology and sociology, qualitative research and journalism, science and politics are not and will probably never be as clearly defined as they were in the past. This complexity is indexed in the ways in which anthropological work across the 20th century has been variously located within various chronotopes of inquiry. Although we have suggested a general movement in the field from *Chronotope I* toward *Chronotope IV*, it is also true that although many anthropologists are engaged in postmodern, poststructural, and postcolonial work, there are also anthropologists engaged in more traditional ethnographic fieldwork and writing. So although we have used our chronotope heuristic primarily to map what we believe to be a plausible trajectory of qualitative inquiry within the field of anthropology, we also want to reiterate that all chronotopes index identifiable and legitimate approaches to inquiry to at least some anthropologists working today. Our chronotopes have fluid, even shape-shifting boundaries. They tend to slip into and transverse each other, and this slippage has both political dimensions and produces political effects. Thus the complex and contradictory representational, epistemological, and political impulses at work within anthropological inquiry today are ones that all of us doing educational anthropology and the linguistic anthropology of education need to understand and take quite seriously. In particular, new researchers in the area of language and literacy studies should be attuned to these impulses as they design and conduct their own research. Being so attuned allows scholars to see them as partial, perspectival, and contingent—and thus open to interrogation and rearticulation.

CHAPTER 4

A Selective History of Inquiry in Sociology

In the last chapter, we looked at key trajectories in the growth and dispersion of qualitative research methods within the discipline of anthropology, paying particular attention to anthropological linguistics and contemporary responses to the crises of relevance, representation, legitimation, and praxis. In this chapter we focus on a parallel trajectory in sociology. As it turns out, this trajectory is considerably more complex, largely due to the constant interanimation within the discipline of social theory, philosophy of science, and empirical research, as well as continual debates about the relative value of qualitative and quantitative approaches to inquiry. To manage the task of reducing the complexity of this history without losing its most important plots and themes, we read it through the more specific history of theoretically informed empirical work in sociology in the 20th century, but we also discuss several key 19th-century scholars or traditions whose foundational insights informed and continue to influence later sociological work. Finally, by our use of *selective* in the chapter title, we mean that we do not present a chronological account but instead focus on key moments or pivot points within sociological theory and the philosophy of science that influenced how empirical work was imagined and enacted.

Nineteenth-Century Roots: Émile Durkheim and Max Weber

Sociology as a science is, in many ways, an outgrowth of continental (especially French and German) philosophy. Émile Durkheim (1858–1917) is usually considered to be the first French sociologist (e.g., Coser, 1971, p. 143). Located primarily within *Chronotope I*, he was very much a holist and a structuralist, or at least a harbinger of structuralism. Basically, structuralism posits that all systems are organized according to an inherent logic that accounts for all of the parts of the system, as well as the rules of combination that account for the possible relations among all these parts. The role of the scientist or researcher is to discover and represent this *a priori* logic. Additionally, from a structuralist perspective, individual or collective subjects do not create the systems of meaning and practice in which they live because these systems are structured *a priori*, and individual and collective subjects are constructed by and within these systems, unable ever to view them with complete objectivity.

Like Sapir (see chapter 3), Durkheim (1976) was fundamentally interested in the logic of social systems, which he argued are constituted by "a whole world of sentiments, ideas and images, which, once born, obey laws all of their own" (p. 424). He went on to say that collective thought and social organization are based on universal wholes or structures and that language, while not the same as these structures, is a system whose laws express the "manner in which society as a whole represents experience" (p. 434). From this perspective, society can never be reduced to the sum total of individual acts, actions, and activities. In fact, all individual acts derive from and operate according to the impersonal structures and forces of social wholes.

In his classic study, *Suicide*, Durkheim (1951) tried to demonstrate the explanatory power of his holism/protostructuralism. Among other things, he argued that all individual acts of suicide are social facts, by which he meant that society created the conditions in which suicide would occur. He supported his argument by showing how psychological constructs and theories could explain neither suicide rates nor the forces that led people to commit suicide. Importantly, for Durkheim the relevant units of analysis for such explanations are always social and cultural rather than psychological or cognitive. Although holism/structuralism provides important insights into how individuals' thoughts, feelings and actions are enabled and constrained by larger social forces and structure, it cannot account for human agency or the fact that individuals are more than just passive dupes in relation to socialization and enculturation processes.

To some extent, the question of agency was more adequately addressed by the German sociologist Max Weber (1864–1920). Located within a conservative variant of *Chronotope II*, he generated theory and conducted research in ways that were more functionalist and interpretivist. Weber was fundamentally concerned with the problem of understanding social life. He was also interested in whether the presumed difference between the interpretive approaches of the human and social sciences (*verstehen*) and the causal explanatory approaches of the natural sciences (*erklären*) was universal or socially constructed. In the end, Weber came to view both approaches to knowledge as operating in both the natural and the human sciences because he saw both kinds of science as involving events constituted by both *nomothetic* (i.e., law-governed) and *ideographic* (i.e., the unique and contingent) forces. Thus, while natural sciences may be more often focused on the *nomothetic* and human sciences on the *ideographic*, both approaches are relevant to both domains of inquiry. However the "scientific method" might be defined, for Weber it was equally applicable to all domains of inquiry in both the natural and social sciences.

For Weber, then, sociology was fundamentally about conducting empirical research on specific social phenomena with an eye toward explaining regularities. Indeed, he spent almost his entire academic life seeking empirical validation for apparent social regularities and developing a methodology that would enable sociologists to do "real" scientific work. But Weber's *verstehen* sociology is also unmistakably interpretive in that it:

> considers the individual and his action as the basic unit. . . . In this approach the individual is also the upper limit and the sole carrier of meaningful conduct. . . . In general, for sociology, such concepts as the "state," "association," "feudalism," and the like, designate certain categories of human interaction. Hence, it is the task of sociology to reduce these concepts to "understandable" action, that is without exception, to the actions of participating men. (Weber, 1970, p. 55)

Whereas Durkheim's primary focus was on social structures, Weber's was on the meanings and values of people interacting with each other. Yet his sociology was not entirely subjective or intersubjective. It attempted "the interpretive understanding of human action in order thereby to arrive at a causal explanation of its course and effects" (Weber, 1968, p. 3). Weber believed that the kind of causality to which the social scientist can lay claim is thus "adequate" and "arguable" rather than "necessary" and "final." He would consider "an interpretation of a sequence of events to be *causally adequate*, if on the basis of past experience it appears probable that it will always occur in the same way" (Weber, 1962, p. 39). A thoroughgoing empiricist-interpretivist, Weber believed in the possibility of interpretive approaches within objectivist epistemological frameworks—again a conservative variant of *Chronotope II.*

The Chicago School of Sociology

The University of Chicago was founded in 1891. Soon afterward, it opened the first sociology department in the country (Hannerz, 1980). This department was home to a stunning range of sociologists and social theorists, including Robert Park, Ernest Burgess, William Foote Whyte, Frederic Thrasher, and many others. All were united in their desire to understand the complexities of contemporary urban life in the city. This work was also motivated by a sincere, if at times problematic, interest in the ills of urban life, especially in relation to immigrant populations.

The school itself was marked by two divergent strands of research. On the one hand, *Chicago School* scholars produced many descriptive studies that were heavily influenced by the anthropological tradition, popular fiction, film, and newspaper reporting and that read like literary texts. The sociologists who conducted these studies were interested in "natural enclaves" such as the Jewish ghetto (Wirth, 1928), Little Italy (Nelli, 1970), hobo jungles (Anderson, 1923), and areas that housed gangs (Thrasher, 1927), and the suicidal (Cavan, 1928).

On the other hand, *Chicago School* scholars produced volumes of theoretical and conceptual treatises about the nature of urban life. This work is exemplified by the writing of Robert Park and Ernest Burgess, both of whom tried to evoke many of the complex conceptual issues related to new groups of immigrants meeting in and across more impersonal cities. This work evoked both the promise and the danger of city life and was centrally concerned with the idea that one could "map" groups and subgroups socially and psychologically.

By and large, *Chicago School* researchers were united in their faith in the possibility of "objective" assessments of reality, in the possibility of a scientific sociology. For them, cities were like laboratories. Yet, at the same time, these researchers grounded their work in the situated interactions of real people. So the *Chicago School* was haunted by a double-edged specter that indexed the tensions between Durkheimian and Weberian approaches to sociology. This tension was embodied in virtually all of the major urban ethnographies produced by the *Chicago School*, including, and perhaps most especially, in William

Foote Whyte's classic *Street Corner Society: The Social Structure of an Italian Slum* (1993), originally published in 1943. A descriptive account of "Cornerville" (a pseudonym for Boston's North End), *Street Corner Society* is the story of two men—the resistant "Doc" and the assimilationist "Chick." These men index two distinct ways that Italian immigrants responded to life in America.

In the revised edition of this book, Whyte (1993) addressed methodological tensions quite explicitly, noting, for example, that much of what happened in the process of researching and writing the book took place in a kind of ad hoc fashion. He confessed, in a sense, that his research was a profoundly human endeavor, taking place at the intersection of different individuals with different social needs, agendas, and goals, all in an intensely local and particular context. Picking up on issues foregrounded in *Chronotope IV*, he also noted that this sort of complexity is typically whitewashed in most sociological studies:

> There are now many good published studies of communities or organizations, but generally the published report gives little attention to the actual process whereby the research was carried out. There have also been some useful statements on methods of research, but, with few exceptions, they place the discussion entirely on a logical-intellectual basis. They fail to note that the researcher, like his informants, is a social animal. (p. 279)

He added that "a real explanation . . . necessarily involves a rather personal account of how the researcher lived during the period of study" (p. 279). And, in fact, Whyte provided just such a narrative—complete with contingencies, unexpected events, failures, and more.

Whyte's musings point to the fact that many early *Chicago School* ethnographers did not have an "extractable" methodology guiding their projects. Their work was more situated, more emergent, and more innovative, and their accounts seldom foregrounded discourse about methodology. In reading these accounts, one gets the sense that these researchers approached their tasks much like investigative reporters—observing events, conducting interviews, collecting archive material, and synthesizing this material into what they believed to be objective accounts. Any sense of a self-consciously marked "scientific" method seems noticeably absent in their work.

However, although Whyte (and others) viewed ethnography as an interpretive, human endeavor, he also believed that research methods can and should be deployed in the service of science. He concluded the appendix to the later edition of his book, for example, by arguing for an epistemological shift away from more interpretive and constructivist approaches—referring to them as "dead ends"—and toward the "pursuit of scientific knowledge" (p. 371). Although Whyte viewed ethnography as a messy human endeavor, he also saw it as a science that could achieve some degree of objectivity. In the end, he developed a hybrid position, arguing that the goal of ethnography should be to explain larger social and cultural structures and functions but that it should do this through descriptions of key figures and stories of their experience. This both/and stance toward epistemology was, in many respects, characteristic of much qualitative work within sociology in the early part of the 20th century. A commitment to objectivity cohabited with the more subjective (or perhaps intersubjective) commitment to verisimilitude and phenomenological description.

Foundationalist/Modernist Strands Within the Chicago School of Sociology

As Denzin and Lincoln (2000) noted, sociology from the 1950s through the 1970s was marked by efforts to make qualitative inquiry "more rigorous" and "to formalize" its methods. Interestingly, this does not seem so much a shift in epistemology as a shift in technique. As we noted in the Introduction, methods do not follow from epistemologies in lockstep ways. Yet foundational philosophies continued to proliferate in sociology, with sociologists trying to "make good" on these epistemologies through "rigorous" research strategies.

Important in this regard is James Short's (1963) preface to the second edition of Thrasher's fascinating book, *The Gang: A Study of 1,133 Gangs in Chicago* (1927). With journalistic enthusiasm, panache, and a sense of presence, Thasher documented a large number of big and small social units he called "gangs." He did not discuss his research strategies in the book, nor did he make it clear where he got his empirical material (including quotations). Like *Street Corner Society, The Gang* reflected the general disposition of qualitative research in sociology of the time. Yet in the new preface to the 1963 edition of the book, Short evoked the anxiety of modernist researchers attempting to come to terms with this tradition. "The study's greatest strength, its comprehensiveness, suffers from lack of analytical sophistication in 'holding constant' variables which might have further elucidated the nature of many aspects of gang variety" (p. xx). He went on to say that Thrasher "does not really concern himself either with building hypotheses or with relating them in systemic fashion. As a consequence, the data are not suitable for hypothesis testing. Often they seem, in fact, confusing, even contradictory, to the student who would attempt to state or test hypotheses" (p. xxii). Among other things, these remarks (and critiques of *Chicago School* sociology generally) reflect many of the methodological anxieties sociologists were registering from the 1940s through the 1970s.

During this time, new approaches to research such as phenomenology, ethnomethodology, conversation analysis, and grounded theory gained prominence within sociology and insinuated themselves into other disciplines (including language and literacy studies). Grounded theory, which was perhaps the least influenced by language and literacy research, ended up having perhaps the greatest influence on such research. Although phenomenology and ethnomethodology would have less influence on language and literacy research per se, they did influence conversational analysis (CA) quite heavily, and CA, in turn, influenced research on language and literacy in ways that were almost diametrically opposed to the influence of the Ethnography of Communication tradition we discussed at length in chapter 3. How these trajectories emerged and affected each other will become more obvious as we describe these modernist approaches in more detail.

Grounded Theory. In a bold and counterintuitive move for the times, Glaser and Strauss (1967) insisted upon drawing together "theory" and "empirical research." They did not ask how data could be used to test hypotheses, but "how the discovery of theory from data—systematically obtained and analyzed in social research—can be furthered" (p. 1). Along with this shift came a more rigorous, systematic, and prescriptive approach to research methodology. The authors advocated what they called a "general method of comparative analysis"—where one would "code" data and compare and contrast categories with the goal of eventually generating explanatory theories. Like the conservative variant of *Chronotope II* that we called interpretivism within objectivism when discussing Weber's sociology, grounded theory developed as an approach to research designed to replace some of the earlier, more holistic ways of conducting qualitative inquiry (e.g., the symbolic interactionism of the *Chicago School*) to give it a more rigor and scientific legitimacy.

Since it is the heart and soul of grounded theory, this "general method of comparative analysis" deserves to be spelled out here. The method involves analyzing multiple forms of data (e.g., texts, observations, interviews) to discover recurrent themes and thematic relations. Three recursive and interdependent phases of data analysis are conducted—open coding, axial coding, and selective coding, along with various forms of cross-checking. Coding and analyzing data begin almost as soon as data collection begins, and the process continues throughout the final write-up. The first phase of analysis involves segmenting and organizing one's data into meaningful (yet preliminary) themes or categories from which more in-depth analysis can occur. Some of these themes or categories may derive from previous theory and research; others emerge from the data themselves. As categories are generated, they are constantly compared, refined, deleted, added, merged, and so on until a relatively small, manageable, and maximally relevant set of categories are settled upon. This process of data collection and comparison continues until a *saturation* point is reached—a point where no new categories emerge and continued data collection and analysis is unlikely to provide additional information that will really amplify one's understanding of focal issues or concerns.

As our description of the "general method of comparative analysis" belies, it is a useful tool for doing exactly what Glaser and Strauss had intended—to add formality, specificity, and rigor to an interpretive research tradition that was often more impressionistic, exploratory, and holistic, in a time when revisiting dimensions of Enlightenment epistemologies was in vogue. Grounded theory is largely a postpositivist endeavor—"with assumptions of an objective, external reality, a neutral observer who discovers data, reductionist inquiry of manageable research problems, and objectivist rendering of data" (Glaser & Strauss, 1967, p. 510). Importantly, grounded theory has become an approach to language and literacy research that is widespread to say the least, a point to which we return in the final chapter of the book.

Ethnomethodology. Like grounded theory, ethnomethodology reflects another iteration of the epistemological struggles of modernist imperatives in sociology. Before unpacking the basic lineaments of ethnomethodology, we thus want to take a detour through a key text that perhaps marks the beginning of the modernist sociology of knowledge tradition—Berger and Luckmann's (1966) *The Social Construction of Reality.* Throughout this landmark text, the authors ask,

"How is it possible that subjective meanings *become* objective factici-
ties?" (p. 18).

Berger and Luckmann's approach is both philosophical and sociological, offering up a grand narrative within which to reconceive some
basic sociological tenets. In this regard, they chart a course somewhere between the twin dangers of unchecked objectivism (in the
form of structuralism) and freewheeling subjectivism. It is worth re-
iterating here that, like most other modernist sociologists, Berger and
Luckmann insisted that even though reality is socially constructed,
this "does *not* imply that sociology is not a science, that its methods
should be other than empirical, or that it cannot be 'value-free'" (p.
189). Straddling across *Chronotopes II* and *III*, they represented a fusion
of Durkheimian and Weberian imperatives, and they foreshadowed
the later work of Pierre Bourdieu, Anthony Giddens, and others.

Drawing largely from the work of Berger and Luckmann, Harold Garfinkel, the founder of ethnomethodology, focused more specifically on the strategies that individuals use for "doing life" in their
ordinary, taken-for-granted social worlds. Ethnomethodology is thus
more "agent-centered" and stresses more microlevel engagement
with data than many of the social-constructionist–oriented approaches that came before it. In this regard, Garfinkel (1967) wrote, "I use
the term 'ethnomethodology' to refer to the investigation of the rational properties of indexical expressions and other practical actions
as contingent ongoing accomplishments of organized artful practices
of everyday life" (p. 11). Importantly, ethnomethodology is neither a
strategy nor a technique for conducting research, but an approach to
inquiry fundamentally concerned with explaining how everyday activities achieve their orderliness and predictability. It thus differs from
ethnography and grounded theory in important ways. For example,
instead of using interpretive strategies to study social life, ethnomethodologists study how people themselves use interpretive strategies to
construct and maintain their unique social lives. Instead of producing
"thick descriptions" of social and cultural formations based on long-
term observations and extensive interviews, ethnomethodologists
examine small slices of social life to understand how specific practices and meanings are constructed moment-to-moment. And unlike
much sociological work, which assumes the validity of prefigured (or
theoretically grounded) social categories, ethnomethodologists insist
on bracketing observable social events or realities and ask, instead,
how these social realities come to be regarded as "natural" or taken

for granted, as well as how people deal with instances in which the natural or the taken-for-granted character of their social realities is threatened or disrupted.

The principle of reflexivity is central to ethnnomethodological analyses. Accounts of experience, for example, are seen as reflexive in the sense that they not only explain reality but also constitute reality. "The ways in which the orderliness of practical action are produced and managed are identical with the ways those orderlinesses are made accountable" (Livingston, 1987, p. 18). An example will help to anchor this idea. In a famous study, Garfinkel looked at how the Los Angeles Suicide Prevention Center (SPC) joined with the Medical Examiner Coroner's Office to produce a practical "warrant" whereby they could determine whether a death could be ruled a "suicide" or not. "Selected cases of 'sudden, unnatural death' that were equivocal between 'suicide' and other modes of death were referred by the Medical Examiner-Coroner to the SPC with the request that an inquiry, called a 'psychological autopsy' be done" (p. 12). Garfinkel and his students documented how case workers sorted through details of deaths, making sense of out of them, making them intelligible, using them to tell a story.

This approach was extended in a study of the U.C.L.A. Outpatient Clinic, where he and his students looked at the process whereby workers "coded" cases to determine the kind of care necessary. In particular, Garfinkel highlighted the role of "ad hocing." Ad hocing occurs "whenever the coder assumes the position of a socially competent member of the arrangement that he seeks to assemble an account of and, when from this 'position,' he treats actual folder contents as standing in a relationship of trusted signification to the 'system' and the clinic activities" (p. 22). This kind of practice is evident, for example, in the use the "et cetera principle," or the tendency of people to rely on each other to fill in what they cannot completely and explicitly convey.

The social reality of suicide was thus continually produced through the ongoing display of these kinds of "typification" activities and the assumption that other members of the social formation would take these displays "for what they are." By continually showing others that they knew what was going on, these social actors contributed to the accumulation and sedimentation of shared certainty and thus to the creation of the "truth" or "reality" of suicide. Moreover, all that was required to validate that shared certainty and "truth" was to refer back to the material and discursive practices that just constituted it. In sum, the primary method of ethnomethodology is to document in careful detail the iterative and reflexive practices used by groups of people to establish, maintain, and justify their social realities as typical, normal, or natural.

Importantly, language plays a central role in these typification activities, especially through the ways in which language *indexes* social context. Expressions like "here" and "there" can only be understood in relation to some continuing ongoing activity in context. This concern with *indexicality* was picked up by Garfinkel and Sacks (1970) in subsequent work in which they showed how understanding what is "indexed" in ongoing activity is central to understanding how activities are socially accomplished:

> The indexical properties of natural language assure to the technology of sociological inquiries, lay and professional, the following unavoidable and irremediable practice as their earmark: Wherever and by whomever practical sociological reasoning is done, it seeks to remedy the indexical properties of practical discourse; it does so in the interests of demonstrating the rational accountability of everyday activities; and it does so in order that its assessments be warranted by methodic observation and report of situated, socially organized particulars of everyday activities, which of course include particulars of natural language. (p. 339)

These three basic principles—reflexivity, ad hocing, and indexicality—are the heart and soul of ethnomethodology. They also informed the development of new approaches to inquiry within sociology, all of which were part of a broader movement to make qualitative inquiry more scientific, to formalize its methods. These approaches, including conversational analysis (CA), focused increasingly on the fine-grained analyses of situated language practices in specific contexts.

Conversation Analysis. Conversation analysis is an "analysis of the practices of reasoning and inference that inform the production and recognition of intelligible courses of action" (Goodwin & Heritage, 1990, p. 287). CA is quintessentially empirical. Instead of theorizing idealized characteristics of social action, CA involves the empirical investigation of the sequential organization of naturally occurring language and social interaction. In this regard, CA has developed/ discovered rules that participants themselves seem to use to make sense of their moment-by-moment interactions and that seem to account for the orderly and collaborative nature of those interactions. CA posits that talk and social interaction are *both* systematic *and* dynamic. They are systematic because there is describable order in the ways in which speaking turns are distributed and sequenced. They are dynamic because each new turn constitutes an opportunity for participants to evaluate and redirect their mutual understanding. Talk and social interaction are thus mediational tools for producing and reproducing intersubjective understandings. Conversely, intersubjective understanding provides certain enablements and constraints for future turn-taking activity.

Context is a fundamental unit of analysis for CA because of its central concern with how participants orient to, manage, and sustain context in actual, real-time interactions. However, context is defined rather narrowly, as the orientations and practices enacted by the participants themselves are considered (Schegloff, 1992). In other words, context includes only the immediate discursive activity of participants. Words, turns, utterances, and interchanges are not treated as isolated, self-contained units but as forms of action situated in specific sequential contexts. They are oriented to these specific contexts, and they have the potential either to maintain or to transform these contexts.

Three other concepts are central to CA. First is the concept of "turn-taking," conceptualized as the rules that govern a local and sequentially managed system and operate on a turn-by-turn basis. This system explains how speaking rights are negotiated and managed, how each speaker is selected for a speaking turn, how overlaps occur and how they are resolved, and how speakers repair problems with developing shared meanings. Another important concept is that of the "adjacency pair" (Schegloff & Sacks, 1973), a sequence of two adjacent utterances produced by different speakers and ordered in such a way that the first utterance requires a particular second utterance or a predictable range of second utterances. A good example of an adjacency pair is the question-answer sequence. Finally, "repair organization" (Schegloff, Jefferson, & Sacks, 1977) refers to instances where trouble occurs in conversation, is noticed, and is corrected, either by the participant whose turn contains the trouble source or by some other participant. Repair can be accomplished in a number of ways, such as defining or clarifying word meanings, apologizing, or revisiting earlier contextual information.

Many of the empirical findings of CA show how parties to talk organize and are sensitive to its sequential arrangement: its openings and closings, turn-taking, overlapping speech, repair structures, and so on (Atkinson, 1988, p. 448). With the emergence of CA in sociology, we see a shift in focus away from "social action" and "meaning" *per se* to the specific ways in which language and language practices establish and maintain the "social order." Above all else, as Atkinson points out, the focus is on the structured logic of unfolding conversation—often separated from meaning almost entirely. "Conversation is regarded as a form of collaborative conduct. There is much less concern with the explication of meaning than with the discovery of competencies or methods whereby speakers generate orderly sequences of activities" (p. 449).

With this microanalytic focus, researchers began to rely much more heavily on extended transcripts as data because such transcripts afford possibilities for fine-tuned and fine-grained analyses of nuances in language that are critical to communication. There was less interest in understanding socialization practices *per se* than in the unfolding language practices and activities that constitute and are constituted by the social order. With its focus on rules and structures, CA embodied positivist epistemological tendencies. These tendencies were clearly evidenced in the anxieties that many CA proponents had about their more interpretive sociological counterparts such as Erving Goffman. In this regard, Schegloff (1988) noted that Goffman's data and his quirky anecdotal methods were quite different from the data and methods typically used in CA:

> Clearly, the differences between Goffman's "data" and CA's are decisive rather than marginal, however indiscriminately "detailed" they may appear to those who work on differently sized worlds. Although he is reported to have, in private conversation, endorsed recording as now the way to work, he never did so publicly, and never systematically incorporated recorded data into his own work. . . . Goffman's attitude toward "real data," in the sense of actual observed occasions, whether taped or not, was equivocal at best, and has not been fully appreciated. (p. 104).

Interestingly, these criticisms index *both* CA's positivist orientations *and* the ways in which social constructionism can animate positivism within certain approaches to research. What we mean here is that CA seems located at the boundary of *Chronotopes I* and *II*, and might be described as a kind of structuralism that does not claim universalism as a necessary part of structure.

Coda: Inquiry Logics Within Foundational/Modernist Approaches

Interestingly, we see a fairly unbroken line in early sociology from Durkheim and Weber through certain stands of the *Chicago School* through the modernist period. Questions of inquiry embodied a struggle to reconcile more scientistic and more interpretive epistemologies, theories, and approaches to research but always with a firm faith in the possibility of objectivity. Throughout, there remained a strong belief in a reality "out there" that can be understood and explained. We see a clear separation, for example, between facts and values, as well as a parallel separation between self and other, and little concern with the precise relations between social structure and individual agency. By and large, language was seen to represent rather than constitute reality. There was little or no agonizing over representing social life or "writing" others. Validity claims were regarded as more or less transparent. One could, quite simply, "get it right" if one paid close enough attention.

Yet occasional blemishes in this smooth veneer were evident as well, such as Weber's reflections on the validity of the distinction between *verstehen* and *erklären* and Whyte's reevaluation of the practices and effects of *Chicago School* fieldwork. Among other things, these blemishes indexed the possibilities for more hermeneutic/interpretive forms of social science inquiry.

Interpretive Strands of Inquiry Within the Chicago School of Sociology

In the previous section, we detailed the rise of modernist imperatives within sociology, which was largely about developing more rigorous empirical methods to legitimate sociology more as a "real" science. Although it straddled *Chronotopes I* and *II*, the modernist trajectory of the *Chicago School* was rooted primarily in positivist epistemologies and reached its height between the 1950s and the 1970s. Throughout its history more interpretive trajectories of the *Chicago School* proliferated as well. And although they remained largely underground during the modernist period, they reemerged with a vengeance in the 1980s. Symbolic Interactionism (SI) is critical here.

Symbolic Interactionism (SI). Symbolic Interactionism is somewhat unique in that it may be regarded both as a theoretical perspective and an approach to research. Many researchers, for example, conduct ethnographic studies grounded in the principles of SI theory. However, within *Chicago School* sociology, SI emerged as a distinct way to study urban life. In many ways, SI grew out of the antibehaviorist tradition of American pragmatism with its insistence that humans are purposive agents who encounter a world that must be interpreted rather than a world of stimuli to which they must simply react.

Since the early work of George Herbert Mead (1863–1931) and his protégé, Herbert Blumer, SI has embodied three basic themes. First, people act in and on the world on the basis of symbol systems that they inherit as a function of being constructed within historically specific social systems. Second, these meanings are historically durable because they are sedimentations of meanings generated over time through interactions among other individuals in these social systems. Third, social systems and society itself are continually (re)constructed from the ongoing situated interactions among people who are active in constructing the limits of experience and behavior. Thus, SI has always been centrally concerned with how interacting individuals create social orders, how individual selves are mediated in and through social interaction, and how, as Denzin (1990) noted, "meanings are acted on collectively, as well, in 'joint acts'—acts which form, dissolve, conflict, merge, and ultimately constitute reality" (p. 25).

Although the history of SI is complex and contested, it is considered to be the predominant interepretive strain of sociological theory and research that emerged from the *Chicago School* and ran alongside the more positivist strains embodied in grounded theory, ethnomethodology, and conversation analysis. Additionally, SI laid the groundwork for the emergence of contemporary ethnographic and even aesthetic, poetic, and performative sociologies, which we will discuss later in this chapter. SI is also associated with what is sometimes called a *"Second Chicago School"* whose heyday was between 1946 and 1960 (Fine, 1995). This school included the work of key figures such as Erving Goffman (e.g., *The Presentation of Self in Everyday Life*, 1959; *Asylums*, 1962), Howard Becker (e.g., *Outsiders: Studies in the Sociology of Deviance*, 1963), and more recently, Gary Alan Fine (e.g., *With the Boys: Little League Baseball and Preadolescent Culture*, 1987; *Kitchens: The Culture of Restaurant Work*, 1996), all of whom set out to understand how interacting individuals create and sustain social orders through everyday interaction. In many respects, the story of sociology in the United States is the story of SI.

Yet this grand narrative has also been traversed and interrupted by other narratives. In 1969, for example, Denzin enthusiastically outlined a kinship between ethnomethodology and SI because "both perspectives posit a link between the person and social structure that rests on the role of symbols and common meaning. . . . Locating the unit of analysis in the individual and interaction separates interactionism and ethnomethodology from other points of view" (p. 22). Although ethnomethodology focuses on the individual, it is grounded in positivist ideals that differ sharply from the more interpretive ideals that largely came to dominate SI. Thus the kinship between the two turned out to be a tenuous one. In fact, 20 years later Denzin (1990) rethought both the likelihood and productivity of connecting ethnomethodology and SI in the context of a profound rereading of Garfinkel's (1967) famous "Agnes" study. The "Agnes" study, originally published in *Studies in Ethnomethodology*, was about a young person trying to have a sex-change operation. "Agnes," who had passed for almost 2 years as a woman, was interviewed by Garfinkel and his colleagues as part of the process of getting approval for the operation. The purpose of the interviews was to allow Agnes to convince (or not convince) them that she had "always really" been a woman. Garfinkel undertook the study to explore how "the experiences of . . . intersexed persons permits an appreciation of these background relevances that are otherwise easily overlooked or difficult to grasp because of their routinized character and because they are so embedded in the background of relevances that are simply 'there' and taken for granted" (p. 118). The concerns of ethnomethodology, outlined above, are clearly reflected here.

Garfinkel described Agnes's physical appearance early on and emphasized it throughout the article. "Agnes's appearance was convincingly female. She was tall, slim, with a very female shape. Her measurements were 38–25–38. . . . At the time of her first appearance she was dressed in a tight sweater which marked off her thin shoulders, ample breasts, and narrow waist" (p. 119). He went on to show how Agnes "passed" as a "natural, normal female" in her everyday life (p. 121). Again, the goal of this study was to show all the ways in which ideas about sexual identity are inscribed in mundane taken-for-granted assumptions and practices. Sexuality, for Garfinkel, was a social accomplishment.

In a passing note in the appendix, however, Garfinkel mentioned that he found out that Agnes had lied throughout the interviews, denying the fact that she had been taking estrogen for several years. He claimed that he would analyze the data again with this new knowledge, but he never did. For Denzin, this is a key fault line in the book, which shows just how precarious Garfinkel's constructions of reality were. Both the article and "Agnes" rested on the idea that the world is "out there" and can be objectively rendered. Yet, as Denzin (1990) pointed out, "the world out there, *as it is known sociologically*, exists only in our texts" (p. 201).

From an SI perspective, texts must be analyzed critically and their transparent claims to reality demystified. The most important question is not about what the texts stand for but how they operate to construct particular realities. "How does Garfinkel's text, which is part detective story (how did she learn to act like a woman?), and part melodrama (how does this poor man/woman find happiness in life?), organize itself so that it gives the appearance of having accounted for Agnes's passing?" (p. 204). Denzin went on to "deconstruct" Garfinkel's account, showing how he "[led] Agnes into femininity" in the narrative in order to tell her (and his) story (p. 205).

This debate is especially interesting for how it evinces tensions within the *Chicago School* such as those between ethnomethodology and SI and even sometimes *within* the patently more interpretive orientation of the latter. As Denzin (1992a) put it elsewhere, "On the one hand, its [the *Chicago School's*] founding theorists argued for the interpretive, subjective study of human experience. On the other hand, they sought to build an objective science of human conduct, a science which would conform to criteria borrowed from the human sciences" (p. 2). In this debate, Denzin places SI squarely in the former camp, arguing for an antifoundational position that calls any *a priori* existence of reality into question. For Denzin, reality is always socially constructed, performative, and intersubjective.

Dispersion and Proliferation of Symbolic Interactionist Imperatives. Denzin also acknowledged the important role played by cultural studies perspectives in late-20th-century iterations of SI, relocating its basic epistemological orientation from *Chronotope II* to *Chronotope IV*. Specifically, he drew together the more interpretive strands of SI (i.e., the idea that we can only understand reality as people in interaction around texts) with the cultural studies insistence on the political nature of texts (i.e., the ideas that texts are key sites of/for the circulation of power). The goal of more recent versions of SI, he argued, has been to show how people make meaning of their lives in and through texts but also to show that the conditions of possibility of these texts are never either of their own making or choosing.

This remaking of SI in and through cultural studies came hand-in-hand with new kinds of rhetorical and performative strategies for the production and dissemination of sociological texts. Sociological poetics, autoethnography, and multimedia performance all rose to prominence as alternative representational strategies in the late 20th and early 21st centuries (Denzin, 1997, 2003). In addition, Denzin (1997) and others attempted to introduce a kind of "postrealist realism" in their reassessment of the so-called "New Journalists" of the 1960s and 1970s—the work of Truman Capote, Norman Mailer, Joan Didion, and others (see Hollowell, 1977). Much of the new journalistic work had to do with changing notions of "objectivity," a changing relationship between "fact" and "fiction," and an attendant attention to the literary and interpretive dimensions of writing. Much of this work also had to do with the social unrest and turmoil of the decade. And in many ways it embodied Geertz's (1973) claim that all ethnographies are "fictions," by which he meant "thick" descriptions aimed at intentionally sorting out the structures of signification that make all social practices intelligible and viable as social practices.

According to Hollowell (1977):

> The most important difference between the new journalism and traditional reporting is the writer's changed relationship to the people and events he depicts. Traditionally, the straight news article is based on an "objectivity" that requires a commitment to telling both sides of the story, and an impartiality on the part of the journalist characterized by the lack of value judgments and emotionally colored adjectives. . . . In sharp contrast to the "objectivity" that the reporter strives for in the standard news article, the voice of the new journalist is frankly subjective; it bears the stamp of his personality. (p. 22)

This more explicitly subjective approach to writing implied a different way of thinking about the literary nature of texts, promoting a series of questions analogous to the questions raised by the crisis of representation theorists. "As a narrative form, the nonfiction novel combines aspects of the novel, the confession, the autobiography, and the journalistic report. This deliberate blending of narrative form prompts such critical questions as: What is a novel? What are the differences between fiction and nonfiction? When is something *literature* and when is it *mere* journalism?" (p. 15).

New Journalists like Tom Wolfe and nonfiction novelists like Truman Capote wrestled with questions of representation as they strove for a morally invested and politically active form of reportage that did not claim any "alibis" for the work they did. As Denzin (1997) noted, "Their legacies are multiple and have yet to be built upon. Ethnography has not embraced, let alone learned from, the many narrative strategies taken by these new writers" (p. 158). This claim is both matter-of-fact and prophetic. Indeed, both theoretical and empirical work continue to proliferate in the field of qualitative inquiry, whose goal is to understand and/or deploy the insights of the new journalism more strategically and effectively.

Exploring and exploiting the affordances of poetic language was another way that sociologists responded to concerns about the literary and political dimensions of representational practices. Laurel Richardson (1994), for example, produced a set of nine poems based on her fieldnotes from an interview study on marriage and the family. These poems interrogate both marriage and family, as well as what it means to be single. The move toward the poetic in sociology both affirms the importance of experience (a traditional SI concern) and implies a more complex and denaturalized relationship between reader and author. Elsewhere, Richardson (1992) offered what she considered "not the only way . . . but a pleasing and credible way to write the postmodern" (p. 23) when she presented her research participant, "Louisa May," through what she called "a poem masquerading as a transcript and a transcript masquerading as a poem" (p. 19). The text's intent was to demand an "analysis of its own production, distribution, and consumption as a cultural object and of itself *as a method* for linking lived interactional experience to the research and writing enterprises . . ." (p. 20).

Poetic conventions call attention to their own artifice and do not appear to transcendently reflect the self. According to Richardson (2000), "When we read or hear poetry, we are continually nudged into recognizing that the text has been constructed" (p. 933). In writing poems, Richardson (1994) also took on the postmodern challenge to be "more fully present" and "more honest; more engaged" in our work (p. 516). It is necessary, she argued, to reflect upon our methods as we explore new ways of knowing and writing (p. 518). These impulses are now constantly embraced in qualitative inquiry. We see sociological poetics regularly in journals such as *Qualitative Inquiry* and *International Journal of Qualitative Studies in Education*. Poetic renderings of events and experiences are often very powerful and can often render dimensions of experience and action in ways not possible through more prosaic forms of academic writing.

Coda: Inquiry Logics Within Interpretive Strands of the Chicago School

The epistemological shift indexed in early SI theory and research and further developed within more recent SI variants during the last several decades is critical. No longer were facts and values seen as separate and unrelated. No longer were self and the social considered as separate and distinct from each other. Instead they were viewed as co-constitutive. No longer was language regarded as merely representational. Importantly, this epistemological shift required the development of new kinds of research strategies and practices, ones that could help to explain the complex relations between facts and values, the co-production of structure and agency, and the constitutive functions of language and fieldwork strategies.

As we suggested in our discussion of the earliest *Chicago School* sociologists, these emerging methods remained largely implicit for most of the century. Since the mid-1980s, however, making them explicit has taken center stage. We return to this issue later in the chapter. Before going there, though, we want to trace another trajectory within sociology that has run parallel to the many variants of *Chicago School* work that have proliferated during the 20th century and that has influenced educational research in powerful ways. Quintessential embodiments of *Chronotope III*, Marxist-inspired critical epistemologies and approaches to research have inhabited the sociological landscape for a long time. Though it is far beyond the scope of this chapter to summarize the vast philosophical thinking of Marx and his followers, we must note some of the central Marxist ideas that have been most relevant to imagining and enacting critical forms of qualitative inquiry.

Marxism and the Emergence of Critical Modes of Inquiry

Both a consummate academic and a fierce and fearless social activist, Marx was praxis—the fusion of theory and practice—incarnate. In his own words, "philosophers have only *interpreted* the world in different ways, the point is to change it" (1961, p. 84). He went on to elaborate this claim:

In direct contrast to German philosophy, which descends from heaven to earth, here we ascend from earth to heaven. That is to say, we do not set out from what men say, imagine, or conceive, nor from what has been said, thought, imagined or conceived of men, in order to arrive at men in the flesh. We begin with real active men, and from their real-life process show the development of the ideological reflexes and echoes of this life-process. The phantoms of the human brain also are necessary sublimates of men's life-process, which can be empirically established and which is bound to material preconditions. . . . Life is not determined by consciousness but consciousness by life. (p. 90)

Among other things, this position constituted a direct challenge to the philosophy of Wilhelm Hegel, who argued that history unfolds as a prefigured and ongoing dialectic of thesis-antithesis-synthesis. Marx retained the dialectical aspect of Hegel's philosophy of history while rejecting its prefigurative and speculative aspects. He replaced Hegel's dialectical idealism with a dialectical historicism/materialism, which regards economic relations between and among people as the most powerful influence on the development of social life and social systems. Central to Marx's dialectical historicism/materialism, then, are the notions of "production" (of goods and services) and "relations of production." Production refers to the actual actions of human beings in the world and what they produce through those actions. It is a "definite form of activity of these individuals, a definite way of expressing their life, a definite *mode of life*" (1961, p. 69). Under capitalism, people's actual labor practices largely influence who they are and what they become. If we are workers who produce automobiles all day, we develop identities as laborers, auto workers, and the like.

Relations of production refer to how different people are related to each other as a function of the material-economic affordances of the production process. So "the hand mill will give you a society with a feudal lord, the steam mill a society with an industrial capitalist" (1961, p.108). Thus, "the multitude of productive forces accessible to men determines the nature of society" (Marx & Engels, 1969, p. 31). Given statements like this one, it is not surprising that Marx is considered by many to be an economic determinist who paid little or no attention to the productive power of nonmaterial forces such as culture, politics, and aesthetics. In many ways, it is true that Marx viewed the material and economic conditions of people's lives as the most important determinants of social life. However, his "sociology" was much more complex than this. For example, he argued that the relations between the material-economic affordances of production (the means of production) and the social relations of production are almost always complex and contested ones for at least two reasons. First, there is always conflict between those who are more or less economically advantaged and powerful. For example, the main purpose of labor unions is to assure that a greater share of profits go to the workers who actually produce goods and thus a smaller share to those who simply own the means of production. Second, the means of production change over time. The advent of the industrial revolution, for instance, rendered the social relations of production characteristic of the feudal system obsolete and unworkable.

The Institute for Social Research and the Frankfurt School of Marxist Thought. Although our discussion of Marx has been quite abstract and focused more on social theory than on research methods, Marx and the Marxist tradition have exerted huge effects on how qualitative research has been imagined and enacted, especially during the past two decades. Before moving on to discuss these specific effects, we would like to outline two particular and particularly important forms of 20th-century Marxist thought—the Frankfurt School and Paulo Freire's critical pedagogy.

What is now most often referred to as the Frankfurt School of Marxist thought grew out of the Institute for Social Research, which was founded at Tübingen in 1924 by socialist political scientist Felix Weil as a forum for discussing and extending Marx's intellectual legacy. Both the Institute and the Frankfurt School have long and complex histories, portions of which are particularly relevant to our goals in this chapter.

Among the scholars who were centrally involved in the Frankfurt School over its 75-or-so year history were Max Horkheimer, Theodor Adorno, Herbert Marcuse, Leo Lowenthal, Henryk Grossman, and Jurgen Habermas. Most of these scholars were Jews who were persecuted during the Nazi regime and fled Germany before or during World War II. They reestablished one or another version of the Institute's agenda in the United Kingdom or the United States. In the 1950s, many of them returned to Germany to continue their work.

Most Frankfurt School scholars were both heavily influenced by the interpretivism of Max Weber and deemphasized Marx's insistence on the almost exclusive power of economic forces to produce social relations and structures. In this regard, the Frankfurt School was largely responsible for the development of what we now know as "critical social theory," or theory designed not merely to represent but to transform social life and social systems. We hear clear echoes of Marx here, but with an emphasis on the theoretical rather than the material. Additionally, like Weber, most in the Frankfurt School believed that the best scientific research combines philosophical reflection and hard-nosed empirical investigation. They had little faith in the general puzzle-solving activities of so-called "normal science" (Kuhn, 1970), nor in philosophy that was not rooted either in idealism or lived experience. Instead, they wanted to understand the conditions of possibility that made particular ideas or lived experiences possible and visible in the first place. This marriage of philosophy and science was embodied in key studies conducted during the 1930s by the scholars from the Institute for Social Research, such as those on authority and the family (e.g., Horkheimer, 1949), which included rigorous empirical analyses and speculative ideas for enacting social change.

As Frankfurt School thought developed, scholars became all but obsessed with understanding and explaining the relations between the material (empirical) and the conceptual (philosophical). This problem of representation (rooted as it is in a correspondence theory of truth) is perhaps most obvious in the work of Theodor Adorno and Max Horkheimer. Adorno (1973), for example, stressed the fact that all concepts fail to capture the richness of the objects and experiences they represent:

> In truth, all concepts, even the philosophical ones, refer to non-conceptualities, because concepts on their part are moments of the reality that requires their formation, primarily for the control of nature. What conceptualization appears to be from within, to one engaged in it—the predominance of its sphere, without which nothing is known—must not be mistaken for what it is itself. Such a resemblance of being-in-itself is conferred upon it by the motion that exempts it from reality, to which it is harnessed in turn. (p. 11)

For Adorno, the key task at hand was always to unseat the dominance of the theoretical that had characterized the Frankfurt School and to retheorize the relations between the material and the conceptual. To accomplish this task, Adorno introduced the idea of "negative dialectics," which is a way to use a concept in such a way as to transcend it. Under traditional dialectics, the goal is to create identity out of difference, to categorize the world so as to make it perceptually and conceptually manageable. The problem with this goal, according to Adorno, is that it overdetermines sameness and underdetermines difference. Under negative dialectics, we continue to categorize the world, but we do so in a way that preserves the tension between the conceptual and the material, realizing that our covering concepts over-simplify and distort reality. This process calls into question traditional notions of originality and genuineness, as well as Enlightenment notions of the self. In this regard, Adorno (1974) noted that:

> . . . the individual is a mere reflection of property relations. In him, the fictitious claim is made that what is biologically one must logically precede the social whole, from which it is only isolated by force, and its contingency is held up as a standard of truth. Not only is the self entwined in society; it owes society its existence in the most literal sense. All its content comes from society, or at any rate from its relation to the object. It grows richer the more freely it develops and reflects this relation, while it is limited, impoverished and reduced by the separation and hardening that it lays claim to as an origin. (pp. 153–154)

With such a notion of the self, authenticity or genuineness as something essential to the individual is rendered hopelessly romantic and obsolete. Our most authentic response to fragmentation, according to Adorno, is to dwell in experience rather than trying to lay claim to it—both as strategies for living one's life and for conducting research. Yet this dwelling is not a phenomenological but a strategic kind of dwelling. Instead of constructing theories of the essences of "things in themselves," he advocated delineating constellations or articulations of social reality. Unlike theories, these articulations are partial, perspectival, and contingent. As such, they are useful primarily for engaging in negative dialectics. Thus, while located primarily in *Chronotope III*, Adorno's work clearly also embodies aspects of the epistemologies and imperatives of *Chronotope IV*.

Marxism and Education: Pedagogies of the Oppressed. Paulo Freire is probably the most well-known scholar to reimagine education and educational inquiry along Marxist lines, laying the foundation for what has come to be known as "critical pedagogy." Because we foregrounded Freire's work in our discussion of *Chronotope III* in chapter 2, we will only briefly review some of his key ideas here.

Freire's work was intensely practical as well as deeply philosophical. His most famous book, *Pedagogy of the Oppressed* (1970), can be read as equal parts social theory, philosophy, and pedagogical method. Throughout this book, Freire argued that the goal of education is to begin to name the world, to recognize that we are all "subjects" of our own lives and narratives, not "objects" in the stories of others. We must acknowledge the ways in which we as human beings are fundamentally charged with producing and transforming reality together. Those who do not acknowledge this, those who want to control and oppress, are committing a kind of epistemic violence. "To surmount the situation of oppression, people must first critically recognize its causes, so that through transforming action they can create a new situation, one that makes possible the pursuit of a fuller humanity. But the struggle to be more fully human has already begun in the authentic struggle to transform the situation" (p. 29).

Freire often referred to these situations as "limit situations," situations that people cannot imagine themselves beyond. Limit situations naturalize people's sense of oppression, giving it a kind of obviousness and immutability. As particularly powerful ideological state apparatuses, schools, of course, play a big role in this naturalization process. Freire argued that most education is based on the "banking model," where educators see themselves as subjects, depositing knowledge into their students, their "objects." This implies an Enlightenment worldview where subject and object are *a priori* independent of each other, and where subjects are objectified and thus dehumanized. "Implicit in the banking concept is the assumption of a dichotomy between human beings and the world: a person is merely in the world, not with the world or with others; the individual is spectator, not re-creator" (p. 56). Among other things, the banking model of education implies that "the teacher teaches and the students are taught" and that "the teacher knows everything and the students know nothing" (p. 54). The model operates according to monologic rather than dialogic logics, serving the interests of the *status quo* and functioning to promote business as usual rather than social change. As problematic as it is politically, the banking model provides the epistemological foundation for most contemporary educational institutions and practices.

In the place of a banking model of education, Freire offered up an alternative model that was based on the elicitation of words (and concomitant ideas) that are fundamentally important in the lives of the people for whom educational activities are designed. He called these words "generative words." He spent long periods of time in communities trying to understand community members' interests, investments, and concerns in order to elicit comprehensive sets of generative words. These words were then used as starting points for literacy learning, and literacy learning was deployed in the service of social and political activism. More specifically, generative words were paired with pictures that represented them and then interrogated by people in the community for what they both revealed and concealed with respect to the circulation of multiple forms of capital. Freire encouraged the people both to explore how the meanings and effects of these words functioned in their lives and also to conduct research on how their meanings and effects do (or could) function in a variety of different ways in different social and political contexts. The primary goal of these activities was to help people feel in control of their words and to be able to use them to exercise power over the material and ideological conditions of their own lives. Thus Freire's literacy programs were designed not so much to teach functional literacy but to raise people's critical consciousness (or *conscientization*) and to encourage them to engage in praxis, or critical reflection inextricably linked to political action in the real world. Freire was clear to underscore the fact that praxis is never easy and always involves power struggles, often violent ones.

Sociology as Politics: Remaking the "Real"

As we have tried to show throughout this chapter, currents of critical social theory in the Marxist tradition have inhabited sociological thinking (sometimes quite boldly) for the past century and a half. Weber, for example, is said to have lived his whole life wrestling with Marx's ghost. More recently, Antonio Gramsci, Pierre Bourdieu, Stuart Hall, Michel Foucault, Gilles Deleuze, Felix Guattari, and others have brought ideas from the Marxist tradition to the very center of sociological thinking and research, constituting a distinct shift from the epistemologies, imperatives, and practices of *Chronotope III* to those of *Chronotope IV*. Driving this shift have been theoretical advances concerned with explaining the constitutive nature and functions of context, as well as intellectual-political imperatives designed to denaturalize objects of study, opening them up to new effectivities. In the next several sections of the chapter we attempt to explain this shift, paying particular attention to the work of Michel Foucault and Gilles Deleuze. Both scholars revised traditional Marxism and the legacy of critical theory to understand how reality is constituted through discursive and material practices in order to transform it in ways that would redistribute power more equally and work against human suffering and oppression. We begin with Foucault.

Discourse and the Production of Reality:
Michel Foucault and His Legacy

More than anything, Foucault was interested in the ways discourses are produced and then produce subjects, allowing for certain meanings and practices to seem perfectly normal and others quite plainly abnormal. Questions of power and the relations between power and knowledge were central to how he theorized these production processes.

According to Foucault, power is always everywhere in institutions and discourses, inscribing their particular "truths" on our bodies themselves. This is what Foucault referred to as "bio-power," the ways we come to physically embody certain regimes of truth. We reproduce these not consciously but in our mundane practices. The case of prisons is a good example. Foucault showed how Jeremy Bentham's model of the *panopticon* rose in prominence during the modern period of punishment. In the panoptic regime, a central tower stands in the middle of the prison with one guard. This guard is able to see everyone, but no one is able to see him. Hence, much of the power of this model lies in the fact that prisoners do not know when they are being watched and thus must self-regulate themselves. They thus sustain and reproduce/produce the panoptic regime, making it seem ever so natural and normal. Discourses operate in this fashion as well. In the first volume of *The History of Sexuality* (1990), Foucault examined how a particular discourse of sexuality was "produced" by the Victorians. In the name of "repressing" sexuality, he argued, the Victorians actually produced a proliferation of discourses around sex. Sex became a site of intense anxiety and a site in which and through which people constructed themselves. Freud, most obviously, constructed a model of "the self" that assumed sexual repression as the dominant "problem" most people would face in coming to full selfhood. A particular kind of sexual(ized) subject was thus "produced" and was allowed to proliferate in numerous ways, all in the name of repression. As we discuss at length in chapter 2, Foucault was fundamentally interested in these kinds of production processes and kinds of questions people are "permitted" to ask within the "common sense" of historically produced cultural systems. He interrogated the ways we sustain and reproduce certain regimes of truth, the ways that certain historical articulations allow us to make certain common sense claims, as well as how these articulations can be dismantled. Genealogy, the practice of making the "present" strange and showing how the seemingly immutable forces that propel us are rooted in historically specific (and often contingent) constellations of material and discursive forces, is most important here.

Critical Discourse Analysis: Conversational Analysis Meets Marx and Foucault. Even though it emerged more within the field of linguistics than of sociology, critical discourse analysis (CDA) is a new and important critical approach to inquiry, especially for the unique ways in which it integrates the rigorous microanalytic strategies typical of all discourse analysis and especially CA (Chronotope I), the emancipatory agendas of critical Marxist approaches to inquiry (Chronotope III), and the postfoundational impulses and analytic strategies typical of more Foucaultian-inspired critical work (Chronotope IV). CDA is an extension of the systemic functional linguistic tradition in Australia (e.g., Halliday, 1994) and the critical language awareness tradition in the United Kingdom (e.g., Clark, Fairclough, Ivanic, & Martin-Jones, 1990). It is a set of theoretical and methodological approaches used by researchers interested in the relationship between language and the construction and maintenance of social identities, social relations, and cultural ideologies.

Unlike some other forms of discourse analysis, CDA is predicated on the idea that language and discourse embody ideologies and are thus constitutive of social identities, social relations, and worldviews. CDA pays particular attention to how power circulates within language and discourse, exerting effects on people and how they relate to each other and to the institutions they inhabit. In this regard, Bloome and Carter (2001) noted that CDA "examines power relations and ideologies embedded in texts through careful and systematic analysis. Although *power relations* can refer to a coercive relationship among people or institutions, we view the term as also referring to the establishment of an ideology, discourse, or world view that makes a particular action or interpretation appear as if it is the only reasonable action or choice to make" (pp. 151–152). Indexing CDA's social justice subtext, van Dijk (1993) noted that CDA focuses "on the role of discourse in the (re)production and challenge of dominance" (p. 249) and that "CDA should deal primarily with the discourse dimensions of power abuse and the injustice and inequality that result from it" (p. 252). Key here is the importance (necessity) of distinguishing between the apparent intentions of situated language and discourse practices and their actual effects. The effects of power and ideology embedded in these practices cannot be assumed but must be studied systematically. CDA helps researchers understand these effects by providing an array of integrated analytic tools for deconstructing the nonnecessary and nontransparent relations of power/knowledge complexes that are hidden in texts and often work on us "behind our backs." The knowledge gained from this deconstructive work positions us to work against asymmetrical power relations, social inequality, nondemocratic practices, and other forms of social and political injustice (Fairclough, 1993).

To study the effects of power/knowledge, CDA includes techniques for analysis at three different levels of discourse organization: text, discursive practice, and social practice (see Fairclough, 1992, 1995, for a diagram of these levels and their relations). Text analyses involve the systematic unpacking of the lexical, grammatical, and semantic structures of texts to determine how they portray social facts as natural or unnatural, normal or abnormal; include (or do not include) the positions, interests, and values of different people or social groups; and are constructed to exert particular kinds of effects on audiences.

Analyses of discursive practices involve mapping the production, distribution, and consumption practices involved in the circulation of texts. These analyses help demonstrate how cultural and economic capital accrue to people involved in these practices, how power circulates as a function of how people are positioned within these practices. For example, whether a text is produced by a lone individual with few economic resources or a corporate mogul matters a great deal. Similarly, the economic and political resources available to distribute a text has serious consequences for its audience range and likely impact. Finally, audiences are not passive consumers or social dupes. So the ways in which texts are heard, read, and talked about by people partially determine their productive power and thus must be studied systematically.

Analyses of social practices involve mapping the conditions of possibility that make particular ideas or lived experiences seem powerful and pervasive for a given social group or society at a given time in history. In mapping social practices, researchers ask questions such as: What are the prevalent societal discourses/ideologies of the time and how might they dispose audiences to have (or not have) an interest in particular texts or to be affected by particular texts in particular ways? Analyses of social practice are designed to deconstruct *power/knowledge*, to show how particular *truth effects* are produced, legitimated, and naturalized with and within specific discourses/ideologies. The particular analytic strategies used to do this work are those of conjunctural analysis, which involve scrupulously mapping the multiple, and often contingent, discursive and material forces that intersect to produce a particular text or event or formation with particular truth effects and not some other text, event, or formation with different truth effects (see chapter 2 for more on conjunctural analysis).

Although these three levels of analysis are central to CDA, practitioners have been fairly criticized for offering overdeveloped analyses of texts but underdeveloped analyses of discursive practices and social practices (e.g., Kamberelis & Jaffe, 2003). They have also been fairly criticized for producing analyses too divorced from the actual social contexts that they purport to interpret and explain, and for making claims about political and social ideologies (and their effects) that do not seem adequately supported by data (e.g., Price, 1998).

These criticisms notwithstanding, the use of CDA within studies of language and literacy is on the rise, and these studies have often produced both interesting and compelling findings. Bergvall and Remlinger (1996), for example, used CDA to show how educators challenged restrictive, reproductive pedagogies. In a more recent study, Ailwood and Lingard (2001) were quite effective in showing how CDA can be used to disrupt naturalized discourses of gender equity, specifically as they are embodied in a recent policy document— *Gender Equity: A Framework for Australian Schools* (Gender Equity Taskforce, 1997)—by attending to both the grammatical and rhetorical construction of the document and to the ways the document has been contextualized within broader social discourses, policy debates, and legislative action. All things considered, CDA is an increasingly powerful force within critical approaches to qualitative inquiry and promises to become even more powerful as it is further developed.

Postcolonial Extensions of Foucault's Work. Although Foucault was not specifically interested in questions of identity politics, his work has been used to generate identity theories that foreground issues of race, ethnicity, gender, and social class. Like Foucault's theories, these theories have foregrounded the social and historical production of the "reality" of such identities. A key example of the extensions of Foucault's work is Edward Said's *Orientalism* (1979), which looked at how the West has traditionally represented the East as a monolithic and "exotic" nowhereland devoid of real humanity and complexity. These representations have proliferated in multiple ways, creating a discursive space that has allowed the West to marginalize large parts of the global populace. They have also allowed the West to create histories that naturalize its global dominance. According to Said (1995):

> I have found it useful here to employ Michel Foucault's notion of a discourse . . . to identify Orientalism. My contention is that without examining Orientalism as a discourse one cannot possibly understand the enormously systematic discipline by which European culture was able to manage—and even produce—the Orient politically, sociologically, militarily, ideologically, scientifically, and imaginatively during the post-Enlightenment period. (pp. 88–89)

Other scholars such as Gilroy (1993) and Omi and Winant (1994) have also looked to denaturalize the idea that race is "essential" or biologically determined, focusing instead on the ways that history allows for certain notions of race and not others. In *The Black Atlantic*, for example, Gilroy examined the ways in which people of the African Diaspora are marked by distinct histories that transcend geographical boundaries. While he explicitly reacted against essentialist positions that ground identity in biology, he also reacted against ahistorical antiessentialist positions, claiming that they "affirm blackness as an open signifier and seek to celebrate complex representations of a black particularity that is *internally* divided: by class, sexuality, gender, age, ethnicity, economics, and political consciousness" (p. 32). Both essentialism and ahistorical antiessentialism, according to Gilroy, ignore historical specificity. Gilroy, in contrast, looked for the ways that particular racial formations are historically produced and what effects they exert on the public imagination.

In their equally famous work on racial formations in the United States, Omi and Winant (1994) interrogated the ways in which "blackness" has signified different things in different historical moments in the United States. They noted, for example, "since racial formation is always historically situated, our understanding of the significance of race, and of the way race structures society, has changed enormously over time" (p. 61). They also compared the ethnic model of racial assimilation that enabled political movements for integration in the 1960s to the more complex and situational models that exist today. Based on their research, they generated principled and warranted explanations for the "social nature of race, the absence of any essential racial characteristics, the historical flexibility of racial meanings and categories, the conflictual character of race at both the 'micro-' and 'macro-social' levels, and the irreducible political aspects of racial dynamics" (p. 4).

Again, the works of Gilroy and Omi and Winant were grounded in the ideas of Foucault, especially his insistence on the productive functions of discourse. Scholars in the Foucaultian tradition have shown how power and knowledge are historically produced and how they, in turn, produce subjects who are enabled and constrained in specific ways. Foucault's historical work has been particularly helpful for looking at the ways in which broad cultural and historical constructs such as insanity or criminality or sexuality register differently in different historical moments. These studies have offered compelling evidence for the imperatives of *Chronotope IV* and raised questions about the purchase of many of the imperatives of *Chronotopes I, II,* and *III*.

Reality as Articulation: From Gramsci to Deleuze and Guattari

Work by Foucault was centrally concerned with how we understand and theorize "the real." This concern has been extended by others, especially through the notion of "articulation." Assembling ideas largely from Gramsci (1971) and Volosinov (1973), Hall (1986) argued that what binds together various practices and effects (which by themselves are not related in any necessary way) into some kind of coherent formation is called an "articulation":

> [A]n articulation is thus the form of connection that *can* make a unity out of two different elements, under certain conditions. It is a linkage which is not necessary, determined, absolute and essential for all time. You have to ask, under what conditions *can* a connection be forged or made? So the so-called "unity" of a discourse is really an articulation of different, distinct elements which can be rearticulated in different ways because they have no necessary "belongingness." The unity which matters is a linkage between that articulated discourse and the social forces with which it can, under certain historical conditions, but need not necessarily, be connected. (p. 53)

Articulations are always constituted through a double process of being "enunciated" or "spoken" and "linked with" or "combined." They are thus always produced as discursive and material structures out of historically available conditions of possibility. Additionally, and also quite Gramscian, Hall argued that articulations are constituted as ongoing struggles to position practices within dynamic fields of forces in order to produce spaces in which certain modes of thought and action are (or remain) possible. In other words, articulations involve continuous production of contexts within which certain practices either are or are not available. For example, although there seem to be no necessary relations among blue jeans, country music, Ford trucks, heartbreak, and a host of other objects and practices, they are all held together by/as an historically produced articulation. Similar examples can readily be proliferated.

Articulations, then, involve the production of unity out of dispersion, identity out of difference, coherence out of apparent randomness. Articulations link particular practices with particular effects (e.g., investing in particular kinds of music and wearing particular kinds of clothing). And these practice-effect constellations themselves get articulated into larger structures or formations (e.g., particular economic, cultural, or political systems or processes). Articulations are ongoing struggles to position practices within dynamic fields of force in particular ways to produce discursive-material geographies within which certain modes of thought and action are possible.

The notion of the collective or the "we" has always been central to most discussions of social action and political activity. For Gramsci (1971), the "we" is always without guarantees. It has to be made and remade, actively articulated in Stuart Hall's (1986) double sense of being both "spoken" (discursively positioned) and "linked with" (temporally and spatially produced). Any "collective" is always a structured (and structuring) field and a set of lived relations in which elements and forces from diverse sources are actively combined, dismantled, and bricolaged to form new politically effective alliances between otherwise fractional groupings. Once articulated, these groupings can no longer be returned to static, homogeneous social categories such as race, class, and gender, which are always configured as hierarchies.

Gramsci insisted on defining hegemony as struggle, as a precarious "moving equilibrium" accomplished through the continual orchestration of conflicting and competing forces by more or less unstable, more or less temporary, more or less contingent, alliances of class fractions (or other relevant social units). From such a perspective, the "we" always favors prescience over science. The "we" is always alert to possibility and emergence. The "we" proceeds knowing/imagining that there are only competing ideologies, which are themselves unstable constellations that are likely to change. The "we" usually works (and works at) the margins, struggling to make more egalitarian ideologies more visible and more viable. The "we" forms alliances. The alliances sometimes strengthen, sometimes weaken, and sometimes dissolve. When alliances dissolve, the "we" forms new alliances committed to new kinds of transgressive, transformative work.

Deleuze and Guattari's (1987) notion of the rhizome is particularly useful for understanding Gramsci's "we" as an articulation with considerable potential for conducting research with political effectivity. For Deleuze and Guattari, the rhizome is an oppositional alternative to what they call arborescent or arboreal ways of thinking, acting, and being, which they claim have defined Western epistemologies at least since the Enlightenment and probably much earlier. As their name suggests, arborescent forms and structures may be imagined metaphorically as trees—linear, hierarchical, sedentary, striated, vertical, stiff, and with deep and permanent roots. They are structures with branches that continue to subdivide into smaller and lesser structures. In their various social and cultural instantiations, arborescent models of thinking, acting, and being amount to restrictive economies of dominance and oppression.

Deleuze and Guattari (1987) oppose the arborescent model because of its inherent totalizing logic. "We're tired of trees. We should stop believing in trees, roots, and radicles. They've made us suffer too much. All of arborescent culture is founded on them, from biology to linguistics" (p. 15). In the place of the tree, they offer up the rhizome as metaphor for an alternative theoretical model. The "rhizome is an acentered, nonhierarchical, nonsignifying system without a General and without an organizing memory or central automaton, defined solely by the circulation of states" (p. 21). Rhizomes are networks. Rhizomes cut across borders. Rhizomes build links between preexisting gaps and between nodes that are separated by categories and orders of segmented thinking, acting, and being.

According to Deleuze and Guattari, rhizomes operate according to six fundamental principles. The first two principles are *connection* and *heterogeneity*. "[A]ny point of a rhizome can be connected to anything other, and must be. This is very different from the tree or the root, which plots a point, fixes an order" (p. 7). Rhizomes are thus ever-growing horizontal networks of connections among heterogeneous nodes of discursive and material force. The third principle of the rhizome is *multiplicity*. A rhizomatic system is comprised of multiple lines and connections. "There are no points or positions in a rhizome, such as those found in a structure, tree, or root. There are only lines" (p. 8), and these lines are organized as ephemeral horizontal relations that are always proliferating. Multiplicity celebrates plurality and proliferative modes of thinking, acting, and being rather than unitary, binary, and totalizing modes. The fourth principle of the rhizome is the principle of *asignifying rupture*. This principle states that "a rhizome may be broken, shattered at a given spot, but it will start up again on one of its old lines, or on new lines" (1987, p. 9). Movements and flows are always rerouted around disruptions in a rhizomatic formation. Additionally, severed sections regenerate themselves and continue to grow, forming new lines, flows, and pathways. The fifth and sixth principles of rhizomatics are *decalcomania* and *cartography*, which ensure that "a rhizome is not amenable to any structural or generative model" (1987, p. 12). Invoking a distinction between maps and tracings, Deleuze and Guattari argue that structural models are reproductive while rhizomes are productive. A tracing (decalcomania) is a copy and operates according to "genetic" principles, evolving and reproducing from earlier forms. In contrast, a map (cartography) is an open system that is contingent, unpredictable, and productive. "The map is open and connectable in all of its dimensions; it is detachable, reversible, susceptible to constant modification. It can be torn, reversed, adapted, to any kind of mounting, reworked by an individual, group, or social formation" (1987, p. 12). In drawing maps, the theorist (like an original cartographer) works at the surface, creating possible realities by producing new articulations of disparate phenomena and connecting the exteriority of objects to whatever forces or directions seem potentially related to them.

Although Deleuze and Guattari see rhizomatics as necessary to any radical political work, they reject utopianism and insist, following Gramsci, that rhizomatic formations are always constructed in the struggle between stabilizing and destabilizing forces. To further explain the nature and functions of rhizomatic formations, Deleuze and Guattari suggest using the linear algebraic metaphors of lines or vectors to think about rhizomes. They posit two basic kinds of lines or vectors: lines of articulation (or consistency) and lines of flight, both of which project their effects across the rhizomatic field. Lines of articulation connect and unify different practices and effects. They establish hierarchies. They define center-periphery relations. They create rules of organization. They encourage stasis. In contrast, lines of flight disarticulate nonnecessary relations between and among practices and effects. They open up contexts to their outsides and the possibilities that dwell there. They disassemble unity and coherence. They decenter centers and disrupt hierarchies.

Finally, every line or vector (of either kind) has its own quality, quantity, and directionality. Thus the effects of any line or vector will vary as a function of these characteristics, as well as the particular densities built up at the intersection of various lines or vectors. From this perspective, rhizomes—as fields or contexts—are produced in the constant struggle between lines of articulation and lines of flight. The coherence and organization of a rhizome are effects of lines of articulation, and the instability and dissolution of a rhizome are effects of lines of flight. Lines of articulation make received models of reality eminently visible. Lines of flight expose these models as historically produced and power-laden (rather than natural and power-neutral). Lines of flight also open up new possibilities for seeing, living, and organizing political resistance. Effects are lines or vectors of force. Reality itself is constituted as configurations of these two kinds of lines or vectors. So deploying or taking up lines of articulation or lines of flight have serious consequences for the production of reality. Taking up lines of articulation ("good student" or "heterosexual parent") helps to keep stable the current organization of a territorialized space and its relations to other territorialized spaces. Taking up lines of flight ("resistant but creative student" or "gay parent") helps open up new configurations of space (i.e., reality) so that new possibilities for thinking, acting, and being may be opened up.

Doing rhizomatics thus requires what Deleuze and Guattari call "a commitment to the real," a commitment to experimenting with and intervening in reality and its relations of power. Rhizomatics is a mapping of the real to challenge and perhaps reconfigure the possibilities of reality itself. Rhizomatics goes beyond representation toward reinvention. To the extent that one is redesigning reality and discourse and to the extent that discourse is an intervention into the real, it may be rhizomatic. Attending to the real and rearticulating the real (not simply reproducing or representing it) is the bottom line.

The work of Deleuze and Guattari has not informed qualitative inquiry to the degree that Foucault's work has. More often, it has been appropriated solely for advancing social theory. For example, William Bogard (1998) argued that Deleuze and Guattari challenge sociologists to rethink traditional connections between "sense" and "meaning," disrupting "an immanent relationship between meaning and reason, between sense and the concept," opening up the possibility for what he calls a "sociology of the inhuman" (p. 53). Deleuze and Guattari's work also helps to disrupt the traditional notions of linear hierarchy that have informed sociological understandings of social stratification. "Class and income strata, status structures, authority relations all involve a scheme of lower to higher" (p. 53). Rhizomatics help us understand the ways in which such segments can be "circular" as well, a point underscored by other recent work on social theory and sociological thinking (e.g., Brown & Lunt, 2002; Toews, 2003).

A small but growing body of educational research has drawn on rhizomatics to disrupt hegemonic notions of the "self" rooted in modernist heterosexist imperatives. Such work has underscored the idea that "the subject does not exist ahead of or outside of language but is a dynamic, unstable effect of language/discourse and cultural practice" (St. Pierre, 2000, p. 502). While these ideas certainly fit with Deleuze and Guattari's insights, they often confuse these insights with more generic (and sometimes anti-Deleuzian) poststructural ideas, and they only begin to exploit the rich affordances of Deleuzian theory.

Scholars have also begun to deploy Deleuze's work to "move beyond" traditional conceptions of interpretive research and writing. Mostly, this has come in the form of revisiting and "rereading" their earlier work. St. Pierre (1997) for example, used the Deleuzian concept of "the nomad" to rethink her attachments to place and to others in the context of her earlier ethnographic work with women from her hometown. Whereas an ethnographic orientation would predispose the researcher to inscribe "some space, some place, some field" (p. 370), a nomadic orientation leads one to deterritorialize "striated space." The tension between these two orientations is central to St. Pierre's work and helps her to disrupt preconceptions about research while "smoothing them over" again in narrative form. In the end, St. Pierre "holds tight to the possibilities of nomadic inquiry," committed to exploring/exploiting it more fully in future work (p. 378).

Drawing on Dimitriadis and Kamberelis's (1997) explanations of the Deleuzian distinction between "tracing" and "mapping," Alvermann (2000) used rhizomatic principles to revisit and reinterpret a series of qualitative studies she conducted on reading groups in public libraries. In the original studies, she had concluded that libraries were spaces where her participants felt freer to challenge and experiment with more "school-like" ways of reading by linking them to abiding interests in popular culture and the media. In her reanalyses, Alvermann tried to generate less predictable connections between and among disparate texts and sources of empirical material, claiming that "in true rhizomatous fashion, then, I have gone from *Pulp Fiction* to popabilly, hip-hop to *South Park*, and all by way of a book on teaching critical media literacy" (p. 121). She further claimed to superimpose this "map" on to her original "tracings," allowing her "to see the original study's findings in a new light" (p. 124).

Wendy Morgan (2000) used rhizomatics in her discussion of Patti Lather's poststructural feminist work on women and AIDS. Of course, Lather herself had already done a certain kind of rhizomatic work by juxtaposing different levels of analysis on the printed page. According to Lather (2000), "Delineating a rhizomatics of proliferations, crossings, and overlaps, all without underlying structures or deeply rooted connections, information in *Troubling the Angels* is organized like a hypermedia environment" (p. 303). Extending these concerns, Morgan (2000) argued that hypertext representation such as this allows feminist scholars to "dismantle the master's house" with the master's tools. Texts like *Troubling the Angels* look outward beyond themselves, drawing lines and proliferating meaning in unpredictable ways that challenge posited links between surface effects and deep meanings.

Clarke and his colleagues (e.g., Clarke, Harrison, Reeve, & Edwards, 2002; Edwards & Clarke, 2002) have used Deleuze's theory of "space " to explain the narratives of lived experiences of university students they studied. Set against corporate discourses of new "flexible" modes of learning and lifelong education, the authors demonstrated the ways in which students themselves picked up and deployed a spatial language to help "map" their own perhaps unpredictable relationship with higher education. These authors noted that students' narratives embodied complex "tensions between the notion of flexibility as a liberation from constraint and the desire to be inside a place" (Clarke et al., 2002, p. 296).

In summary, so far rhizomatics has been appropriated and deployed in sporadic, selective, and often tentative ways within qualitative inquiry. Most of the attention to Deleuze and Guattari's trenchant social theories has been a matter of trying to figure out what they mean. Importantly, this was also true of Foucault's work for quite some time. If history repeats itself here, we may see more and more interesting uses of rhizomatics in the service of empirical work.

Coda: Inquiry Logics Within Critical Sociological Theory and Research

Critical approaches to qualitative inquiry within sociology have situated themselves variously within and across *Chronotopes III* and *IV*. Looking across the many lines of thought that we have drawn under the sign of the "critical," several tenets emerge that are directly related to understanding the logics of critical modes of inquiry. First, the basic goal of these modes is to change the world by exposing social, economic, and political forces that have been socially and historically constructed and have produced asymmetrical distributions of power and goods in society.

Epistemologically, critical modes of inquiry are based on a rejection of instrumental notions of rationality, arguing that such notions focus on "correct" methods rather than desirable and just ends. Concomitantly, the distinction between facts and values is also rejected because facts are regarded as emanating from the values of dominant groups in society and "naturalized" within the discourses of various ideological state apparatuses so that they seem unquestionably real. Redistributions of power can thus produce new sets of facts. Related to this point, the relations between signs and their referents (whether material or social) are seen as contingent and unstable because they have been produced/mediated within specific sets of social, cultural, and economic relations with specific value valences. Language and discourse are thus seen not so much as representational tools as productive ones. No value-neutral interpretations or explanations of reality—even those developed by critical social theorists—are possible. Because language and discourse function in this way, new languages and new discourses can contribute to the redistribution of power/ knowledge and material goods and thus new articulations of reality.

Just as they reject the distinction between fact and value and unproblematic relations between signs and concepts and their referents, critical modes of inquiry are suspicious of phenomenological accounts of experience because these accounts are always already constructed within specific discourses of power/knowledge that, in Marx's words, operate "behind people's backs." Recall Marx's insistence on the fact that economic and social conditions determine consciousness rather than the converse. So whereas researchers working within more hermeneutic/interpretive modes of inquiry embrace accounts of "lived experience" as genuine and authentic (as discussed in chapter 2, *Chronotope II*), researchers working within more critical modes are suspicious of such accounts because they see experience itself as enabled and constrained by discourses that produce the conditions of possibility for certain kinds of experience (and not others) in the first place. Similarly, they see individuals as constructed by and within discourses, which, in turn, "speak through" these individuals. Experiences and the individuals that are posited from them are thus constructions of specific social/economic/cultural forces rather than original "essences."

Given the rejection of the fact/value distinction and the veracity of "accounts of lived experience," the primary rhetorical goal (or the mode of explanation) central to critical forms of inquiry is to interrogate, deconstruct, and then reconstruct discourses and concomitant relations between power and knowledge. Whether it takes the abstract, radical form of "negative dialectics" or the more humanistic form of "pedagogy of the oppressed," critical social research is always about detecting particular articulations of reality that privilege dominant groups to set the groundwork for disarticulating and rearticulating them in ways that result in more equitable distributions of power/ knowledge and material well-being.

Critical modes of inquiry are thus motivated by what we call a "politics of possibility" wherein researchers work *with* research participants toward emancipation and self-empowerment. Research practice is thus radically dialogic, which means that researchers share in the cultural practices of the people they research, suggest ways in which their lives may be re-imagined and transformed, and are themselves transformed in the process. In this regard, critical modes of research always require attention not only to the pragmatic sense of praxis but to its political sense as well, wherein researchers and research participants enter into reciprocal relationships of common work to advance both of their points of view and interests. Developing and maintaining such reciprocal relationships, however, is extraordinarily difficult work and can easily go awry because it requires being uneasy in one's skin (Probyn, 1993, p. 80), and being uneasy in one's skin demands self-defamiliarization, self-reconstruction, and sometimes painful redistributions of economic, social, cultural, and symbolic capital (e.g., Behar, 1993).

Critical qualitative research is evaluated and validated according to the logic of praxis as well, the extent to which it is effective in alleviating oppression and redistributing economic and symbolic capital. Patti Lather (1986), for instance, argues that "emancipatory knowledge increases awareness of the contradictions hidden or distorted by everyday understandings, and in doing so directs attention to the possibilities for social transformation inherent in the present configuration of social processes" (p. 259). She goes on to propose a form of justification for critical qualitative research that she calls "catalytic validity," which involves the examination of "the degree to which the research process reorients, focuses, and energizes participants toward knowing reality in order to transform it" (p. 272).

Summary and Conclusions

In this chapter, we mapped the complex social field of sociological inquiry during the last 150 years or so. This social field has been marked by the almost constant intersecting, traversing, and colliding of social theory and empirical investigation. We could have discussed many other figures who were clearly influential in the development of various modes of sociological theory and approaches to inquiry. Habermas, for example, exerted a strong influence on the hermeneutic strand in sociological theory, and Bourdieu has been absolutely central to the development of the practice theories (e.g., Lave & Wenger, 1991) and social linguistics/literacies (e.g., Gee, 1996) that have recently become so popular in educational research.

Our approach, though, was more selective. We started with a discussion of the foundational/modernist strains and the hermeneutic/interpretive strains of sociological thought that reached their apex in the work of the *Chicago School* of sociology. We argued that grounded theory, ethnomethodology, and conversational analyses represent the most powerful embodiments of foundational/modernist theory and research in 20th-century sociology and that symbolic interactionism represents the most powerful embodiment of the hermeneutic/interpretive trajectories of thinking and practice. We then noted that some contemporary (post-1980s) spinoffs of symbolic interactionism have adopted a more critical stance that involves a stronger praxis orientation and more experimental forms of fieldwork and representation. Finally, because "critical" modes of inquiry arrived rather late on the scene within *Chicago School* work, we discussed Marx and the Marxist tradition of critical social theory, and we noted some of the ways in which this tradition has influenced qualitative inquiry. Basically, we argued that this tradition transformed inquiry into a venture concerned primarily with interrogating and remapping reality itself to produce more equitable distributions of economic and symbolic capital. From this perspective, reality is produced historically through articulations.

It is important to note, however, that the more foundational and interpretive approaches to sociological inquiry, the kinds reflected in *Street Corner Society* and *The Gang*, have not simply given way to more critical approaches in the late 20th and early 21st centuries. These later forms of inquiry remain alive and well, albeit in evolved forms. Work of current literacy scholars such as Brandt (1992), Bauman and Ivey (1997), and Cicourel (1992), for example, follow in the footsteps of modernist/foundational approaches. Work of scholars such as Dunier (1992), Lofty (1987), Schaafsma (1993), and Finders (1997) build upon and extend more hermeneutic/interpretive ones. And the work of scholars like Luke (1992), Dressman (1997), and Lewis (2001) clearly take up critical approaches.

Except for our discussion of critical approaches to sociological inquiry, the *Chicago School* of sociology figured most prominently in our account because of the tremendous impact it has had on qualitative inquiry in virtually all disciplines, especially in the United States. We want to remind readers, however, that this was a strategic choice, designed to simplify an almost unmanageable amount of complexity in the ways in which sociological inquiry has been imagined and enacted during the last century. Another history might tell a slightly different story with a slightly different cast of characters, but we maintain that an examination of the development and dispersion of *Chicago School* ideas and practices offers productive (if idiosyncratic and incomplete) ways to understand many of the central ideas related to imagining and practicing qualitative inquiry that have circulated within sociology for some time and have influenced qualitative inquiry in other disciplines in profound ways.

The same goes for the more critical strains of social theory and sociological research we discussed. Although almost any author writing a book such as this one would likely begin with Marx, he or she might offer accounts that differ from ours about the proliferation and dispersion of Marxist thought in the 20th century. Whereas we foregrounded the work of Theodor Adorno, Paulo Freire, Michel Foucault, and Gilles Deleuze, other authors might have foregrounded the work of

Louis Althusser, Herbert Marcuse, and especially Jürgen Habermas, whom we mentioned in passing but did not assign central roles. We did this partly because we discussed some of these scholars in chapter 2 and partly because we had to make certain strategic cuts to create a manageable account. As we noted at the beginning of the chapter, our rhetorical task here was to offer a selective (not comprehensive) history various trajectories of thought and to outline their key tropes and their relevance for those of us who find them useful in imagining and conducting critical qualitative research.

CHAPTER 5

Qualitative Inquiry:
A Transdisciplinary Metadiscourse

In the first major section of this book, we discussed the philosophical foundations of qualitative inquiry. In the second major section of the book, we mapped the histories of qualitative inquiry as they have emerged within anthropology and sociology. In this chapter, we (re)present and draw together many of the central themes of the book but in a "new key" (Langer, 1957). First, we revisit the idea that qualitative inquiry has become a transdisciplinary metadiscourse, and we discuss some of the implications of this social fact. Second, we offer annotations of key language and literacy studies located within and across various chronotopes and conducted from within and across different approaches to qualitative inquiry. Third, we argue that qualitative researchers can and should remain sensitive to the complex and uneven terrain of epistemologies, theories, approaches, and strategies that constitute the "blooming buzzing confusion" of qualitative inquiry while still adopting "postures" (Wolcott, 1992) that allow us all to get some work done. It is through this kind of pragmatic reflexivity that qualitative inquiry has become a powerful force within the human sciences, and it will be this kind of reflexivity that pushes its theoretical and empirical boundaries in the 21st century.

We noted in the Introduction to this book that although qualitative inquiry was born and matured within specific disciplinary contexts, it has become a transdisciplinary metadiscourse. A subtext that runs throughout this book is that its language and organizational schemes can be used to talk productively about the diverse range of approaches we have discussed, from traditional ethnography to genealogy/rhizomatics. Creating this subtext was a strategic gesture designed to signal both the possibilities and dangers of qualitative inquiry's present state of affairs. As we noted in the Introduction, these are indeed generative times for the field, marked by new journals, new book series, a myriad of handbooks, and many other synoptic volumes. Although we have tended to highlight these generative dimensions of qualitative inquiry, we would be remiss if we did not mention some of their attendant dangers. Most specifically, there is an increasing risk, especially given certain reactionary political flows, that qualitative inquiry will become "ghettoized" (for lack of a better term), marked off as different from and less legitimate than other forms of inquiry. In other words, the forceful emergence of qualitative inquiry as a transdisciplinary metadiscourse (especially in education) may have enabled, even fueled, the dangerous and (now) highly politicized split between "hard" and "soft" sciences—a split with particularly serious implications and consequences for graduate students and junior scholars.

This danger was brought into high relief in a 1999 cover story in the *Chronicle of Higher Education* by D. W. Miller entitled "The Black Hole of Educational Research: Why Do Academic Studies Play Such a Minimal Role in Efforts to Improve the Schools?" Despite rhetoric to the contrary, Miller noted that a sharp quantitative/qualitative distinction still informs much of the debate around school reform. He went on to claim that leading scholars are increasingly polarized, and many bemoan a lack of common goals and standards in conduct of educational inquiry, including the following quotation by Ellen Condliffe Lagemann of New York University and the National Academy of Education: "There are no common patterns of training. If you don't have common patterns of training, it's hard to reach agreement on what research is, much less what good research is" (p. A18). Although implicit, the answer to the general question posed in the article—why doesn't educational research seem to make a difference in improving schools?—seems to come down to the fact that "mushy" qualitative approaches are eroding the scientific integrity of educational research. In this regard, Diane Ravitch, also quoted in the article, contends that schools should be more like hospitals, with rigorous scientific research informing their daily practice. Importantly, rigorous scientific research is defined quite narrowly here, referring primarily to the use of randomized experiments to evaluate the effectiveness of classroom practice. Largely absent from these debates is the fact that qualitative inquiry is often constructed according to facile stereotypes and the fact that qualitative empirical research was both instrumental and effective in responding to the *crisis of relevance* indexed by the Coleman Report. For a set of trenchant critiques of this reactionary turn, see the special issue of *Qualitative Inquiry, 10* (1), published in 2004 and featuring essays by scholars as diverse as Yvonna Lincoln, Joseph Maxwell, Katherine Ryan, Kenneth Howe, and Thomas Popkewitz.

These kinds of countervailing voices notwithstanding, we are in the midst of a backlash against qualitative inquiry, fueled largely by the promotion within mainstream discussions of facile stereotypes about its nature and functions, as well as the exclusion of critique in mainstream journals and books. Magnifying this tendency are recent moves to link federal policymaking and funding almost exclusively to "scientifically based research," usually defined as replicable experimental studies designed to improve outcomes on high-stakes tests. Needless to say, qualitative approaches to inquiry have little or no place here. At best, they are viewed as unnecessary and unaffordable luxuries in a time of societal crisis. As a result, most qualitative work is now done with little funding (at least federal funding) and has largely proliferated in other than mainstream venues, including those noted in the Introduction.

The state of affairs in which qualitative inquiry finds itself is further complicated by some internal tensions, including an increasing proliferation and dispersion of approaches within the field itself. In the face of such proliferation and dispersion, there is little consensus about what counts as the "best" kinds of qualitative work being conducted today. On one level, the diversity of approaches and the generative impulses of the field are clearly strengths, producing a certain richness and complexity that opens up new dialogues and debates. On another level, though, they are dangerous because they suggest disunity, an absence of "common patterns of training," and a lack of clear guidelines for evaluating research quality.

Another pressing set of concerns for qualitative research(ers) are the increasing and increasingly powerful structural constraints that work against us. To begin with, much of the best qualitative research has traditionally relied on long-term immersion in field sites. With rapidly shrinking funding venues, this kind of work becomes less and less possible. The ever-increasing pressure on junior scholars to publish articles and books early and often has further exacerbated this problem. Building a career (never mind having a personal life) is virtually impossible if one spends years on a long-term research project with no funding and few, if any, publications.

A parallel concern is the implicit mandate in the field to negotiate reciprocal and ethical relationships with our research participants.

Although we fully support this mandate, it constitutes time-consum-
ing and personally taxing work, with uncertain outcomes—a point
sometimes lost on key gatekeepers. To make things worse, the concerns for reciprocity and ethical integrity adopted by many qualitative researchers often clash with what is expected by the institutional
review boards of academic institutions. These boards often translate
relational and ethical concerns into legal concerns defined in quite
narrow ways. These translations reflect a lack of understanding of the
contingent, complex, relational, moral, and political dimensions of
qualitative inquiry—dimensions that define its key strengths.

Given how politically charged, powerful, and pervasive the quantitative-qualitative debates in education have been, it is perhaps not
surprising that teasing out and mapping the richness and complexity
of qualitative inquiry has not been prioritized. Recall our criticisms in
this regard from chapter 1. Part of the reason we wrote this book in the
way we did was to work against this tendency and contribute to the
nascent but "complicated conversation" (Pinar, 2004) about the nature
and functions of qualitative inquiry. By arguing that qualitative inquiry has become a transdisciplinary metadiscourse and by offering a
principled transdisciplinary language for thinking and talking about
it, we hope we have provided some ideas for how to work within,
through, and across various approaches to inquiry and to create new
epistemology-theory-approach-strategy articulations that are as ele-
gant, interesting, and productive as those created during the past few
decades.

Approaches to Qualitative Inquiry Revisited: Language and Literacy Exemplars

Research on language and literacy, typically located within the discipline of education, has been a key site for the growth of qualitative inquiry as a transdisciplinary metadiscourse. Recall our earlier
observations about how pioneering scholars in our field had to go to
journals in other disciplines to get their qualitative work published. It
is fitting, then, for us to end the book with annotations of key studies
of language and literacy conducted within and across many of the approaches to research we have discussed throughout. Because our goal
here is to be illustrative and not comprehensive, our annotations are
selective—we do not cover each and every approach to research discussed in the book, and we offer only one or two annotations for each

of the approaches we include. This means we had to leave out the work of many outstanding scholars, for which we apologize. Taken together, though, these annotations fairly well represent the exciting range of ways in which qualitative inquiry has been taken up and developed by language and literacy scholars.

Because one of our goals in creating these annotations is to draw together many of the themes developed throughout the book, we highlight—sometimes directly, sometimes obliquely—the ways in which epistemology, theory, approach, and strategy were considered and deployed in these studies. We do this to remind ourselves and our readers that research decisions and practices partially constitute the objects we study and the claims we make from/about our studies. It would be interesting to imagine what some of these studies might have looked like or what conclusions might have been drawn from them were they situated within different epistemological, theoretical, or approach frameworks.

Besides functioning as a review of the book's key themes, our annotations also serve as reminders that, like the field of qualitative inquiry itself, the actual practice of qualitative work is often less monolithic than hybrid, marked as much, if not more than, by breaks and ruptures from the rules of specific approaches as by adherence to them. Importantly, this impulse has always been at the heart of qualitative inquiry—resistance against any and all forms of instrumental rationality and engagement in multiple forms of informed bricolage.

Ethnography of Communication. Shirley Brice Heath's classic work (see chapter 2) is certainly a wonderful example of the ethnographic impulse within language and literacy studies. John Lofty's *Time to Write* (1992) and David Schaafsma's *Eating on the Street* (1993) are two more recent studies that represent and broaden the ethnography of communication tradition.

In *Time to Write*, John Lofty returned to a familiar site to do his work—a fishing community in Maine where he had previously taught before leaving for graduate school. Like Heath, his ethnographic study was located pretty firmly in *Chronotope II*, informed by hermeneutic theory and involving long-term participant observation and interviewing. He met up with former students, some graduates, some still in high school, and their younger siblings "in their homes, on the clam flats, and in lobster boats. . . . in a corner of the library and in empty classrooms" (p. 258). In many respects, Lofty positioned himself as an

impartial observer here. His goal was to situate local language practices in context, though he was concerned about power imbalances
between school and nonschool settings.

Informed by Heidegger's (1962) hermeneutics of *time*, Lofty demonstrated how these students, many of whom were fishers and would
be fishers later in life, had a sense of time that did not resonate with
the way time was organized in school. School time was regulated by
the clock. Rooted in late 19th- and early 20th-century imperatives,
this organization was designed to prepare people for work in an industrial manufacturing workplace. He compared this organization of
time with the "sea time" of fishing people, with its much more fluid,
open, and even circular characteristics, as well as the ways in which
it was always articulated with weather and the seasons. School time
(along with many other school practices) had no relevance in students'
lives when they were out working on their boats. These two temporal worlds conflicted with each other. Because they privileged work
over school, and because they saw no payoff in adopting school time
and school tasks, they experienced conflicts and enacted resistance in
school. Indeed, what is most unique and powerful about Lofty's work
is the way in which he combines hard-nosed ethnographic research
with theoretical and philosophical knowledge of *time* and its central
relevance in everyday life to render an account of students' experiences of school and work that would not have been possible without
such an articulation. His methodological and theoretical positioning
here were crucial, and we daresay he would have written a very different book had he positioned himself otherwise.

David Schaafsma's *Eating on the Street* reported on a community-
based summer writing program in Detroit—the Dewey Center Community Writing Project. Drawing from *Chronotopes II* and *IV*, Schaafsma used sociocultural theory to understand how texts were negotiated and produced, as well as how these processes were imbricated
within power relations between and among teachers and students. In
doing so, he highlighted which narrative forms were acceptable/ac-
cepted at which times, under which circumstances, and why. Schaafsma also drew upon key elements of *Chronotope III* in that he was a key
collaborator in the program and participated in and documented the
conversations teachers had about students, framing them with examples of student writing. More self-consciously than Lofty, Schaafsma
attended carefully to the emergent nature of collaboration and its implications for the production, distribution, and consumption of texts.

Schaafsma's narrative is devoted to unfolding different perspectives about the issue of whether teachers should confront poor Black children about "eating in the street." The fact that Black teachers often uphold strict modes of public behavior for Black children while White liberals often see these modes as unnecessary and constraining produced palpable tensions. In the end, Schaafsma argues that "collaborative learning is messy" and that "the story of our teaching collaboration, unlike most carefully written stories, has no fixed beginning or ending" (p. 201). The text itself is a unique account, largely because it is genuinely ethnographic at the same time that it reimagines ethnographic work by locating it within more critical chronotopes. How Schaafsma assembled and deployed theoretical constructs from narrative theory, translinguistics, and poststructuralism to construct complex interpretations and explanations of key events around which the book's narratives pivot is particularly interesting and portends several impulses that are now common in literacy research.

Grounded Theory. Located on the cusp of *Chronotopes I* and *II*, James Baumann and Gay Ivey's 1997 article, "Delicate Balances: Striving for Curricular and Instructional Equilibrium in a Second-Grade, Literature/Strategy-Based Classroom," is an excellent example of the sophisticated use of a grounded theory approach to investigate the nature and effects of literacy teaching and learning. The authors set out to examine how strategy instruction influenced reading and writing in a literature-rich learning setting. They found that literature-rich learning settings helped young people develop into better and more engaged readers. The students made gains in vocabulary, fluency, comprehension, and writing ability. The setting for this study was a second-grade classroom where one of the authors worked as a teacher. In true grounded theory fashion, the authors collected a wide range of empirical material—field notes, videotaped interviews, and videotapes of classroom literacy activities, as well as several different kinds of reading and writing assessments (p. 257). They analyzed these data using the constant comparative method and working through all three forms of grounded theory coding to build a theory from "the ground up." They "looked across all the cases to find recurring patterns among the data" and "induced and defined categories and properties" (p. 258). The researchers then compared and contrasted categories to help refine and sharpen their emerging theory. All this helped to expand their understandings of the breadth and depth of children's learning,

which they then read against their *a priori* assumptions and categories. Recall that grounded theory approaches highlight the ways data
"speak back" to us in surprising ways. In this study, we see a suspicion of *a priori* understandings coupled with a deep faith in empirical
methods for discovering what is really "there."

Ethnomethodology. There have been very few efforts to bring ethnomethodology to bear within language and literacy research, but one
stands out as exemplary. In her article "The Cognitive and the Social:
An Ethnomethodological Approach to Writing Process Research,"
Deborah Brandt (1992) explicated the ways in which ethnomethodology can help breach a longstanding fissure in the field, between those
who study only (or primarily) cultural influences and those who study
only (or primarily) cognitive processes. In her words, she used "ethnomethodological perspectives to translate the language of Flower
and Hayes's cognitive theory of writing into a more thoroughly social
vocabulary as a way of articulating the role of social context and social structure in individual acts of writing" (p. 315). Like the cognitive
think-aloud studies of Flower and Hayes, ethnomethodology stresses the emergent nature of composition, while also asking the question, "what know-how is in use here" (p. 324). The latter is, largely, a
cultural question. To examine the interaction of the cultural and the
cognitive, Brandt conducted an empirical study of how an advanced
doctoral student assembled a proposal abstract for an MLA conference. She highlighted the think-aloud procedure the student used as
well as the cultural conventions he employed. Relying largely on the
ethnomethodological principles of reflexivity, indexicality, et cetera,
and reciprocity of perspective, she showed how ethnomethodology is
a powerful tool for investigating the processes by which people make
sense out of themselves and their writing in context.

   Although this study does a tremendous job of showing the reflexivity of agents in practice, it does not turn the reflexive lens back on
the researcher or the research process, perhaps because "ethnomethodologists refuse to invoke generalizations that arise from an observer's perspective independent of the perspectives of the participants
themselves" (p. 346).

   Located on the cusp of *Chronotopes I* and *II*, this ethnomethodological study is clearly motivated by modernist imperatives. However,
in discussing the limitations of an ethnomethodological approach,
Brandt gestures toward *Chronotope IV* with extraordinary insight and

reflexivity. She suggests, for example, that researchers need to attend more closely to distal social and cultural forces rooted in institutionalized forms of race, class, and gender. "Rather than focusing on the contingent, unfolding of events in real time" researchers should focus on "the cultural forms and materials which are antecedent to the situations of their use, recognizing that in their situated, contingent use those forms and materials will be reshaped, reflexively reproduced anew" (Heap, 1991, p. 112, cited in Brandt, 1992, p. 351).

Discourse Analysis/Conversation Analysis. We discuss two examples of discourse analysis in this section: Marjorie Goodwin's *He-Said-She-Said* (1990), and Niko Besnier's *Literacy, Emotion, and Authority: Reading and Writing on an Polynesian Atoll* (1995). As we noted above, Goodwin's *He-Said-She-Said* reports on a conversational analytic study embedded in an ethnography of adolescent peers in Philadelphia. It is a well-known study in which Goodwin treats conversation as "action," as a way in which young people achieve certain social ends. The book focuses on conflicts and resolutions among Goodwin's participants, especially how local social orders are created and sustained through conversation. To conduct the study required a deep investment in participant observation as well as recording and carefully attending to naturally occurring conversation. Throughout, Goodwin was at pains to "disturb as little as possible the activities [she] was studying" (p. 23), and did not make any "effort to systematically elicit any particular speech genre" (p. 22). These impulses betray CA's modernist tendency to separate self and other, subject and object, as well as the idea of the researcher as an objective instrument. Goodwin focused on several kinds of discursive tools, the most notable of which is the "he-said-she-said" pattern. Here, one youth tells another that a third party was talking behind her back. The offended party then confronts the offender to "get something straight" (p. 190). As Goodwin shows, these kinds of activity structures are highly consequential. "While some he-said-she-said disputes can be brief and even playful, on other occasions accusations can lead to an extended dispute which the girls treat as quite consequential for the social organization of their group . . . as well as an event of high drama within which character and reputation can be gained or lost" (p. 190). Conversation instantiates key participation structures through which young people live their lives. That young people actively draw upon these structures to create and sustain particular orders is an important theme of this

book. Such a rendering of social activity is structuralist and modernist, firmly rooted in *Chronotope I*. However, the firmness of this rooting
is loosened somewhat by the ethnographic perspectives (*Chronotope
II*) Goodwin brings to bear on her work as well.

Niko Besnier's *Literacy, Emotion, and Authority: Reading and Writing on a Polynesian Atoll* (1995) is a fascinating study of the Nukulaelae
and their uses of literacy. The study on which this book is based was
primarily concerned with the relationships among literacy (especially
letter writing and reading), affect, and gender. Substantively, Besnier's
work argues against notions that literacy is "restricted" (e.g., Goody,
1977) on the atoll, a claim commonly leveled against many language
and literacy practices of poor and so-called "primitive" peoples. Introduced through missionaries and preserved in part through sermons,
the communicative practices of the Nukulaelae were rooted in a rich
and multifarious system of "incipient literacy" that embodies multiple technological tools from the West and mediates complex constructions of selfhood, gender, and social relationships.

Besnier's study was located primarily within *Chronotope II* and
constituted as another interesting hybrid combining ethnographic
and discourse analytic (especially but not only CA) strategies. In his
descriptions of the local "events" around which reading and writing
took place, Besnier clearly drew on EOC to contextualize his work.
His analyses of spoken language, however, are clearly indebted to CA,
especially its concern with "indexicality." However, he also flirts with
the impulses of *Chronotope IV* when he concludes that "gender and literacy practices do not map onto one another in a rigid fashion. Rather,
the indexical nature of the mapping opens the possibility for leakages,
as when men are 'allowed' to take on 'women-like' social roles, as they
do in letters, and for some contestation, as when women appropriate
some (but not all) of the authority embedded in written in sermonic
performances" (pp. 184–185). Like *He-Said-She-Said*, this book largely
embodies modernist imperatives, evidencing a clear split between self
as researcher and other as research object, as well as a sense of having
"got it right." However, Besnier's work also has clear intimations of
more constructionist and even poststructural impulses.

Linguistic Anthropology of Education Approaches. Several of the
studies we have discussed so far have drawn data collection and/or
analysis strategies from more than one approach to research. Goodwin's and Besnier's research are exemplary in this regard and marked

early (and to some extent tacit) efforts to contextualize microanalyses of discursive activity within macroanalyses of context. Several recent studies have even more intentionally and explicitly been designed to exploit the potentials of micro-macro integrations. Betsy Rymes's *Conversational Borderlands: Language and Identity in an Alternative Urban High School* (2001), which integrates strategies of ethnography, narrative theory/analysis, and discourse analysis (especially CA), is an exceptional example of this imperative. She looked "at *genre, narrative, grammar, naming,* and *indexicality* as linguistic resources students and teachers used to establish individual identity and negotiate their social roles" at an alternative charter school (p. 13). Much of her account revolves around narratives of dropouts and how they functioned at an alternative school. Among other things, she traced the uses of what she calls the "discourse genre" of dropping out, focusing especially on the ways young people positioned themselves in the narratives of school and the moral imperatives that seemed to motivate these stories. She contrasted these narratives with those of young people who decided to stay in school.

Throughout this all, Rymes situated students' stories within the complex fabric of institutional life at the school and in the district, and she demonstrated how certain kinds of stories were enabled by this context while others were constrained or negated. Much more than Goodwin or Besnier, Rymes attempted to be self-reflexive about her work, discussing how the different "selves" she adopted with different participants and in different school contexts affected what she saw and what she came to understand about her participants and their language and literacy practices. All in all, Rymes's work is a wonderful example of careful empirical work located within *Chronotope II* but informed by many of the ethical, praxis-oriented, and reflexive impulses so central to *Chronotope IV*.

Narrative and Life History Approaches. We now turn to two studies that embody narrative and life history approaches to research—Amy Shuman's *Storytelling Rites* (1986) and Wendy Luttrell's *Schoolsmart and Motherwise* (1997). Primarily located within *Chronotope II*, Shuman's *Storytelling Rights* is based on a two-and-a-half-year ethnographic study of middle-school students in Philadelphia and focused both on their written and oral communication. In particular, Shuman examined how young people used these media to communicate "fight stories," including their sense of what kinds of stories were appropriate and what narrative forms were sanctioned. Besides using the traditional ethnographic strategies of participant observation and interviewing, Shuman used her ever-present tape recorder to capture stories *in vivo*. To analyze her data she used strategies developed by narrative theorists such as Vladmir Propp and William Labov. Based on her work, Shuman concluded, "The adolescents transformed the conventional uses of writing and speaking for their own purposes. They had their own understanding of what could be written but not said, and vice versa" (p. 3). In tracing these storytelling activities, Shuman demonstrated how young people transformed fights into stories about fights and what effects these transformations had on the organization of their social lives. The variability Shuman documented with respect to how events get transformed into narratives and how these narratives function in communities is at the heart of this book.

Moving back and forth across *Chronotopes II, III,* and *IV,* Wendy Luttrell's *Schoolsmart and Motherwise* reports on a study of the life histories of women from Pennsylvania and North Carolina who returned to school to get GEDs, focusing largely on the short- and long-term effects of their school experiences on their developing sense of self. Unlike Shuman, Luttrell was not positioned as a "researcher" alone. She was also the adult education teacher of the women she studied. She used this role to organize interviews and focus groups, and her work quickly became both collaborative and praxis-oriented. Interested in the ways women "story" their "selves" and the consequences of this process for how they are positioned and position themselves in their social worlds, Luttrell highlighted "the controlling images and ambivalent feelings that were evoked as the women recounted their lives" (p. xiv). According to Luttrell, "these images and feelings were bound up together in institutional, cultural, and psychological ways of knowing." She argued that understanding these "life stories may help us see ourselves better . . . they function for our protection, renewal, or transformation" (p. xiv).

Like Shuman, Luttrell explored a particular kind of recounting—the narration of school experiences and their perceived effects. She also worked with the women to deconstruct these stories and to see some of the oppressive structural forces they occluded. "What the women emphasized and what they omitted in their stories provide insight into the multiple positions, sometimes as victims of, sometimes as rebels against, and sometimes unaware of oppressive cultural conditions" (p. 4). Integrating psychological and critical social theories,

Luttrell also chronicled the ways that her participants often "split" themselves in their tellings and how this splitting process enabled or constrained their efforts to forge what they imagined to be better lives. All in all, Luttrell's work is a brilliant example of bricoleurship. She locates and relocates herself in multiple epistemological frameworks; she assembles and deploys multiple theoretical tools; and she uses multiple strategies of data collection and analyses to render an account that is both empirically solid and complex, contingent, and contradictory.

Critical Marxist Approaches. We have already discussed the Marxist, praxis-oriented literacy research of Paulo Freire. There have been many other ways in which critical Marxist perspectives have been turned into research orientations. Paul Willis's *Learning to Labor* (1977), now a classic, is one of the earliest and perhaps the best examples of such efforts. This book reports on a critical ethnography of working-class youth ("lads") conducted between 1972 and 1975 in an industrial town Willis calls Hammertown. For this study, Willis followed a small group of about 12 working-class youth throughout their school and work days. He attended classes and leisure activities and, at points, accompanied them onto the shop floor. He recorded interviews as well as group discussions. He also interviewed the lads' parents and teachers, as well as senior masters and career officers at the school. Although he relied more or less on traditional ethnographic techniques to collect his data, Willis's study was far ahead of its time—a great example of a multisited ethnography (e.g., Marcus, 1998) that embodied collaborative and praxis impulses. Located primarily within *Chronotope III*, *Learning to Labor* occasionally pushes up against *Chronotope IV* in almost prophetic ways.

Willis's findings are well known. These working-class boys created a culture of resistance and opposition to authority. "The opposition [was] expressed mainly as style. It [was] lived out in countless small ways which [were] special to the school institution, instantly recognized by the teachers, and an almost ritualistic part of the daily fabric of life for the kids" (p. 12). "Opposition to the school [was] principally manifested in the struggle to win symbolic and physical space from the institution and its rules and to defeat its main perceived purpose: to make you 'work'" (p. 26). Ironically, their actions led students to reproduce the lives of their parents and thus their place in the class structure of the United Kingdom. A brilliant study, *Learning to Labor* betrays a deep faith in empirical methods, yet gestures toward a kind of research that is more genealogical, praxis-oriented, and political.

   The New Journalism. Jonathon Kozol's *Savage Inequalities: Children in America's Schools* (1991) is an excellent example of the New Journalism. Throughout this book, Kozol blurs the line between "reporting" and activism as he counterposes school systems (and their effects) in wealthy and less wealthy districts around the country. A master storyteller, he chronicles the economic segregation that marks cities like East St. Louis, Illinois, and he maps the effects this segregation has on children and families. The violence, pollution, sickness, general depression, and disaffection he describes all evoke a sense of the Third World within our national borders. Besides offering eyewitness accounts of dilapidated school buildings with peeling paint, leaking roofs, broken toilets, no heat, and virtually no learning materials, Kozol convincingly shows how conditions beyond the school walls are no better, leaving children and families with little hope.

   In addition to describing these material conditions and their effects, Kozol adopts a Ted Koppel–like stance, offering statistical information on differential levels of school funding across adjacent communities and disclosing the various ways in which community leaders, business owners, and even school officials justify their actions morally, usually with one or another form of a "blaming the victim" argument. He also explores how children and parents who live in these very poor communities and go to these schools account for their lives. Often they respond with resentment, which often leads to lives of violence and crime. Grounded in the transformative possibilities of Freirean ethics, Kozol's narratives become morality plays about democratic imperatives and their visible absence in the wealthiest, most democratic country in the world. "Surely there is enough for everyone in this country. It is a tragedy that these things are not more widely shared. All our children ought to be allowed a stake in the enormous richness of America" (p. 233). In a refreshing way, the book contains no claims for reflexivity or self-reflexivity in relation to research processes or participants. Instead, Kozol positions himself as a reporter in the field, collecting and exhibiting "facts" and commenting on their implications for the children and families he came to know, the future of education, and the ongoing health of the nation. Sometimes objective, sometimes interpretive, sometimes polemic, always poetic, Kozol moves seamlessly across *Chronotopes I, II,* and *III.*

Autoethnography. Mike Rose's *Lives on the Boundary* (1989) is an excellent example of autoethnography used as a way into understanding the complexities of literacy and education for many of the nation's disenfranchised youth. Rose begins this book by talking about the anxieties around educating people from diverse social, economic, and cultural backgrounds in a democratic country for which education and schooling are microcosms. What we think about the country, he argues, is reflected in and through our ideas about school. This is seen broadly in debates around standards and education, testing and sorting, tracking, and other key issues that vary depending on the social, economic, and political tenor of the times. Importantly, Rose reads the practices and politics of schooling through his own biography. As an "underprepared" student from a working-class family, Rose always experienced school as somehow "strange." His experience of school became even stranger when, due to a clerical error, he was accidentally placed in a remedial class where he remained for over a year. This experience shaped his orientation toward school for years to come, which might be characterized in much the same way as Lutrell's participants—a matter of "splitting" the world of school from the world of everyday life and work. Also like Lutrell's participants, the tension between these two worlds always ended up propelling him back toward school and the promises it seemed to hold.

Although Rose was an "at risk" student in the vocational track throughout many of his school years, he connected at one point with an important mentor, Mr. McFarland, a beat poet who excited him both by his life(style) and his love of language and learning. Through McFarland's example, Rose was able to see what living a practiced life of the mind might be. With his mentor's guidance and help, Rose ended up going to college and graduate school, but he still felt an outsider to school, left out of its ongoing conversation.

Eventually, Rose became involved in the Teacher Corps, where he tutored adults. Through his involvement in the Teacher Corps, Rose began to see and celebrate the complexity of the lives of young people, and he became what he would be for the rest of his life—a teacher. In the second half of the book, Rose documents some of his own teaching efforts as he analyzes the politics of educational remediation. Rose argues that education should be culturally vibrant, and offers several principles that must be in place. These principles insist upon a view of literacy teaching and learning as social, and of the academy as a unique community with rules, languages, and practices that must be explicitly taught and learned. All of this needs to be done in a context of personal connection and care among teachers and students.

What makes *Lives on the Boundary* uniquely compelling is how Rose spins his theories from/through the threads of his own life history—locating himself in the text and struggling to articulate inquiry with the promises of a democratic society. His work is simultaneously novelistic, journalistic, and political; self-reflexive, objective, and praxis-oriented. Unlike more poststructural, poetic versions of autoethnography, Rose's version is both more modernist and more Marxist. Whereas the latter autoethnographies celebrate partiality, instability, the fragmentary nature of human experience, and ruptures between self and other, Rose's celebrates the emergence of self-knowledge and the possibilities of collective commitment. It is an amazingly hopeful book rooted in the objectivist yet transformative impulses of *Chronotope III*.

Symbolic Interactionism in a New Key. We turn now to a very recent study located within the symbolic interaction (SI) tradition but conducted in a postfoundational moment. Since its inception, SI has been centrally concerned with the ways interacting individuals helped constitute social orders through the use of symbolic resources. In this regard, SI work has often embodied the interpretive dispositions of *Chronotope II*. Recently, however, research inspired by SI has become more critical and deconstructive, invoking many of the impulses of *Chronotopes III and IV*. Denzin (1992b), for example, has promoted a postfoundational transformation of SI, with calls for sparser, more narrative-driven writing that both evokes emotion-laden experiences and hails people to political action. SI's traditional concern with how symbols circulate and construct social orders is still present, but SI's quasi-objectivist orientation, its subject-object split, its quasi-representational view of language, and its political neutrality are all gone.

Drawing on Denzin's work, Christopher Dunbar's (2001) *Alternative Schooling for African American Youth: Does Anyone Know We're Here?* is an excellent example of an SI ethnography in a new key. Ostensibly, the book is about a local alternative school in a small Midwestern city, but it indexes the many failures of public schooling in the United States. Dunbar spent several months at this site, conducting observations and collecting stories of experience from the perspectives of students, teachers, and administrators. In this regard, his work embodies the ethnographic impulses of a traditional SI approach. Yet Dunbar stories his account of the school and its students, creating narrative and dramatic vignettes that evoke the complexity, ambivalence, and nuance of his subject(s) while also calling attention to their own artifice. For example, he opens the book with a *portrait* of the school that unfolds in three *acts*, each of which contains several *scenes*, with his *transcription* presented as scripted dialogue. The effect of this rhetorical work is to give the reader the sense of experiencing an unfolding drama. And like a drama, Dunbar evokes tensions through his writing. More specifically, he does not reduce his participants' stories to single, extractible messages. Instead, he allows dialogic tensions to live and speak. For example, he talks about how the word "bitch" circulated freely among the students during a movie-watching activity, in plain earshot of all adults (including himself) present (p. 6). Dunbar neither condemns the students as misogynists nor the adults for lack of control or interest. Instead, he uses this example to evoke the *normalcy* of life in school, in all its tangled and uncomfortable complexity.

Dunbar then highlights twelve interlocking stories, each of which captures a key, even epiphanal, moment in a youth's life. He also displays other students' reactions to these events. Importantly, Dunbar never resolves the conflict(s) in these stories, nor does he extract any singular significance from them. Instead, he evokes the complexity of the events and the lives they affect.

Dunbar situates his unfolding narrative in his own story as a young black male—someone who might have easily wound up in the kinds of systems in which these youths are enmeshed. He discusses his own early difficulties with school, as well as his (and his parents') choices to leave his local urban school system to attend a more elite school across town. Yet he also historicizes and contextualizes his own experience, noting that the "open enrollment" that saved him is not available to many young black men (p. 20). Among other things, this is an act of defamiliarization that signals the poststructural claim that one cannot know "the other" without situating "the self." Dunbar presents his story as one of many intersecting stories, related in contingent and often counterintuitive ways. Reading his story against those of others, he acknowledges, "It could have been me!" (p. 19) consigned to a very different kind of life and to a second-class education.

Dunbar's book is marvelously intertextual—stories within and against other stories. Theory and "related research" are included sparingly. His own lived experience is used to impel analyses of his differential relations to different levels of the social formations in which he finds himself. Though obliquely, he shows how experience without theory can mask the construction of its own ground, and how theory without experience tends to privilege structural determinants of knowledge. Also obliquely, he shows how the *subject* is an ideological illusion because it is not strictly personal but also designates various levels of the social and points out potential sites for critical intervention. Finally, Dunbar's multiply laminated accounts draw attention to their situated, partial, and constructed nature while also propelling their readers toward reflection and action. It is praxis in one of its most subtle forms.

    Critical Discourse Analysis. Squarely situated in *Chronotope IV*, Alison Lee's *Gender, Literacy, Curriculum: Re-writing School Geography* (1996) is a powerful example of critical discourse analysis conducted within a framework of poststructural feminist imperatives. The study shows how "students are positioned and take up positions within a gender/power/knowledge dynamic in and through literate practices in the classroom" (p. 23). Invoking the work of Patti Lather, Lee celebrates the need for "a more hesitant and partial scholarship capable of helping us to tell a better story in a world marked by the elusiveness with which it greets our efforts to know it" (Lather, 1991, p. 15, quoted in Lee, 1996, p. 23). The study on which the book is based involved four months of intense participant observation of a senior high school geography class in Western Australia and the multiple institutional contexts and imperatives that helped to constitute it. Combining genealogical strategies (e.g., Foucault, 1977), strategies from systemic functional linguistics (e.g., Halliday, 1994), and critical discourse analysis strategies (e.g., Fairclough, 1989, 1992), Lee analyzed her various data (student writing, interview transcripts, transcripts and field notes from classroom observations, curriculum materials, policy documents, etc.) contextually, intertextually, and intercontextually "to evoke a complex sense of the curriculum context within which student writings [were] embedded and that they help[ed] to constitute" (p. 22). Lee's goals here were multiple—to "engage the specificity and density of actual texts produced by material processes in actual curriculum contexts, and also situate them within curriculum and wider social and political concerns" (p. 25).

    Lee adopted a highly self-reflexive stance in her work, claiming that the interpretations and explanations in the book are "as much an evocation of the specificity of [her]institutional and theoretical history and consequent reading position as of the classroom itself as a social site" (p. 22). Her findings are thus unabashedly "produced" rather than "reported."

Lee's work was also motivated by praxis concerns, "produced under the hypothesis that a different reality is possible" (p. 22). She offers many interesting and complex findings such as how female students, often marginalized in classroom discussions, turn to writing as an alternative communication medium. In almost palpable ways, she demonstrates throughout how gender is constructed through "practice" and how gender, power, and knowledge relations are "not purely binary or linear . . . [but] are complex and indeterminate relations specific to local sites" (p. 205). All in all, Lee's work is as interesting and as complex as any we have discussed, welding rigorous empirical analytic strategies with poststructural imperatives and seventh-moment bricoleurship in powerful and compelling ways.

Genealogy/Rhizomatics. Allan Luke's work on "discourse and inscription," which we discussed at length in chapter 2, is certainly a key early exemplar of the genealogical impulse within language and literacy research. In this section we discuss two studies that in many ways have tried to extend Luke's work. Straddling *Chronotopes III* and *IV*, Mark Dressman's research, reported in "Preference as Performance: Doing Social Class and Gender in Three School Libraries" (1997), took a critical approach to the study of young people's preferences in school libraries. Dressman challenged the idea that young people's book preferences can be mapped easily onto class and gender backgrounds. For Dressman, the act of choosing a book was seen as a performative act. In his words, "the acts of preferring . . . do not merely reflect, but reflexively constitute a reader's performance of her or his sociocultural identity by enacting the cultural logic of consensually agreed-upon norms, or 'tastes' for readers of a particular social category such as gender, ethnicity, or social class" (p. 321).

Using the fairly traditional strategies of participant observation and interviews in three third-grade libraries, Dressman looked at the ways "preference" is both predictable and unpredictable, personal and political. He highlighted, in particular, how complicated personal desires often superceded expected gender and class performances. In addition, Dressman interrogated his own "preferences" for literature as a child, and how they influenced his own interpretive horizons (p. 328), enacting the self-reflexivity that is a key part of recent critical work.

In a recent book chapter entitled "The Rhizome and the Pack: Liminal Literacy Formations with Political Teeth," George Kamberelis (2004) demonstrated how certain marginalized literacy formations achieve political effectivity through rhizomatic activity. He provided two key examples of the work of such formations: the subversive activities of African Americans in the fight for freedom, especially in the *antebellum* period, and current literacy practices on/of the Internet, especially within radical sites designed to promote public dialogue linked to political work. Importantly, he did not argue that formations that are organized and function rhizomatically are the only or the most politically effective kinds of assemblages. He simply claimed that because they have unique histories of effectivity, they are worth attending to more closely and more seriously for the ways in which they might help us reconceptualize collective affiliation and action and political motivations and outcomes.

Kamberelis ended the chapter with some reasons why literacy formations organized as rhizomes seem to have such effectivity. Among other things, they deterritorialize systems of authority by disrupting, circumventing, or subverting instruments of surveillance and regulation, and they reterritorialize the spaces in which these instruments operate. They are also local, mobile, and agile. They involve transmogrification, multiple codings, utopian visions, and a commitment to intervening in reality and its relations of power to enact those visions. They also involve mapping the real to challenge and perhaps reconfigure the possibilities of reality. These formations use binaries strategically to create new binaries that are more effective for egalitarian and transformative purposes. They generate action, thought, and desire by proliferation, juxtaposition, and disjunction rather than by subdivision and pyramidal hierarchization. These formations do not engage in political activity to discredit any line of thought on speculative grounds alone. Instead, their political activity functions to intensify thought, and their political analyses multiply the forms and domains available for the intervention of political action. They strive to "deindividualize" by means of multiplication, displacement, and diverse/diversifying combinations, and do not celebrate power or the will to power. These formations operate according to an anti-method or anti-logic. They regard discourse in terms of its dissolution into lines of flight and its organization into lines of articulation. In doing so, they open up new ways of understanding the world and therefore new ways of organizing political resistance. In short, their activity/activism is a constant flow of pedagogical politics and political pedagogy.

Final Thoughts

Through this book, we attempted to tell a somewhat more complex story about the constitution of the field of qualitative inquiry than is sometimes told, denaturalizing some of the linear and static ways the domain has been characterized and trying to look at it with new eyes. In the first major section of the book, we argued that qualitative inquiry must be imagined and enacted at several different levels of abstraction (epistemology, theory, approach, and strategy) and that researchers must engage continuously in intense reflection about the relations among these levels. Next, we suggested that qualitative research tends to gel around four key chronotopes (i.e., objectivism and representation; reading and interpretation; skepticism, conscientization, and praxis; and power/knowledge and defamiliarization). We also noted that our chronotopes are nomenclatural, arbitrary instances of naming (and thus stabilizing and simplifying) complex, ongoing social practices. Other authors might suggest more or fewer chronotopes, or they might assign them different (perhaps more felicitous) names. Finally, we acknowledged that in practice there is considerable leakage among and movement across our various chronotopes. This, of course, problematizes efforts to create neat systems of relations between and among the four dimensions of inquiry we need constantly to consider (i.e., epistemology, theory, approach, and strategy).

In the second major section of the book, we looked at how qualitative research emerged and gained steam in partially unique ways in two disciplinary contexts—anthropology and sociology. In choosing to write our account in this way, we analytically separated disciplinary histories from the more general intellectual histories within which the disciplines were always embedded.

Finally, in this chapter we returned to the larger intellectual history of the past century or so and argued that it is as productive to construct "qualitative inquiry" as a transdisciplinary metadiscourse as it is to construct it as a set of distinct (though interanimating) trajectories within multiple disciplinary domains. Because research on language and literacy figured prominently in the emergence and legitimation of qualitative inquiry, we used it to illustrate what we mean by a transdisciplinary metadiscourse. Specifically, we showcased key language and literacy studies that seem to "represent" many of the various approaches to research discussed throughout the disciplinary chapters of the book, while also indexing how disciplinary imperatives and chronotopic impulses are almost always taken up in actual practice in complex, transversing, and even contradictory ways. Many, if not most, of the studies involved one or another form of creative syncretism—(a) blending research strategies from ostensibly different approaches to research, (b) integrating approaches to form new and productive hybrids, (c) assembling constructs from multiple theoretical perspectives to frame new problems in new ways, and (d) even moving strategically across heretofore incommensurable epistemological boundaries. Indeed, in a very real sense, qualitative inquiry has always been and will always be practical inductive work. Every study is partially unique and calls for a unique configuration of the epistemology-theory-approach-strategy nexus. Thus, exploring how disciplines have organized themselves over time and how individual researchers have gone about their work is invaluable preparation for designing and conducting new qualitative studies in inventive, strategic, and powerful ways.

So where does this all leave us and our fellow qualitative researchers today? How might our philosophical and historical reflections inform the ways in which we imagine and enact research practices as we move through the 21st century? Many metaphors have recently been proposed to describe the possible futures of qualitative inquiry. Each is predicated on particular ontological and epistemological assumptions, and each calls attention to the complexities and difficulties of conducting research in a globalized, fast-capitalist, media-saturated world. We conclude with brief descriptions of a subset of these metaphors.

Locating themselves primarily within *Chronotope IV*, Denzin and Lincoln (1994, 2000) urged qualitative researchers to become "bricoleurs," mixing and matching the multiple logics and tools of qualitative inquiry in pragmatic and strategic ways to "get the job done," whatever one imagines that job to be. The goal of research, according to this metaphor, is to produce "a complex, dense, reflexive collage-like creation that represents the researcher's images, understandings, and interpretations of the world or phenomenon under analysis" (2000, p. 3).

Locating himself more in *Chronotopes I* and *II*, Hammersley (1999) responded to this metaphorically informed call with another one rooted in more cautionary, pragmatic, neomodernist impulses. Briefly, he argued that qualitative researchers should imagine themselves not as bricoleurs but as "boat builders." This metaphor derives from what is known as Neurath's boat, named after the German sociologist Otto Neurath, who compared the work of scientists with the work of sailors who must often rebuild their ships at sea, never able to start from scratch and always aware that their reconstructions must result in a coherent whole that floats. Hammersley went on to argue that producing collage and pentimento can never be a basis for good boat building and that the impulse toward bricolage threatens to "sink" the qualitative inquiry ship. "A central message that ought to be taken from Neurath's metaphor," Hammersley claimed, "is that because we are always faced with the task of rebuilding our craft at sea, everything cannot be questioned at once" (p. 581). He argued further that "those who want to be poets or political activists, or both, should not pretend that they can simultaneously be social researchers" (p. 583). Unabashedly modernist, Hammersley urges that we "develop a coherent sense of where we are going and of how we need to rebuild our vessel to sail in the right direction" (p. 579), which, among other things, will require thoroughgoing knowledge of where we have been.

A third metaphor, and the one that motivated many of our arguments in this book, is the "genealogist." Thinking genealogically forces us to see disciplines as the ongoing work of invested actors, not as paradigms we must uncritically occupy. Traditionally, researchers have been encouraged to see research traditions and approaches as immutable, with parameters that are defined *a priori*. Genealogists have no given lineages, but different histories at their disposal. Using these histories, they attempt to understand how any "subject" (e.g., a person, a social formation, a social movement, an institution) has been constituted out of particular intersections of forces and systems of forces by mapping the complex, contingent, and often contradictory ways in which these forces and systems of force came together to produce the formation in the precise way that it did and not in some other way.

Guided by Foucault's genealogical imperative that knowledge is "for cutting," researchers choose methodological directions strategically and with full knowledge that there are no safe spaces, no alibis for our decisions. While genealogists call into question naïve realism and the authority of experience, they also try to deploy such constructs in thoughtful and partial ways. Deleuze and Guattari (1987), for example, do not claim to rid the world of binaries but to create new ones that are more productive for achieving democratic ideals.

Genealogists realize that they need to appropriate extant epistemologies, theories, approaches, and strategies to do their work, but they are aware that there are no "pure" choices, no guarantees about what these appropriations will produce or how they will produce it. To understand such outcomes requires intense retrospective analysis, constantly looking back and trying to understand how our accounts were constructed in the ways they were and not in other ways.

In closing we want to underscore the fact that we have presented these three metaphors because we believe that all of them (as well as others we might have discussed) are powerful and productive tools for thinking about the central topic of this book—the logics of qualitative inquiry—past, present, and future. These metaphors index tensions that have always existed in the field of qualitative inquiry and will probably always exist. Together they map the many imperatives and impulses that we, as qualitative researchers, must struggle with in our daily work, especially with respect to locating ourselves strategically within and across chronotopes and creating epistemology-theory-approach-strategy assemblages that are both principled and pragmatic.

Notes

Chapter 1

1. For an excellent set of analyses of the objectivism inherent in classic ethnographies, see James Clifford's (1988) *The Predicament of Culture*.

Chapter 2

1. We struggled to decide on a conceptual frame to use for this chapter. Besides Birdwhistell's *logics-of-inquiry* and Strike's *expressive potential*, we considered Bakhtin's (1981) *chronotope*, Foucault's (1977) *discourse*, and Bourdieu's (1977, 1990) *habitus/field*. We finally settled on the *chronotope* because it seemed more comprehensive to us, combining the connotative valences of the various other candidates. Although we discuss *discourse* and *habitus* elsewhere in the book, we want to define them briefly here to index some of these connotative valences. In brief, Foucault claimed that discourses create, shape, and bound social life. They are naturalized over time and become the implicit rules about what counts as knowledge, who may use such knowledge, and how individuals and collectives are constructed within such knowledge schemes. In other words, discourses function to create, sustain, and reproduce particular versions of reality and to render others obscure. In the context of conducting research, discourses delimit what counts as research, the kinds of questions that are asked, and how answers to those questions may be "properly" pursued.

Bourdieu used the term *habitus* to emphasize the fact that how people think, talk, and act is the result of sedimented experiences and practices within specific fields of practice over long periods of time. According to Bourdieu, all of social life is closely linked to historically constituted and durable yet dynamic structural tendencies that operate at multiple levels of social organization both horizontally and vertically. He referred to these tendencies as social fields, and he defined these fields as particularly determining but open-ended sets of material, historical, and social forces that prescribes their particular values and possess their own regulative principles. Thus, Bourdieu's notion of field is quite similar to Foucault's notion of discourse, except perhaps that it functions more locally within particular disciplines or communities of practice. The principles of a social field (or a discourse) delimit a socially structured space in which agents struggle, depending on the positions they occupy in the space, either to change or to preserve its boundaries and form. *Habitus* is the structuring mechanism that gets internalized and operates from within agents, though it is neither strictly individual nor itself fully determinative of conduct. Because *habitus* is always historically constituted and institutionally grounded, it is creative or inventive only within the limits of its own structures—structures that are themselves historically produced and thus always structures-in-the-making.

2. Much of poststructuralist theorizing and critique has targeted the foundational metanarratives that have functioned to ground and perpetuate Enlightenment versions of the self, knowledge, truth, validity, and so on. Within this view, concepts are placed under erasure. Following Derrida, this erasure is often represented in the following way: ~~foundational~~. The strikethrough, which both crosses out and leaves the word or phrase visible, indicates the fact that we still need to use this term (or some synonym) but that we also need to understand its usage as problematic, naturalized, and in need of deconstruction or interrogation.

3. Readers interested in learning more about the distinction between within-discipline and across-discipline structuring tendencies and the consequences this distinction has for understanding the historical and philosophical foundations for qualitative inquiry may want to study the distinction Foucault makes between archaeology and genealogy (e.g., Foucault, 1977, 1984a, 1984b; Dreyfus & Rabinow, 1982).

4. Other, less politically charged examples include Mehan's (1979) work on classroom discourse structures, Flower and Hayes's (1981) work on the composing process, and Langer's (1986) work on genres and genre learning. All are predicated on the key assumptions of a chronotope of objectivism and representation. We urge you to read or reread Hirsch's work on cultural literacy as you ponder our use of his work as an exemplar here. Similarly, we urge you to read or reread the exemplars we link to the other chronotopes we discuss in subsequent sections of this chapter.

5. See Shannon and Weaver's (1949) mathematical model of communication for an excellent treatment of language as fundamentally representational.

6. "Being-in-the-world" is the most common translation of the German word *dasein*, which Heidegger (1962) used to refer to the individual human being. *Dasein* is not primarily a signifying subject but a situated one. Heidegger chose the term *dasein* strategically to connote the fact that we always know the world in a practical/situated and not an abstract/absolute way; hence his argument that "present-at-hand" or abstract knowledge is always predicated on "ready-to-hand" or practical situated knowledge. Knowing

always begins in practice or in mucking around with others in the world. We consulted a number of German dictionaries about the denotative meaning of *dasein*. Although variants abound, most include "existence" as a defining characteristic. This is important because in the history of philosophy and philosophy of science, the difference between "essence" and "existence" has been crucial. Positivist and postpositivist perspectives regard existence as epiphenomenal, biased, and deceptive, and they celebrate essence as ultimately true and real, hence the separation of subject and object and the separation of epistemology (the study of knowing) from ontology (the study of being). One assumption from this perspective is that there is a real world out there that, with increasing exactitude, we can know in some unmediated fashion. Science, then, is a discovery of essences. One of Heidegger's major contributions was to suggest that even if there is a real world out there (and he agreed that there is), we nevertheless only understand it as a function of our experience of it (e.g., playing with our kids, observing classroom interactions, working in a chemistry lab, or solving a complex equation) and never "in-itself."

7. Other relevant examples abound. Most, but not all, are literacy ethnographies such as Bissex (1980), Lofty (1987), Fishman (1988), and Dyson (1989).

8. Gadamer does not use the term "prejudices" in its everyday sense here. Instead he uses the term to refer to habituated ways of thinking that make historically constructed ways of being, thinking, and acting seem normal or "natural." Analogues of this construct within philosophy and social theory would include Foucault's *discourse* and Bourdieu's *habitus*, both of which we discussed earlier.

9. For an exceptional set of discussions about the relevance of Habermas's systematic theory of communicative action for contemporary qualitative research practice, see Carspecken (1999).

10. For an analogous taxonomy, see Grice's (1975) work on conversational implicature.

11. Another theory that bears a family resemblance to Habermas's theory of communicative action is the philosophical anthropology at the heart of Bakhtin's (1993) *Toward a Philosophy of the Act*. Also worth noting here is the fact that theories with strong parallels to Habermas's theory of communicative action were also developed within American pragmatics and symbolic interactionism. Dewey's (1938) insistence that "warranted assertibility" constitutes the end of controlled inquiry (p. 9) belongs to one such theory. Predicated on a nonfoundational epistemological stance, Dewey argued for the possibility of achieving collective agreement about the most plausible interpretation of a phenomenon or event based on the available evidence. He referred to this form of collective agreement as a "warranted assertion."

12. *Communitas* figures prominently in Turner's (1967, 1969) discussions of the processes of community renewal. To Turner, *communitas* is freedom coexisting within structure in ways that disrupt and dissolve the norms that

govern institutionalized relationships and make way for potent forms of social critique and transformation. Wisdom is the achievement of balanced productive relations between *communitas* and structure within any specific situated social field. *Communitas* is thus a moment of renewal and transformation,
not a permanent condition. It is possibility in dialogue with reality.

13. Other good examples of research conducted within the chronotope of
skepticism, conscientization, and praxis include Carspecken's (1991) research
on Croxeth Comprehensive School and Edelsky's (1991) work on literacy and
social justice.

14. Unpacking the meanings of postmodernism and poststructuralism
and arguing about the differences between them has become a virtual cottage
industry during the past two decades (e.g., Best & Kellner, 1991; Dunn, 1998;
Ebert, 1996; Roseneau, 1992; Sarup, 1988; Shapiro, 1992).

15. Bourdieu's (1977, 1990) construct of *habitus* is also quite useful for
understanding such dispositions and how they become predispositions over
time.

16. Two interesting empirical illustrations of these phenomena may be
found in Lyn Mikel Brown's (1999) book, *Raising Their Voices: The Politics of
Girls' Anger*, and Alison Lee's (1996) book, *Gender, Literacy, Curriculum: Re-
writing School Geography*.

17. Bakhtin's (1981) theory of the *utterance* is instructive here as well.

18. Also important to note here is the fact that forms of postmodern and
poststructural cultural analysis predicated on models of texts, readers, and
the perpetual slippage of the signifier have not exerted any sustained influence on qualitative modes of empirical inquiry in language and literacy even
though they have been quite influential within literary criticism and literature
studies for quite some time.

19. It is important to note here that exactly what Foucault meant by "discourses," "discursive formations," and the precise difference between the two
is the subject of intense debate. For excellent though somewhat different treat-
ments of this debate, see Grossberg (1992) and Sawyer (2002).

20. In *The Postmodern Condition*, Lyotard (1984) also insists that discourse
is fundamentally agonistic and not dialogic.

References

Abu-Lughod, L. (1993). *Writing women's worlds: Bedouin stories*. Berkeley: University of California Press.

Adorno, T. (1973). *Negative dialectics* (E. B. Ashton, Trans.). New York: Continuum.

Adorno, T. (1974). *Minima moralia: Reflections from a damaged life*. London: NLB.

Ailwood, J., & Lingard, B. (2001). The endgame for national girls' schooling policies in Australia? *Australian Journal of Education, 45*(1), 9–22.

Alasuutari, P. (1995). *Researching culture: Qualitative method and cultural studies*. Thousand Oaks, CA: Sage Publications.

Alcoff, L. (1988). Cultural feminism versus post-structuralism: The identity crisis in feminist theory. *Signs: Journal of Women and Culture, 13*(3), 405–436.

Althusser, L. (1971). *Lenin and philosophy*. New York: Monthly Review Press.

Alvermann, D. (2000). Researching libraries, literacies, and lives: A rhizoanalysis. In E. St. Pierre and W. Pillow (Eds.), *Working the ruins: Feminist poststructural methods in education* (pp. 114–129). New York: Routledge.

Anderson, N. (1923). *The hobo: The sociology of the homeless man*. Chicago: University of Chicago Press.

Anzaldua, G. (1987). *Borderlands*. San Francisco: Spinsters/Aunt Lute Press.

Atkinson, J. M., & Heritage, J. (Eds.). (1984). *Structures of social action: Studies in conversation analysis*. Paris: Cambridge University Press.

Atkinson, P. (1988). Ethnomethodology: A critical review. *Annual Review of Sociology, 14*, pp. 441–465.

Atkinson, P., Coffey, A., & Delamont, S. (1999). Ethnography: Post, past, and present. *Journal of Contemporary Ethnography, 28*(5), 460–471.

Bakhtin, M. M. (1981). *The dialogic imagination* (C. Emerson & M. Holquist, Trans.). Austin: University of Texas Press.

Bakhtin, M. M. (1993). *Toward a philosophy of the act* (V. Liapunov, Trans.). Austin: University of Texas Press.

Barton, D., & Ivanic, R. (Eds.). (1991). *Writing in the community*. London: Sage.

Baudrillard, J. (1983). *Simulations*. New York: Semiotext(e).

Bauman, J., & Ivey, G. (1997). Delicate balances: Striving for curricular and instructional equilibrium in a second-grade, literature/strategy-based classroom. *Reading Research Quarterly, 32*(3), 244–275.

Baynham, M. (1995). *Literacy practices: Investigating literacy in social contexts*. Boston: Addison-Wesley.

Becker, H. S. (1963). *Outsiders: Studies in the sociology of deviance*. New York: Free Press.

Behar, R. (1993). *Translated woman: Crossing the border with Esperanza's story*. Boston: Beacon Press.

Berger, P., & Luckmann, T. (1966). *The social construction of reality: A treatise in the sociology of knowledge*. New York: Doubleday.

Bergvall, V., & Remlinger, K. (1996). Reproduction, resistance, and gender in educational discourse: The role of critical discourse analysis. *Discourse & Society, 7*(4), 453–479.

Bernstein, R. (1983). *Beyond objectivism and relativism: Science, hermeneutics, and praxis.* Philadelphia: University of Pennsylvania Press.

Bernstein, R. (1992). *The new constellation: The ethical/political horizons of modernity/post-modernity.* Cambridge, MA: MIT Press.

Besnier, N. (1995). *Literacy, emotion, and authority: Reading and writing on a Polynesian atoll.* Cambridge, UK: Cambridge University Press.

Best, S., & Kellner, D. (1991). *Postmodern theory: Critical interrogations.* New York: Guilford Press.

Birdwhistell, R. L. (1970). *Kinesics and context: Essays on body motion communication.* Philadelphia: University of Pennsylvania Press.

Bissex, G. L. (1980). *Gnys at wrk: A child learns to read and write.* Cambridge, MA: Harvard University Press.

Bloome, D., & Carter, S. P. (2001). Lists in reading education reform. *Theory into Practice, 40*(3), 150–157.

Bogard, W. (1998). Sense and segmentarity: Some markers of a Deleuzian-Guattarian sociology. *Sociological Theory, 16*(1), 52–74.

Bogdan, R., & Biklen, S. K. (1992). *Qualitative research for education: An introduction to theory and methods* (2nd ed.). Boston: Allyn and Bacon.

Bourdieu, P. (1977). *Outline of a theory of practice* (R. Nice, Trans.). Cambridge, UK: Cambridge University Press.

Bourdieu, P. (1990). *The logic of practice* (R. Nice, Trans.). Stanford, CA: Stanford University Press.

Bourdieu, P. (1998). *Practical reason* (R. Nice, Trans.). Stanford, CA: Stanford University Press.

Brandt, D. (1992). The cognitive and the social: An ethnomethodological approach to writing process research. *Written Communication, 9*(3), 315–355.

Brown, L. M. (1999). *Raising their voices: The politics of girls' anger.* Cambridge, MA: Harvard University Press.

Brown, S., & Lunt, P. (2002). A genealogy of the social identity tradition: Deleuze and Guattari and social psychology. *British Journal of Social Psychology, 41,* 1–23.

Bruner, J. (1986). *Actual minds, possible worlds.* Cambridge, MA: Harvard University Press.

Burke, K. (1966). Terministic screens. In K. Burke, *Language as symbolic action: Essays on life, literature, and method* (pp. 44-62). Berkeley: University of California Press.

Carspecken, P. F. (1991). *Community schooling and the nature of power: The battle for Croxteth Comprehensive School.* London: Routledge.

Carspecken, P. F. (1999). *Four scenes for posing questions of meaning and other essays in critical philosophy and critical methodology.* New York: Peter Lang.

Cavan, R. (1928). *Suicide.* Chicago: University of Chicago Press.

Cazden, C. (1982). Four comments. In P. Gilmore & A. Glatthorn (Eds.), *Children in and out of school* (pp. 209–226). Washington, DC: Center for Applied Linguistics.

Cazden, C., John, V., & Hymes, D. (Eds.). (1972). *Functions of language in the classroom.* New York: Teachers College Press.

Cicourel, A. (1992). The interpretation of communicative contexts: Examples from medical encounters. In A. Duranti & C. Goodwin (Eds.), *Rethinking context: Language as an interactive phenomenon* (pp. 291–310). New York: Cambridge University Press.

Clark, R., Fairclough, N., Ivanic, R., & Martin-Jones, M. (1990). Critical language awareness. Part 1: A critical review of three current approaches. *Language & Education 4*(4), 249–260.

Clarke, J., Harrison, R., Reeve, F., & Edwards, R. (2002). Assembling spaces: The question of "place" in further education. *Discourse, 23*(3), 285–297.

Clifford, J. (1986). Introduction: Partial truths. In J. Clifford & G. Marcus (Eds.), *Writing culture: The poetics and politics of ethnography* (pp. 1–26). Berkeley: University of California Press.

Clifford, J. (1988). *The predicament of culture: Twentieth-century ethnography, literature, and art.* Cambridge, MA: Harvard University Press.

Clifford, J., & Marcus, G. (Eds.). (1986). *Writing culture: The poetics and politics of ethnography.* Berkeley: University of California Press.

Cortazzi, M. (1993). *Narrative analysis.* London: Falmer Press.

Coser, L. A. (1971). *Masters of sociological thought: Ideas in historical and social context.* New York: Harcourt Brace Jovanovich.

Crotty, M. (1998). *The foundations of social research: Meaning and perspective in the research process.* Thousand Oaks, CA: Sage.

deCerteau, M. (1984). *The practice of everyday life* (S. F. Rendall, Trans.). Berkeley: University of California Press.

Deleuze, G., & Guattari, F. (1987). *A thousand plateaus: Capitalism and schizophrenia.* Minneapolis: University of Minnesota Press.

Denzin, N. K. (1969). Symbolic interactionism and ethnomethodology: A proposed synthesis. *American Sociological Review, 34*, 22–34.

Denzin, N. K. (1990). Harold and Agnes. *Sociological Theory, 8*(2), 198–216.

Denzin, N. K. (1992a). Who's Cornerville is it anyway? Two versions of Whyte's *Street Corner Society. Journal of Contemporary Ethnography, 21*(1), 120–132.

Denzin, N. K. (1992b). *Symbolic interactionism and cultural studies: The politics of interpretation.* Oxford, UK: Blackwell Press.

Denzin, N. K. (1997). *Interpretive ethnography.* Thousand Oaks, CA: Sage.

Denzin, N. K. (2003). *Performance ethnography: Critical pedagogy and the politics of culture.* Thousand Oaks, CA: Sage.

Denzin, N., & Lincoln, Y. (Eds.). (1994). *Handbook of qualitative research.* Thousand Oaks, CA: Sage.

Denzin, N., & Lincoln, Y. (Eds.). (2000). *Handbook of qualitative research* (2nd ed.). Thousand Oaks, CA: Sage.

Derrida, J. (1976). *Of grammatology* (G. Spivak, Trans.). Baltimore: Johns Hopkins University Press.

Dewey, J. (1938). *Experience and education.* New York: Collier Books.

Dilthey, W. L. (1976). *Selected writings.* Cambridge, UK: Cambridge University Press. (Original work published 1900)

Dimitriadis, G., & Kamberelis, G. (1997). Shifting terrains: Mapping education within a global landscape. *The Annals of the American Academy of Political and Social Sciences, 551*, 137-150.

Dressman, M. (1997). Preference as performance: Doing social class and gender in three school libraries. *Journal of Literacy Research, 29*(3), 319–361.

Dreyfus, H., & Rabinow, P. (1982). *Michel Foucault: Beyond structuralism and hermenutics.* Chicago: University of Chicago Press.

Dunbar, C. (2001). *Alternative schooling for African American youth: Does anyone know we're here?* New York: Peter Lang.

Dunier, M. (1992). *Slim's table: Race, respectability, and masculinity.* Chicago: University of Chicago Press.

Dunn, R. G. (1998). *Identity crisis: A social critique of postmodernity.* Minneapolis: University of Minnesota Press.

Durkheim, E. (1951). *Suicide, a study in sociology.* New York: Free Press. (Original work published 1897)

Durkheim, E. (1976). *The elementary forms of religious life.* London: George Allen & Unwin.

Dyson, A. (1989). *Multiple worlds of child writers: Friends learning to write.* New York: Teachers College Press.

Ebert, T. L. (1996). *Ludic feminism and after: Critical perspectives on women and feminism.* Ann Arbor: University of Michigan Press.

Eckert, P. (1989). *Jocks and burnouts: Social categories and identity in the high school.* New York: Teachers College Press.

Edelsky, C. (1991). *With literacy and justice for all: Rethinking the social in language education.* Bristol, PA: Falmer Press.

Edwards, R., & Clarke, J. (2002). Flexible learning, spatiality, and identity. *Studies in Continuing Education, 24*(2), 153–165.

Eisenhart, M. (2001). Educational ethnography past, present, and future: Ideas to think with. *Educational Researcher, 30*(8), 16–27.

Fairclough, N. (1989). *Language and power.* London: Longman.

Fairclough, N. (1992). *Discourse and social change.* Cambridge, UK: Polity Press.

Fairclough, N. (1993). Critical discourse analysis and the marketization of public discourse: The universities. *Discourse & Society, 4*(2), 138–168.

Fairclough, N. (1995). *Critical discourse analysis: The critical study of language.* New York: Longman.

Finders, M. (1997). *Just girls: Hidden literacies and life in junior high.* New York: Teachers College Press.

Fine, G. A. (1987). *With the boys: Little League baseball and preadolescent culture.* Chicago: University of Chicago Press.

Fine, G. A. (1995). *A second Chicago School: The development of a postwar American sociology.* Chicago: University of Chicago Press.

Fine, G. A. (1996). *Kitchens: The culture of restaurant work.* Berkeley: University of California Press.

Fine, M. (1994). Working the hyphens: Reinventing self and other in qualitative research. In N. K. Denzin & Y. S. Lincoln (Eds.), *The handbook of qualitative research* (pp. 70–82). Newbury Park, CA: Sage.

Fishman, A. (1988). *Amish literacy: What and how it means.* Portsmouth, NH: Heinemann.

Flower, L., & Hayes, J. (1981). A cognitive process theory of writing. *College Communication and Composition, 32*, 365–387.

Foucault, M. (1975). *The birth of the clinic: An archaeology of medical perception* (A. Sheridan, Trans.). New York: Vintage.

Foucault, M. (1977). *Discipline and punish: The birth of the prison* (A. Sheridan, Trans.). New York: Vintage Books.

Foucault, M. (1979). *Michel Foucault: Power, truth, strategy* (M. Morris & P. Patton, Eds.; P. Foss & M. Morris, Trans.). New York: Prometheus Books.

Foucault, M. (1980). *Power/knowledge: Selected interviews and other essays.* New York: Pantheon Books.

Foucault, M. (1984a). Truth and power. In P. Rabinow (Ed.), *The Foucault reader* (pp. 51–75). New York: Pantheon.

Foucualt, M. (1984b). Nietzsche, genealogy, history. In P. Rabinow (Ed.), *The Foucault reader* (pp. 76–100). New York: Pantheon Books.

Foucault, M. (1988). Technologies of the self. In L. H. Martin, H. Gutman. & P. H. Hutton (Eds.), *Technologies of the self: A seminar with Michel Foucault* (pp. 16–49) . Amherst: University of Massachusetts Press.

Foucault, M. (1990). *The history of sexuality: An introduction* (Vol. 1) (R. Hurley, Trans.). New York: Vintage. (Original work published 1978)

Foucault, M. (1996). History, discourse and discontinuity. In S. Lotringer (Ed.), *Foucault live (Interviews, 1961–1984)* (pp. 33–50). New York: Semiotext(e). (Original essay published 1972)

Freire, P. (1970). *Pedagogy of the oppressed*. New York: Continuum.

Gadamer, H. G. (1968). *Truth and method* (J. Weinsheimer & D. G. Marshall, Trans.). New York: Continuum.

Gadamer, H. G. (1972). *Knowledge and human interests* (J. J. Shapiro, Trans.). Boston: Beacon.

Garfinkel, H. (1967). *Studies in ethnomethodology*. Englewood Cliffs, NJ: Prentice-Hall.

Garfinkel, H., & Sacks, H. (1970). On formal structures of practical actions. In J. McKinney & E. Tiryakian (Eds.), *Theoretical sociology: Perspectives and developments* (pp. 338–366). New York: Appleton Century Crofts.

Gee, J. P. (1996). *Social linguistics and literacies: Ideology in discourses* (2nd ed.). London: Falmer Press.

Geertz, C. (1973). *The interpretation of cultures: Selected essays*. New York: Basic Books.

Gender Equity Taskforce. (1997). *Gender equity: A framework for Australian schools*. Canberra, Australia: Ministerial Council on Education, Employment, Training, and Youth Affairs.

Giddens, A. (1979). *Central problems in social theory*. Berkeley: University of California Press.

Gilmore, P., & Glatthorn, A. (Eds). (1982). *Children in and out of school: Ethnography and education*. Washington, DC: Center for Applied Linguistics.

Gilroy, P. (1993). *The black Atlantic: Modernity and double consciousness*. Cambridge, MA: Harvard University Press.

Glaser, B., & Strauss, A. (1967). *The discovery of grounded theory: Strategies for qualitative research*. Chicago: Aldine.

Goffman, E. (1959). *The presentation of self in everyday life*. New York: Doubleday.

Goffman, E. (1962). *Asylums: Essays on the social situation of mental patients and other inmates*. Chicago: Aldine.

Goodwin, C., & Heritage, J. (1990). Conversation analysis. *Annual Review of Anthropology, 19*, 283–307.

Goodwin, M. H. (1990). *He-said-she-said: Talk as social organization among black children*. Bloomington: Indiana University Press.

Goody, J. (1977). *The domestication of the savage mind*. Cambridge, UK: Cambridge University Press.

Gramsci, A. (1971). *Selections from the prison notebooks of Antonio Gramsci* (Q. Hoare & G. N. Smith, Eds. and Trans.). New York: International Publishers.

Grice, H. P. (1975). Logic and conversation. In P. Cole & J. Morgan (Eds.), *Syntax and semantics III: Speech acts* (pp. 41–53). New York: Academic Press.

Grossberg, L. (1992). *We gotta get out of this place: Popular conservatism and postmodern culture*. New York: Routledge.

Gumperz, J., & Hymes, D. (Eds.). (1972). *Directions in sociolinguistics: The ethnography of communication*. New York: Holt, Rinehart and Winston.

Habermas, J. (1984). *The theory of communicative action: Reason and the rationalization of society* (Vol. 1) (T. McCarthey, Trans.). Boston: Beacon Press.

Habermas, J. (1987). *The theory of communicative action: Lifeworld and system* (Vol. 2) (T. McCarthy, Trans.). Boston: Beacon.

Hall, S. (1986). On postmodernism and articulation: An interview. *Journal of Communication Inquiry, 10,* 56–59.

Hall, S. (1992). Cultural studies and its theoretical legacies. In L. Grossberg, C. Nelson, & P. Treichler (Eds.), *Cultural studies* (pp. 277–294). New York: Routledge.

Hall, S. (1996). The meaning of new times. In D. Morley & K. Chen (Eds.), *Stuart Hall: Critical dialogues in cultural studies* (pp. 223–237). London, UK: Routledge.

Halliday, M. A. K. (1994). *An introduction to functional grammar* (2nd ed.). London: Edward Arnold.

Hammersley, M. (1999). Not bricolage but boatbuilding. *Journal of Contemporary Ethnography, 28*(5), 574–585.

Hannerz, U. (1980). *Exploring the city: Inquiries toward an urban anthropolgy*. New York: Columbia University Press.

Heath, S. B. (1972). *Telling tongues: Language policy in Mexico colony to nation*. New York: Teachers College Press.

Heath, S. B. (1982). Ethnography in education: Defining the essentials. In P. Gilmore & A. A. Glatthorn (Eds.), *Children in and out of school: Ethnography and education* (pp. 33–55). Washington, DC: Center for Applied Linguistics.

Heath, S. B. (1983). *Ways with words: Language, life, and work in communities and classrooms*. Cambridge, UK: Cambridge University Press.

Heath, S. B., & McLaughlin, M. W. (Eds.). (1993). *Identity and inner city youth: Beyond ethnicity and gender*. New York: Teachers College Press.

Hebdige, R. (1979). *Subculture: The meaning of style*. London: Routledge.

Heidegger, M. (1962). *Being and time* (R. MacQuarrie, Trans.). New York: Harper & Row.

Hicks, D. (2002). *Reading lives: Working class children and literacy learning*: New York: Teachers College Press.

Hirsch, E. D. (1987). *Cultural literacy*. Boston: Houghton Mifflin.

Holdaway, D. (1979). *The foundations of literacy*. London: Ashton Scholastic.

Holland, D., Lachiotte, W., Skinner, D., & Cain, C. (1998). *Identity and agency in cultural worlds*. Cambridge, MA: Harvard University Press.

Hollowell, J. (1977). *Fact & fiction*. Chapel Hill: University of North Carolina Press.

Horkheimer, M. (1949). Authoritarianism and the family today. In R. N. Anshen (Ed.), *The family: Its function and destiny*. New York: Harper.

Horkheimer, M., & Adorno, T. (1988). *The dialectic of enlightenment* (J. Cummings, Trans.). New York: Continuum.

Hornberger, N. H. (Ed.). (1997). *Indigenous literacies in the Americas: Language planning from the bottom up*. Hawthorn, NY: Mouton de Gruyter.

Hull, G. A., & Schultz, K. (2002). *School's out: Bridging out-of-school literacies with classroom practice*. New York: Teachers College Press.

Hymes, D. (Ed.). (1972). *Reinventing anthropology*. New York: Vintage.

Hymes, D. (1974). *Foundations in sociolinguistics: An ethnographic approach*. Philadelphia: University of Pennsylvania Press.

Hymes, D. (1985). Epilogue. In D. Mandelbaum (Ed.), *Selected writings of Edward Sapir in language, culture, and personality* (pp. 598–600). Berkeley: University of California Press.

Hymes, D., & Cazden, C. (1980). Narrative thinking and story-telling rights: A folklorist's clue to a critique of education. In D. Hymes (Ed.), *Language in education: Ethnolinguistic essays* (pp. 126–138). Washington, DC: Center for Applied Linguistics.

Kamberelis, G. (2004). The rhizome and the pack: Liminal literacy formations with political teeth. In K. Leander & M. Sheehy (Eds.), *Space matters: Assertions of space in literacy practice and research* (pp. 161–215). New York: Peter Lang.

Kamberelis, G., & Jaffe, A. (2003). *Imagining and enacting the linguistic anthropology of education* (final report). New York: National Academy of Education.

Knobel, M. (1999). *Everyday literacies: Students, discourse, and social practice*. New York: Peter Lang.

Kozol, J. (1991). *Savage inequalities: Children in America's schools*. New York: HarperPerennial.

Kuhn, T. (1970). *The structure of scientific revolutions*. Chicago: University of Chicago Press.

Lacan, J. (1977). *Écrits: A selection* (A. Sheridan, Trans.). New York: W. W. Norton & Co.

Laclau, E., & Mouffe, C. (1985). *Hegemony and socialist strategy: Towards a radical democratic politics*. New York: Verso.

Langer, J. (1986). *Children reading and writing: Structures and strategies*. Norwood, NJ: Ablex.

Langer, S. (1957). *Philosophy in a new key: A study in the symbolism of reason, rite, and art* (3rd. ed.). Cambridge, MA: Harvard University Press.

Lather, P. (1986). Research as praxis. *Harvard Educational Review, 56*(3), 257–277.

Lather, P. (1991). *Getting smart: Feminist research and pedagogy with/in the postmodern*. New York: Routledge.

Lather, P. (1997). Drawing the lines at angels: Working the ruins of feminist ethnography. *Qualitative Studies in Education, 10*(3), 285–304.

Lather, P. (2000). Drawing the line at angels: Working the ruins of feminist ethnography. In E. St. Pierre & W. Pillow (Eds.), *Working the ruins: Feminist poststructural methods in education* (pp. 284–311). New York: Routledge.

Lather, P. (2001). Postbook: Working the ruins of feminist ethnography. *Signs: Journal of Women in Culture and Society, 27*(1), 199-227.

Lather, P., & Smithies, C. (1997). *Troubling the angels: Women living with HIV/AIDS*. Boulder, CO: Westview Press.

Latour, B., & Woolgar, S. (1986). *Laboratory life*. Princeton, NJ: Princeton University Press.

Lave, J., & Wenger, E. (1991). *Situated learning: Legitimate peripheral participation*. New York: Cambridge University Press.

Lee, A. (1996). *Gender, literacy, curriculum: Re-writing school geography*. London: Taylor & Francis.

LeFebvre, H. (1991). *The production of space*. Oxford: Blackwell Publishers.

Lenzo, K. (1994, April). Reinventing ethos: Validity, reliability, and the transgressive self. Paper presented at the annual meeting of the American Educational Research Association, New Orleans, LA.

Lewis, C. (2001). *Literary practices as social acts*. Mahwah, NJ: Erlbaum.

Livingston, E. (1987). *Making sense of ethnomethodology*. New York: Routledge.

Lofty, J. (1992). *Time to write*. Albany: State University of New York Press.

Lovejoy, A. O. (1970). *The great chain of being: A study of the history of an idea*. Cambridge, MA: Harvard University Press.

Lukács, G. (1971). *History of class consciousness: Studies in Marxist dialectics* (R. Livingstone, Trans.). Cambridge, MA: MIT Press.

Luke, A. (1992). The body literate: Discourse and inscription in early literacy training. *Linguistics and Education, 4*(1), 107–129.

Luttrell, W. (1997). *Schoolsmart and motherwise: Working-class women's identity and schooling*. New York: Routledge.

Lyotard, F. (1984). *The postmodern condition: A report on knowledge* (G. Bennington & B. Massumi, Trans.). Minneapolis: University of Minnesota Press.

Marcus, G. (1998). *Ethnography through thick and thin*. Princeton, NJ: Princeton University Press.

Marcus, G., & Fischer, M. (1986). *Anthropology as cultural critique: An experimental moment in the human sciences*. Chicago: University of Chicago Press.

Marx, K. (1961). *Selected writings in sociology and social philosophy*. (2nd ed., T. B. Bottomore & M. Rubel, Eds.). Harmondsworth, UK: Penguin.

Marx, K., & Engels, F. (1969). *Selected works* (Vol. 1). Moscow: Progress Publishers.

McLaren, P. (1998). *Life in schools* (3rd ed.). New York: Longman.

Mehan, H. (1979). *Learning lessons: Social organization in the classroom*. Cambridge, MA: Harvard University Press.

Merriam, S. B. (2001). *Qualitative research and case studies applications in education*. San Francisco: Jossey-Bass.

Michaels, S. (1981). "Sharing time": Children's narrative styles and differential access to literacy. *Language in Society, 10*, 423–442.

Miller, D. W. (1999). The black hole of education research. *Chronicle of Higher Education, 45*(48), A17–A18.

Mills, C. W. (1959). *The sociological imagination*. New York: Oxford University Press.

Moermann, M. (1988). *Talking culture: Ethnography and conversation analysis*. Philadelphia: University of Pennsylvania Press.

Morgan, W. (2000). Electronic tools for dismantling the master's house: Poststructural feminist research and hypertext poetics. In E. St. Pierre & W. Pillow (Eds.), *Working the ruins: Feminist poststructural methods in education* (pp. 130–149). New York: Routledge.

Morrow, R. (2000). Social theory and educational research: Reframing the quantitative-qualitative distinction through a critical theory of methodology. In K. McClafferty, C. Torres, & T. Mitchell (Eds.), *Challenges of urban education: Sociological perspectives for the next century* (pp. 47–77). Albany: State University of New York Press.

Morson, G., & Emerson, C. (1990). *Mikhail Bakhtin: Creation of a prosaics*. Stanford, CA: Stanford University Press.

Nelli, H. (1970). *Italians in Chicago, 1880–1930: A study in ethnic mobility*. New York: Oxford University Press.

Nietzsche, F. (2003). *The genealogy of morals*. Mineola, NY: Dover. (Original work published 1887)

Ochs, E. (1988). *Culture and language development: Language acquisition and language socialization in a Samoan village*. Cambridge, UK: Cambridge University Press.

Omi, M., & Winant, H. (1994). *Racial formation in the United States: From the 1960s to the 1990s*. London: Routledge.

Ortner, S. (1999). (Ed.). *The fate of "culture": Geertz and beyond*. Berkeley: University of California Press.

Packer, M., & Addison, R. (Eds.). (1989). *Entering the circle: Hermeneutic investigation in psychology*. Albany, NY: State University of New York Press.

Philips, S. (1972). Participant structures and communicative competence. In C. Cazden, V. John, & D. Hymes (Eds.). *Functions of language in the classroom* (pp. 370–394). New York: Teachers College Press.

Philips, S. (1983). *The invisible culture: Communication in classroom and community on the Warm Springs Indian Reservation*. New York: Longman.

Pinar, W. (2004). *What is curriculum theory?* Hillsdale, NJ: Lawrence Erlbaum.

Popper, K. (1959). *The logic of scientific discovery*. New York: Basic Books.

Price, S. (1998). Critical discourse analysis: Discourse acquisition and discourse practices. *TESOL Quarterly, 33*(3), 581–595.

Probyn, E. (1993). *Sexing the self: Gendered positions in cultural studies*. London & New York: Routledge.

Richardson, L. (1992). The consequences of poetic representation: Writing the other, rewriting the self. In C. Ellis & M. G. Flaherty (Eds.), *Investigating subjectivity: Research on lived experience* (pp. 125–137). Newbury Park, CA: Sage.

Richardson, L. (1994). Writing: A method of inquiry. In N. Denzin & Y. Lincoln (Eds.), *Handbook of qualitative research* (pp. 516–529). Thousand Oaks: Sage Publications.

Richardson, L. (2000). Writing: A method of inquiry. In N. Denzin & Y. Lincoln (Eds.), *Handbook of qualitative research* (2nd ed.) (pp. 923–948). Thousand Oaks, CA: Sage.

Ricoeur, P. (1970). *Freud and philosophy: An essay on interpretation*. New Haven: Yale University Press.

Roman, L. G. (1993). Double exposure: The politics of feminist materialist ethnography. *Educational Theory, 43*, 279–308.

Rorty, R. (1979). *Philosophy and the mirror of nature*. Princeton, NJ: Princeton University Press.

Rosaldo, R. (1989). *Culture and truth: The remaking of social analysis*. Boston: Beacon.

Rosch, E. (1978). Principles of categorization. In E. Rosch & B. L. Lloyd (Eds.), *Cognition and categorization*. Hillsdale, NJ: Erlbaum.

Rose, M. (1989). *Lives on the boundary: A moving account of the struggles and achievements of America's educational underclass*. New York: Penguin Books.

Rosenblatt, L. (1983). *Literature as exploration*. New York: Modern Language Association. (Original work published 1938)

Roseneau, P. M. (1992). *Postmodernism and the social sciences*. Princeton, NJ: Princeton University Press.

Rymes, B. (2001). *Conversational borderlands: Language and identity in an alternative urban high school*. New York: Teachers College Press.

Said, E. (1979). *Orientalism*. New York: Vintage.

Said, E. (1995). *Culture and imperialism*. New York: Vintage.

Sapir, E. (1909). *The Takelm language of southwestern Oregon*. Unpublished doctoral dissertation, Columbia University.

Sapir, E. (1985). Why cultural anthropology needs the psychiatrist. In D. Mandelbaum (Ed.), *Selected writings of Edward Sapir in language, culture, and personality* (pp. 569–577). Berkeley: University of California Press. (Original work published 1938)

Sarup, M. (1988). *Introduction to poststructuralism and postmodernism*. New York: Harvester.

deSaussure, F. (1959). *Course in general linguistics* (W. Baskin, Trans.). New York: Philosophical Library. (Original work published 1900)

Sawyer, K. (2002). A discourse on discourse: An archaeological history of an intellectual concept. *Cultural Studies, 16*(3), 433–456.

Schaafsma, D. (1993). *Eating on the street: Teaching literacy in a multicultural society.* Pittsburgh: University of Pittsburgh Press.

Schegloff, E. (1988). Goffman and the analysis of conversation. In P. Drew & A. Wootton (Eds.), *Erving Goffman: Exploring the interaction order* (pp. 89–135). Cambridge, England: Polity.

Schegloff, E. (1992). Repair after next turn. *American Journal of Sociology, 92*(5), 1295–1345.

Schegloff, E., Jefferson, G., & Sacks, H. (1977). The preference for self-correction in the organization of repair in conversation. *Language, 53*(2), 361–382.

Schegloff, E., & Sacks, H. (1973). Opening up closings. *Semiotica, 8,* 289–327.

Schensul, J. J., & LeCompte, M. D. (1999). *Ethnographers' toolkit.* Lanham, MD: Rowman and Littlefield.

Schieffelin, B., & Gilmore, P. (1986). *The acquisition of literacy: Ethnographic perspectives.* Norwood, NJ: Ablex.

Searle, J. R. (1969). *Speech acts: An essay in the philosophy of language.* Cambridge, UK: Cambridge University Press.

Shannon, C. E., & Weaver, W. (1949). *The mathematical theory of communication.* Urbana: University of Illinois Press.

Shapiro, M. J. (1992). *Reading the postmodern polity: Political theory as textual practice.* Minneapolis: University of Minnesota Press.

Short, J. (1963). Preface. In F. Thrasher, *The gang: A study of 1,313 gangs in Chicago* (abridged with a new introduction by James Short). Chicago: University of Chicago Press.

Shuman, A. (1986). *Storytelling rights: The uses of oral and written texts by urban adolescents.* Cambridge, England: Cambridge University Press.

Socolovsky, M. (1998). Moving beyond the mint green walls: An examination of (auto)biography and border in Ruth Behar's *Translated woman. Frontiers, 19*(3), 72–97.

Soja, E. (1989). *Postmodern geographies: The reassertion of space in critical and social theory.* London: Verso.

Sparkes, A. (1994). Life histories and the issue of violence: Reflections on an emerging relationship. *International Journal of Qualitative Studies in Education, 7*(2), 165–183.

St. Pierre, E. (1997). Nomadic inquiry in the smooth space of the field: A preface. *International Journal of Qualitative Studies in Education, 10*(3), 365–383.

St. Pierre, E. (2000). Poststructural feminism in education: An overview. *International Journal of Qualitative Studies in Education, 13*(5), 477–515.

Street, B. (1995). *Social literacies: Critical approaches to literacy learning, ethnography, and education.* Boston: Addison-Wesley.

Strike, K. (1974). On the expressive potential of behaviorist language. *American Educational Research Journal, 11*(2), 103–120.

Taylor, C. (1979). Interpretation and the sciences of man. In P. Rabinow & W. Sullivan (Eds.), *Interpretive social science: A reader* (pp. 25–71). Berkeley: University of California Press.

Thompson, J. B. (1990). *Ideology and modern culture.* Stanford, CA: Stanford University Press.

Thrasher, L. (1927). *The gang: A study of 1,313 gangs in Chicago*. Chicago: University of Chicago Press.

Toews, D. (2003). The new trade: Sociology after the end of the social. *Theory, Culture & Society, 20*(5), 81–98.

Turner, J. C. (1995). The influence of classroom contexts on young children's motivation for literacy. *Reading Research Quarterly, 30*, 410–441.

Turner, V. (1967). *The forest of symbols*. Ithaca, NY: Cornell University Press.

Turner, V. (1969). *The ritual process: Structure and anti-structure*. Chicago: Aldine.

van Dijk, T. (1993). Principles of critical discourse analysis. *Discourse and Society, 4*(2), 249–283.

Volosinov, V. N. (1973). *Marxism and the philosophy of language* (L. Matejka & I. R. Titunik, Trans.). New York: Seminar Press.

Weber, M. (1962). *Basic concepts of sociology*. London: Peter Owen.

Weber, M. (1968). *Max Weber on charisma and institution building: Selected papers* (S. N. Eisenstadt, Ed.). Chicago: University of Chicago Press.

Weber, M. (1970). *From Max Weber: Essays in sociology* (H. H. Gerth & C. W. Mills, Eds.). New York: Oxford University Press.

Wells, G. (1985). *Language and learning: An interactional perspective*. London, UK: Taylor & Francis.

Whyte, W. F. (1993). *Street corner society: The social structure of an Italian slum* (4th ed.). Chicago: University of Chicago Press. (Original work published 1943)

Willis, P. (1977). *Learning to labor: How working class kids get working class jobs*. New York: Columbia University Press.

Winch, P. (1963/1958). *The idea of a social science and its relation to philosophy*. London: Routledge & Kegan Paul.

Wirth, L. (1928). *The ghetto*. Chicago: University of Chicago Press.

Wittgenstein, L. (1958). *Philosophical investigations* (G. E. M. Anscombe, Trans.). Oxford, UK: Basil Blackwell.

Wolcott, H. (1992). Posturing in qualitative inquiry. In M. D. LeCompte, W. L. Millroy, & J. Preissle (Eds.), *Handbook of qualitative research in education* (pp. 3–52). San Diego: Academic Press.

Wolf, M. (1992). *A thrice told tale: Feminism, postmodernism & ethnographic responsibility*. Stanford, CA: Stanford University Press.

Wortham, S. (2001). *Narratives in action: A strategy for research and analysis*. New York: Teachers College Press.

Wortham, S., & Rymes, B. (Eds.). (2002). *Linguistic anthropology of education*. New York: Praeger.

Index

Abrahams, Roger, 5
Abstracted empiricism (Mills), 73
Abu-Lughod, L., 27–28
Acquisition of Literacy, The (Schieffelin & Gilmore), 68–69
Addison, R., 13, 61, 82
Adjacency pairs (Schegloff & Sacks), 103
Adorno, Theodor, 38–39, 51, 113–115, 133–134
Agents of change, researchers as, 67–71
"Agnes" study (Garfinkel), 107–108
Ailwood, J., 121
Alasuutari, P., 17
Alcoff, L., 49
Alternative Schooling for African American Youth (Dunbar), 150–152
Althusser, Louis, 38, 133–134
Alvermann, D., 128–129
Anderson, N., 95
Anthropology, 60–91
    Chronotope I and, 62–66, 74, 82–83, 91
    Chronotope II and, 62–67, 74–76, 79–80, 82–83, 87–90
    Chronotope III and, 67, 74–76, 79–80, 82–83, 87–90
    Chronotope IV and, 76, 79–80, 87–88, 90, 91
    crisis of evaluation and, 61, 82
    crisis of praxis and, 61, 82
    crisis of relevance and, 60, 88–89
    crisis of representation and, 60–61, 75–87
    emergence as discipline, 6
    Ethnography of Communication (EOC) tradition and, 60, 63–64, 66, 67, 71–75, 76, 79–80, 87–88, 89–90
    inquiry logics in, 87–89
    new approaches to research in, 64–67
    rapprochement with education, 6
    researcher as agent of change in, 67–71
    separation of subject and object in, 31
    in the twentieth century, 61–63

Anthropology and Education Quarterly (journal), 34
Anzaldua, G., 49
Approaches, 17–18
Aristotle, 16, 40
Articulation, 123–130
Asylums (Goffman), 106
Atkinson, J. M., 19
Atkinson, P., 9, 103–104
Autoethnography, 149–150

Bakhtin, M. M., 24–25, 52, 159 n. 1, 161 n. 11, 162 n. 17
Banking model of education (Freire), 42–43, 116–117
Barton, D., 71
Bateson, Gregory, 24
Baudrillard, J., 45, 51
Bauman, James, 133, 141
Baynham, M., 71
Becker, Howard S., 106
Behar, Ruth, 7, 80, 83–85, 88, 91, 131
Bentham, Jeremy, 118
Berger, P., 99–100
Bergvall, V., 121
Bernstein, R., 13, 39
Besnier, Niko, 7, 143–145
Best, S., 162 n. 14
Biklen, S. K., 19
Birdwhistell, R. L., 24, 159 n. 1
Bissex, G. L., 161 n. 7
Black Atlantic, The (Gilroy), 122–123
Blaming the victim, 148
Bloome, D., 119
Blumer, Hubert, 106
Boas, Franz, 62
Bogard, William, 128
Bogdan, R., 19
Bourdieu, Pierre, 5–6, 15, 22, 25, 46, 54, 58, 100, 117, 132, 159 n. 1, 162 n. 15
Brandt, Deborah, 133, 142–143
Brown, Lyn Mikel, 162 n. 16

About the Authors

George Kamberelis is an Associate Professor in the School of Education at the State University of New York at Albany. He teaches and conducts research on the history and philosophy of science, qualitative inquiry, social theory, and literacy studies. His work has appeared in many journals including *Qualitative Inquiry*, *Reading Research Quarterly*, *Research in the Teaching of English*, *Journal of Literacy Research*, *Journal of Contemporary Legal Issues*, and *The Annals of the American Academy of Political and Social Sciences*. Currently, he is also working with scholars from the National Center for Education and the Economy to produce a book on literacy performance standards for fourth- and fifth grades.

Greg Dimitriadis is Associate Professor in the Department of Educational Leadership and Policy at the State University of New York at Buffalo. He is the author of *Performing Identity/Performing Culture: Hip Hop as Text, Pedagogy, and Lived Practice* (Peter Lang) and *Friendship, Cliques, and Gangs: Young Black Men Coming of Age in Urban America* (Teachers College Press). He is also a co-author or co-editor of several other books. He has two forthcoming books, *Studying Urban Youth Culture* (Peter Lang) and *Race, Identity, and Representation in Education* (Second Edition) (co-edited with Cameron McCarthy, Warren Crichlow, and Nadine Dolby) (Routledge Falmer).